Lecture Notes of the Institute for Computer Sciences, Social Informatics and Telecommunications Engineering 176

More information about this series at http://www.springer.com/series/8197

Carlos Vaz de Carvalho · Paula Escudeiro
António Coelho (Eds.)

Serious Games, Interaction and Simulation

6th International Conference, SGAMES 2016
Porto, Portugal, June 16–17, 2016
Revised Selected Papers

Springer

Editors
Carlos Vaz de Carvalho
Instituto Superior de Engenharia do Porto
Porto
Portugal

António Coelho
University of Porto
Porto
Portugal

Paula Escudeiro
Instituto Superior de Engenharia do Porto
Porto
Portugal

ISSN 1867-8211 ISSN 1867-822X (electronic)
Lecture Notes of the Institute for Computer Sciences, Social Informatics and Telecommunications Engineering
ISBN 978-3-319-51054-5 ISBN 978-3-319-51055-2 (eBook)
DOI 10.1007/978-3-319-51055-2

Library of Congress Control Number: 2016959800

Printed on acid-free paper

This Springer imprint is published by Springer Nature
The registered company is Springer International Publishing AG
The registered company address is: Gewerbestrasse 11, 6330 Cham, Switzerland

Preface

SGAMES 2016, the 6th EAI International Conference on Serious Games, Interaction and Simulation, was a multidisciplinary event dedicated to research, practice and validation in the fields of serious games, interaction, and simulation.

The serious games area focuses on the design, development, use, and application of games for other purposes than entertainment. The most striking reported effect from the use of serious games is an increased user motivation and engagement toward the "serious" objectives. Interaction and simulation are fundamental tools for this motivation and engagement: providing intuitive and innovative forms of interaction with the game captures the user interest and creating intelligent game play maintains that interest.

However, in spite of the existing evidence of success, there is still limited use of serious games. This has mainly to do with social concerns and stereotypes about the relation of games and serious purposes. But it is also related to the lack of extended evidence of effective application. This is where SGAMES plays a crucial role as a forum to exchange knowledge and best-practices and to disseminate that evidence.

The program of SGAMES 2016 reflected the contributions to core issues of serious game design and development and their application in distinct areas. The keynotes presented state-of-the-art information about two major topics in this field:

- Sylvester Arnab presented the need to harness the potential of hybrid spaces in teaching and learning resulting from the merging of digital and physical experiences and the potential of the playful nature of games and gamification to create contexts for that pervasive learning process.
- Rui Prada analyzed the use of AI characters with socio-emotional agency that increase the range of social situations that players can explore in the application of games to learn social skills.

The definition of models for the collection of usage data (game learning analytics) was a major concern together with the automatic extraction of gameplay design expertise, and the development of a requirements definition model for pervasive games-based learning systems:

- Cano et al. introduce the GLAID (game learning analytics for intellectual disabilities) model that describes how to collect, process, and analyze videogame interaction data in order to provide an overview of the user learning experience, from an individualized assessment to a collective perspective.
- Vahldick et al. propose a model to identify the students' progress by recording (through game learning analytics) their performance in programming tasks. They demonstrate the model through an implementation in a casual computer programming serious game.

- Raies et al. propose a process to extract and represent the necessary specialized knowledge required to design game-based learning systems in order to transfer that knowledge to novice actors. The process uses ontology techniques based on the semantic annotation of gameplay descriptions.
- In a related approach, Mejbril et al. propose a model, also based on ontology techniques, to define a requirements engineering process in order to improve the development of pervasive game-based learning systems.

Accessibility and social inclusion applications deserved special attention. Articles in these areas addressed aspects like the phonetics awareness of children with Down syndrome, the improvement of the learning of child movements, neurocognitive stimulation and assessment for older people, digital skill building for individuals at risk, older people's interaction with digital gaming on consoles and tablets, sign language learning support and task-specific training for rehabilitation purposes:

- Markham et al. present a study where they examined skill acquisition and retention of a non-injured population performing a sensorimotor navigation task in the computer-assisted rehabilitation environment (CAREN), driving a virtual boat through a scene using weight shifting and body movement. They conclude that task-specific training in immersive VEs may be effective for warfighter operational skills training and the rehabilitation of wounded warriors, by utilizing tasks that lead to long-term retention.
- Jali and Arnab present a study investigating the correlation between the challenges associated with older people, their existing engagement with digital gaming, the andragogical perspectives and existing game design attributes. Their preliminary results demonstrated that older people's initial perspectives and perceptions toward digital gaming and gameplay were influenced by perceived or assumed difficulties, but they were changed once they had broken the confidence barrier associated with engaging with new technologies and experienced the enjoyment from the social aspects of the engagement.
- Costa et al. present a serious game aiming to analyze neurocognitive deficits and stimulate the players' neurocognitive processes. This game is built on top of sound neurocognitive psychotherapy for adults, mainly addressing the cognitive processes of attention and memory. The game simulates real-world scenarios, allowing a better generalization process due to the application of the ecological validity concept.
- Tsalapatas et al. presented the EMPLOY project that addresses the development of digital skills among young learners with the objective of enhancing their future employment opportunities in innovation-related sectors. They conclude that the integration of technology and pedagogies offer broad learning benefits to both students and teachers by enhancing motivation, promoting long-term engagement with the learning process, providing timely and constructive feedback, and promoting critical and entrepreneurial thinking mindsets.
- Simão et al. present a research work that proposes a computer-assisted education application that aims to teach talking and reading through games. The work described was carried out in close cooperation with a child-care institution that works with children with distinct growth disorders, namely, Down syndrome.

- Raposo et al. present a serious game that tackles developmental coordination disorders that can be identified when children show motor skills below the expected levels considered adequate for their physical age and through the creation of a systematic collection of exercises children are able to perform frequently using the user-friendly game.
- Escudeiro et al. present the evaluation methods and techniques applied to a serious game developed within the VirtualSign project, a Portuguese sign language bi-directional translator. The serious game aims to make the process of learning sign language easier and enjoyable.
- From a more technical perspective, Lopes et al. present a research work that introduces a new generic software layer between the gesture capture device and the application level, therefore hindering lower-level, software/hardware details from a developer and letting him or her focus directly on the application level. This work is also planned to be used in the context of sign language support.

Other application areas included intelligence analysis and energy efficiency.

- Bourazeri et al. present the Social Mpower game, a representation of an autonomous energy community for local power generation and distribution in which the participants have to avoid a collective blackout by individually reducing their energy consumption by synchronizing and coordinating their actions.
- Rudnianski et al. present LabRint, a serious game that provides intelligence analysts with a set of learning experiences The game focuses on three stages of intelligence analysis: information collection and structuring, inference schemes development, and determination of inferences about the issue under scrutiny.
- Cesário et al. present ClueKing a children's pervasive game that encompasses context-aware and parent mediation to create an informal learning environment. The basic concept of ClueKing is an interactive environment where teachers define the learning goals and challenges and parents mediate their application on the home setting, on the children's schedule, and on how to promote their engagement.

Gamification was also approached and its use in software development contexts was presented.

- Silva et al. present the use of gamification to encourage software developers to use agile methodologies and tools with the necessary regularity. The main focus of this work is on the task completion and the regular use of the project management tool, while insuring the respect of the values proposed by the agile manifesto to software development.
- Jurado et al. describe a model for the design of game strategies based on related works in the field of gamification and its applications, composed of three components: a game environment process, a game environment, and a component for measurement and evaluation. This proposition seeks to offer a methodological tool for the design of game strategies in the field of gamification, applied to knowledge management.

SGAMES 2016 was also meant to foster interaction and informal networking between researchers. Taking advantage of the fact that several European R&D project coordinators attended the conference, an expert panel was organized to discuss several topics related to the submission and management of these projects, namely:

- How to successfully prepare a project proposal
- How to lead and manage such a complex project
- How to monitor and assess the project development
- How to disseminate and make widely public project results
- How to sustain project results after the life of the project

Finally, another innovation in SGAMES 2016 was the presentation of exemplary serious games developed in the context of academic studies. The selected serious games for this show were:

- No Bug's Snack Bar: A Casual Serious Game to Support Introductory Computer Programming Learning, by Adilson Vahldick, a game to help learn the initial topics in introductory computer programming courses
- English Is Cool, by Ana Sousa Silva and Sandra Patricia Queirós, an educational game to learn basic concepts of English
- Car Driving Simulator, by Vasco Vaz and Alexandre Bastos, a car driving simulator that helps in learning the basic traffic rules
- Nutrigame, by Francisco Fernandes and Orlando Neves, an adventure game that develops competences in nutrition
- VirtualSign Game, by Marcelo Norberto, a game aiming to aid the learning of Portuguese Sign language
- Cognitive Stimulation Game, by Jorge Neto and João Costa, a game that stimulates the players' cognitive processes
- Escalada Musical, by Augusto Manuel Bilabila, Fábio Amarante and Mariana Derigi Ambrózio, a game of musical perception that fits the music education curricula

SGAMES 2016 was once again an excellent opportunity to be in contact with the most recent research and development in the serious games domain. The quality of the contributions and discussions clearly showed tremendous potential for evolution, which we expect will continue in the next few years. We look forward to seeing you in 2017.

November 2016

Carlos Vaz de Carvalho
António Coelho
Paula Escudeiro

Organization

Steering Committee

Imrich Chlamtac	Create-Net and University of Trento, Italy
Carlos Vaz de Carvalho	Instituto Superior de Engenharia do Porto, Portugal

Organizing Committee

General Chairs

Carlos Vaz de Carvalho	Instituto Superior de Engenharia do Porto, Portugal
Antonio Coelho	University of Porto, Portugal

Technical Program Chair

Paula Escudeiro	ISEP, Porto, Portugal

Workshops Chair

Joze Rugelj	University of Ljubljana, Slovenia

Publicity Chair

Martin Sillaots	Tallinn University, Estonia

Demos and Tutorials

Ivan Martinez-Ortiz	Complutense University of Madrid, Spain

Committee Chair

Panels Chair

Hariklia Tsalapata	University of Thessaly, Greece

Posters and PhD Track Chair

Gavin Sim	University of Central Lancashire, UK

Publications Chair

Leonel Morgado	Universidade Aberta, Portugal

Web Chair

Antonio Andrade	Virtual Campus Lda., Porto, Portugal

Local Organizing Committee

Ana Barata	Instituto Superior de Engenharia do Porto, Portugal
Bertil Marques	Instituto Superior de Engenharia do Porto, Portugal
António Castro	Instituto Superior de Engenharia do Porto, Portugal
Rosa Reis	Instituto Superior de Engenharia do Porto, Portugal
Dulce Mota	Instituto Superior de Engenharia do Porto, Portugal
Ricardo Batista	Universidade do Porto, Portugal

Technical Program Committee

Alfredo Pina	Universidad de Navarra, Spain
Ana Barata	Instituto Superior de Engenharia do Porto, Portugal
Andreea Molnar	Portsmouth University, UK
Anthony Brooks	Aalborg University, Denmark
Antonio Andrade	Virtual Campus Lda., Porto, Portugal
António Castro	Instituto Superior de Engenharia do Porto, Portugal
Antonio Coelho	University of Porto, Portugal
Baltasar Fernandez-Manjon	Complutense University of Madrid, Spain
Bertil Marques	Instituto Superior de Engenharia do Porto, Portugal
Carina Gonzalez	Universidad de la Laguna, Spain
Carlo Bartolini	e-Campus, Novedrate, Italy
Carlos Vaz de Carvalho	Instituto Superior de Engenharia do Porto, Portugal
Cristiano da Costa	Unisinos, Brazil
Diana Xu	University of Central Lancashire, UK
David Gouveia	Virtual Campus, Portugal
Dulce Mota	Instituto Superior de Engenharia do Porto, Portugal
Elvira Popescu	University of Craiova, Romania
Etelberto Costa	APG, Portugal
Francesco Napoli	e-Campus, Novedrate, Italy
Gavin Sim	University of Central Lancashire, UK
Hariklia Tsalapata	University of Thessaly, Greece
Ivan Martinez-Ortiz	Complutense University of Madrid, Spain
Janet Read	University of Central Lancashire, UK
Joze Rugelj	University of Ljubljana, Slovenia
Leonel Morgado	Universidade Aberta, Portugal
Lucia Bertolini	e-Campus, Novedrate, Italy
Manuel Caeiro Rodriguez	Universidad de Vigo, Spain
Manuela Cantoia	e-Campus, Novedrate, Italy
Martin Sillaots	Tallinn University, Estonia
Martin Llamas-Nistal	Universidad de Vigo, Spain
Olivier Heidmann	University of Thessaly, Greece
Paula Escudeiro	ISEP, Porto, Portugal
Pascual Lahuerta	Universidad de Valencia, Spain
Pedro Cardoso	Universidade do Porto, Portugal

Peter Van Rosmalen	Welten Institute, The Netherlands
Ricardo Batista	Universidade do Porto, Portugal
Roberto Guerrero	Universidad de San Luís, Argentina
Romain Raffin	Aix-Marseille University, CNRS, France
Rosa Reis	Instituto Superior de Engenharia do Porto, Portugal
Rui Nóbrega	University of Porto, Portugal
Rui Rodrigues	University of Porto, Portugal
Sandra Baldassarri	Universidad de Zaragoza, Spain
Sandro Rigo	Unisinos, Brazil
Stefano Za	eCampus University, Italy
Tobias Mülling	Universidade Federal de Pelotas, Brazil
Wouter Sluis-Thiescheffer	Fontys Applied University of ICT, Germany

Contents

Using Games for the Phonetics Awareness of Children with Down Syndrome

José Simão[1], Luísa Cotrim[2], Teresa Condeço[2], Tiago Cardoso[1(✉)], Miguel Palha[2], Yves Rybarczyk[1,3], and José Barata[1]

[1] UNINOVA, DEE, FCT, Universidade Nova de Lisboa, 2825-516 Caparica, Portugal
j.simao@campus.fct.unl.com, {tomfc,jab}@uninova.pt, y.rybarczyk@fct.unl.pt

[2] Centro Diferenças – Centro de Desenvolvimento Infantil, 2825-516 Caparica, Portugal
{luisacotrim,miguelpalha}@diferencas.net, tcondeco@appt21.org.pt

[3] MIST, Universidade Tecnológica Indoamérica, Quito, Ecuador

Abstract. Computers and technology can play a key role in supporting learning, namely for students with special educational needs. Nevertheless, despite the emphasis the society puts on the use of technology and its fast proliferation in the area of education, few initiatives focus on the specific needs of children with disabilities. Motivated by this gap, this research work proposes a computer assisted education application that targets to teach talking and reading through games. The work described herein was carried out in close cooperation with *Centro Diferenças - Centro de Desenvolvimento Infantil*, a child-care institution that works with children with distinct growth disorders, namely the Down syndrome.

Keywords: Down syndrome · Multi-platform · PhaserJS · Educational games · Neuro-development · E-learning

1 Introduction

The availability and accessibility to technology is rapidly growing. In Portugal, during the year 2014 it was registered that 70% of Portuguese households had internet access within the home and 66% were able to access the internet outside the home and workplace with the use of mobile devices [1]. Taking into account the large amounts of existing devices, the opportunity arises to make use of technology to solve day-to-day problems.

Technological advances as related to educational tools is one key area that has received increased attention. With this, several applications and tools have been devised to assist in both the accessibility to information as well as in the education element itself [8–10].

Learning to read is a complex and challenging task which requires explicit teaching and considerable practice to acquire. It involves two interacting, but separate,

C. Vaz de Carvalho et al. (Eds.): SGAMES 2016, LNICST 176, pp. 1–8, 2017.
DOI: 10.1007/978-3-319-51055-2_1

components which are key to effectively reading: word recognition and language comprehension. Work with typically-developing children has identified phonological awareness and letter knowledge to be essential for the development of alphabetic reading. Phonological awareness being defined as the ability to reflect on the sound structure of speech and is assessed by tasks which require children to separate words into syllables, identify and produce rhymes, match words that begin with the same sound, and to manipulate individual sounds (or 'phonemes') in words, for example by blending, segmenting and deleting them. As evidenced, there is clearly a need for further research to evaluate those methods which appear promising for supporting reading in children with Down syndrome, using well-designed and controlled research methods. In addition, despite recent advances in knowledge, it remains significant areas in which our understanding is lacking, and this is particularly true for comprehension. More research is needed to explore the comprehension skills of children with Down syndrome, and to evaluate methods of instruction which may support the development of this skill [2]. The number and quality of existing electronic tools to assist these children in their learning process have proved to be limited.

To help address this problem, specialized associations have begun to partner with universities. One example of this type of initiative is the partnership formed between the "Centro Diferenças" and the "Faculdade de Ciências Tecnologias da Universidade Nova de Lisboa". Through such partnerships, commitments to create and continue the development of several tools to help in the education and integration of these children have been initiated, some of them within the area of neuro-development. In Portugal, 1 in 800 children are born with Down syndrome [3]. These children face day-to-day learning challenges, such as attention deficit disorders, difficulties in associating objects with words, etc. Despite these statistics and facts, as dispelled within the "Down Syndrome Fact Sheet" of the National Down Syndrome Society (www.NDSS.org), although all people with Down syndrome experience cognitive delays, the effect is usually mild to moderate and is not indicative of the many strengths and talents that each individual possesses. People with Down syndrome attend school, work, participate in decisions that affect them, have meaningful relationships, vote and contribute to society in many wonderful ways. Inclusively life expectancy for people with Down syndrome has increased dramatically in recent decades – from 25 in 1983 to 60 today [4].

Perhaps the most important lesson learned through the course of this project, is one also shared within another study on online learning tools for individuals with Down syndrome, whereas in spite of the many unknowns and challenges in embarking on such endeavor if time is taken to value and understand design from the user's perspective, one can chart unknown territory and yield transformational results. This view embodying and setting forth the overarching goal of this work [2].

2 Proposal

As part of this project, a set of functional and non-functional requirements were devised. According to Makesys, the functional ones define a software function or a part thereof. The non-functional ones are related to the performance of the application while it is being used, as well as restrictions on the functional requirements [5].

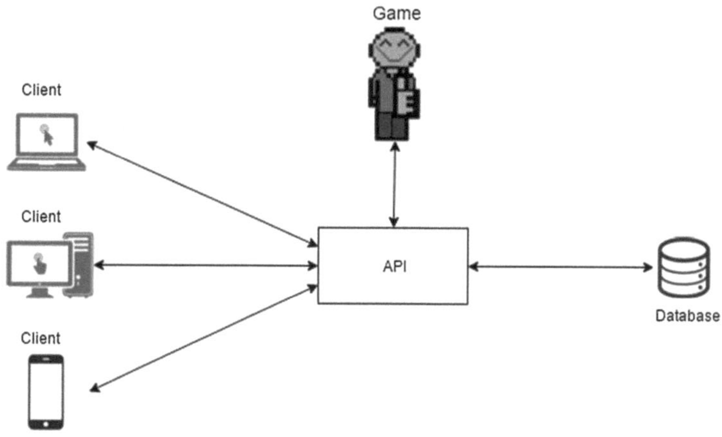

Fig. 1. Architecture description, where it can be observed how the clients will access the application as well as how their communication will work.

Considering all specified requirements, an architecture was created with the following components: one database, one Application Program Interface (API) and one game (Fig. 1). The use of the API was essential to establish the connection between all the components as previously described, as well as allowing for changes to each one of these without affecting the behavior of the other components.

Game The game consists of several mini-games that are designed to address a specific issue in order to most effectively teach the individual player. There are 7 mini-games:

- 2 designed to teach the association of images with words or phrases.
- 2 intend to teach the child how to separate components present in the sounds of the images and to force them to count the number of previously-separated components.
- 2 intend to teach the child how to associate words and objects - in this particular case, associating words and similar objects based on their sound.
- Finally, the last mini-game aims to teach the child how to make associations between a grapheme (smallest meaningful contrastive unit in the writing system [7]) and a phoneme (any of the perceptually distinct units of sound in the specified language that distinguishes one word from another [7]).

The application should be equipped with a data recording process which provides for the recording of data at the end of each level, so as to avoid excessive use of memory. This process should be fluid and must never interrupt the natural flow of the game.

2.1 Mini-Games: "Palavra-a-Palavra" and "Fraseando"

The model presented by the "Centro Diferenças" for the mini game "Palavra-a-Palavra and Fraseando"is based on the repetition of a word or phrase, while the child is being shown a picture (Fig. 2). The image display will be chosen at random and displayed in

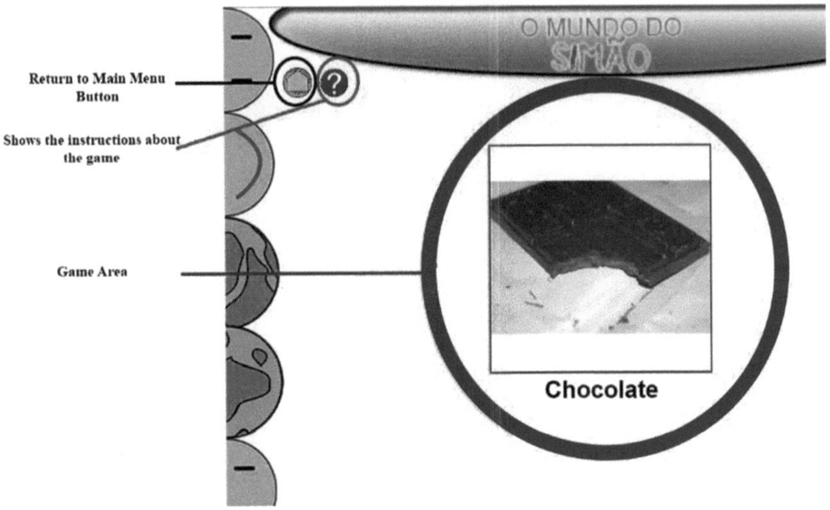

Fig. 2. Screenshot from the mini-game "Palavra-a-Palavra" with layout explained

the center of the screen. The goal of this exercise is to teach the child to speak using images as corresponding to the text in order to provide a visual support. This method was previously tested and is proven to increase the child's understanding and information recall [6].

2.2 Mini-Games: "Palavras a Rimar" and "Sons Iniciais"

The main objective of these mini-games is to prompt the user to find a relationship between the referenced image and options provided. In both games, several images are displayed to the user. One will be the reference and the remaining will be the options that may be selected. In the mini-game "Palavras a Rimar", the user must identify the images that have rhyming sounds. For the "Sons Inicias" mini-game, the user must identify the images that have words that begin with the same sound (Fig. 3).

In this mini-game two buttons, one in green and another in yellow is utilized to record the responses. The yellow is used to lock the answer and the green button is used to confirm the answer as entered.

2.3 Mini-Games: "Contar as Palavras" and "Contar Os Bocadinhos"

The mini-games "Contar as Palavras" and "Contar os Bocadinhos" aims to divide a word and force the student to count the number of words which can be divided into phonemes or syllables. The game "Contar as Palavras" will divide words into phonemes and will force the student to count the number of phonemes (Fig. 4). In the case of the game "Contar os Bocadinhos", the word is divided into syllables. Students may proceed to the next image once you have chosen the right amount of syllables or phonemes.

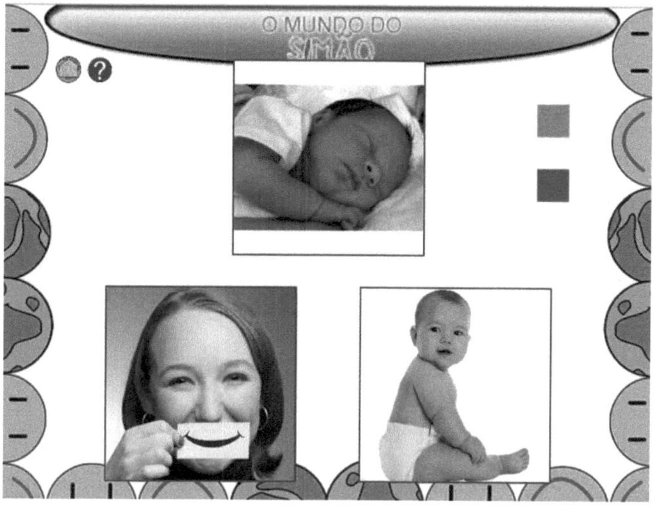

Fig. 3. Screenshot from the mini-game "Sons Iniciais" (Color figure online)

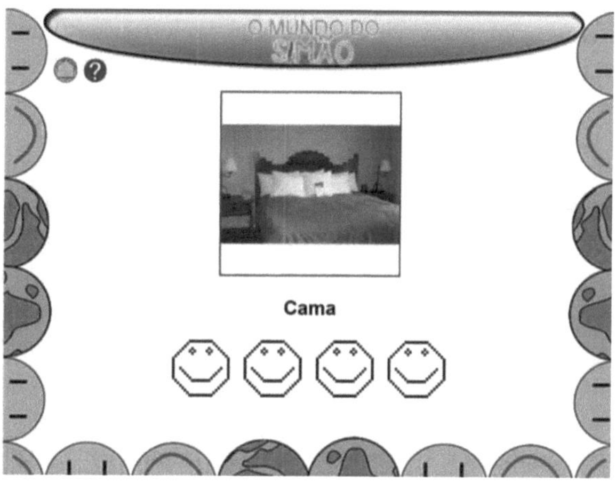

Fig. 4. Screenshot from the mini-game "Contar as Palavras"

2.4 Mini-Game: "Guardar os Sons"

"Guardar os Sons" is a mini-game to teach the user to make associations between a grapheme and a phoneme (Fig. 5). After the start of this mini-game, two random figures together with an associated sound are presented. The child will then have the opportunity to drag the image to one of the chests that represents the corresponding grapheme. If the child drags the image to an incorrect chest, the image will return to its original position.

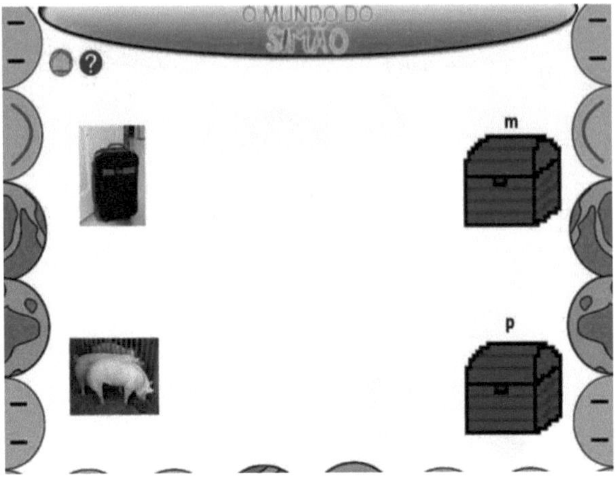

Fig. 5. Screenshot from the mini-game "Guardar os Sons"

3 Validation

This research initiative took place within the Social Tech Booster (http://stb.uninova.pt) branch from the Robotics and Industrial Complex Systems (RICS) research group, trying to solve a concrete problem and pursuing the real deployment of the result, as illustrated in [11].

The validation of this research work was divided into two phases: 1 - the development of a prototype system with the above-mentioned seven mini-games; and 2 – the testing of these games with learning impaired children, i.e., with Down syndrome.

Implementation - Different methods and tools were considered as part of this project. The tools as selected included PhaserJS. This was primarily due to being an open-source system coupled with the level of support provided to the users either by tutorials, or examples as included in its official website. The need to create an API using RESTful Web Services was identified during the project development. It was responsible for the communication between different components. The API also served as a possible interface for the user, in a manner that s/he could access their information along with its restricted modifications within its security parameters.

Validation of the Experimental Data - Between the period of the 5th of October and the 2nd of December, data for three children with Down syndrome from the "*Centro Diferenças*" was gathered as part of this project. The data as collected, represented a total of 3 sessions for each child with varying spacing between the individual sessions. The sessions contained information from the various mini-games.

Every correct answer from the player received a score of 10 points, and every wrong answer received 0 points. The evaluation of the improvement is based on comparing scores between individual sessions. If the score is higher, the child improved and learned something, if the score is lower, the child did worse and did not demonstrate any improvement. The statistics of three children are shown in Tables 1, 2 and 3.

Table 1. Sample results for child number 1

Mini games\Days	Day 1	Day 2	Day 3	Analysis
Palavra a Palavra	50	50	50	Maintained
Fraseando	0	0	10	Improved
Guardar os Sons	40	40	x	Maintained
Contar os Sons	50	10	x	Diminish
Palavras a Rimar	10	20	x	Improved
Contar os Bocadinhos	50	50	50	Maintained

Table 2. Sample results for child number 2

Mini games\Days	Day 1	Day 2	Day 3	Analysis
Palavra a Palavra	10	10	50	Improved
Fraseando	0	10	10	Improved
Guardar os Sons	0	10	x	Improved
Contar os Sons	x	x	x	No Data
Palavras a Rimar	0	10	0	Diminish
Contar os Bocadinhos	0	40	30	Improved

Table 3. Sample results for child number 3

Mini games\Days	Day 1	Day 2	Day 3	Analysis
Palavra a Palavra	0	50	x	Improved
Fraseando	0	10	x	Improved
Guardar os Sons	40	x	x	Not enough Data
Contar os Sons	x	x	x	No Data
Palavras a Rimar	0	10	x	Improved
Contar os Bocadinhos	0	50	x	Improved

4 Conclusions and Future Work

The conclusions drawn were that:

- In a universe consisting of 6 distinct mini-games, 83.3% of the mini-game universe showed an improvement in the children's scores between individual sessions. The total universe of the mini-games should have been 7, however, one mini-game was excluded as data was not available.
- Two mini-games were subject of negative results, but only one had 100% negative results, the other game had 2 children showing improvement and one negative performance.
- In 5 of the 6 mini-games (83.3%), 2 of the 3 children (66.67%) showed improvement in their overall results.

- The activities that demonstrated the most improvement were those as specific to the image association with the object and the separation of the image into sounds along with its count.

For final consideration, it should be noted that based on results obtained, great success was highlighted and continued initiatives should be undertaken to improve the mini-game that was subject of negative results.

References

1. Instituto Nacional de Estatística, Statistical Yearbook of Portugal (2014). http://www.ine.pt
2. Assadour, K., Matthew, M.: Web Fun Central: Online Learning Tools for Individuals with Down Syndrome. John Wiley & Sons, Ltd., Hoboken. ISBN: 13:978-0-470-01866-8
3. Correio da Manhã. http://www.cmjornal.xl.pt/nacional/sociedade/detalhe/trissomia-21-afeta-15-mil-em-portugal.html
4. National Down Syndrome Society. http://www.ndss.org/
5. Makesys Fábrica de Software. http://www.makesys.com.br
6. Kelly, B.: Reading interventions for children with Down syndrome, Down Syndrome Research and Practice, pp. 1–6. Advance Online Publication
7. Oxford Leaner's Dictionaries. http://www.oxfordlearnersdictionaries.com
8. Sybenga, S., Rybarczyk, Y.: Using machine learning and image processing for character recognition: an application for teaching handwriting. In: 28th International Conference on Computer Applications in Industry and Engineering, San Diego, USA (2015)
9. Gameiro, J., Cardoso, T., Rybarczyk, Y.: Kinect-Sign: teaching sign language to "listeners" through a game. In: Rybarczyk, Y., Cardoso, T., Rosas, J., Camarinha-Matos, L.M. (eds.) eNTERFACE 2013. IFIP AICT, vol. 425, pp. 141–159. Springer, Heidelberg (2014). doi:10.1007/978-3-642-55143-7_6
10. Carrasco, G., Rybarczyk, Y., Cardoso, T., Martins, I.P.: A serious game for multimodal training of physician novices. In: 6th International Conference of Education, Research and Innovation, Seville, Spain (2013)
11. Cardoso, T., Santos, V., Santos, C., Barata, J.: Games' "Social Tech Booster". Serious Games, Interaction, and Simulation, pp. 119–126 (2016)

Playful and Gameful Learning in a Hybrid Space

Sylvester Arnab(✉)

Disruptive Media Learning Lab, Coventry University, Coventry, UK
s.arnab@coventry.ac.uk

Abstract. There is a need to harness the potential of a hybrid space in teaching and learning as digital and physical experiences are merging and it is essential that the experience empowers the minds and practices, bridges formal and informal contexts and deepens the learning process. This paper elaborates on the playful nature of the use of games and gamification in creating contexts to a pervasive learning process including the Horizon 2020 Beaconing project as an example.

Keywords: Serious games · Gamification · Playful learning · Pervasive learning

1 Introduction

Key to reducing the barriers of time and physical space in learning is to open up education in such a way that formal and informal learning contexts, and digital and physical experiences are blended – a hybrid learning space. Exploiting current advances in digital technologies allow for learning processes to be better situated in a learner's context, needs and surroundings, where many different forms of learning experience can be combined in working toward the desired learning outcomes. Learning should be pervasive in order to exploit the values different learning preferences, environments and contexts can collectively bring into the experience.

This paper touches on the need to support learning in a hybrid space, specifically the initiative within the Beaconing project funded by the European Horizon 2020 programme. The pervasive nature of anytime-anywhere learning investigated in the project aims to provide an avenue for self-regulated learning to be nurtured, where the role of learners will be amplified in the process of knowledge curation, application and sharing framed under investigative, collaborative and exploratory scenarios.

2 Learning Experience in a Hybrid Space

Recognition of informal learning as an extension to formal methods is an important means for promoting anytime anywhere and lifelong learning and, subsequently, for reshaping learning to better match the needs of the 21st century knowledge economies and open societies. To support this extension, it is important for educational institutions to evaluate and possibly re-design how formal spaces are being used in teaching and

C. Vaz de Carvalho et al. (Eds.): SGAMES 2016, LNICST 176, pp. 9–14, 2017.
DOI: 10.1007/978-3-319-51055-2_2

learning and how digital platforms can help facilitate delivery, application and assessment of learning in informal context.

Through the years, digital platforms ranging from e-learning and simulation platforms to game-based learning and mobile applications have provided alternative means for the way learning contents are being delivered. The inclusion of digital tools in learning has to be holistic as the learning experience may focus too much on digital and virtual activities, which could lead to disparities between virtual/digital and real capabilities [1, 2], confidence and self-awareness.

Therefore, there is a need to harness the potential of a hybrid space in teaching and learning. Digital and physical experiences are merging, and it is essential that the experience empowers the minds and practices, and deepens the learning process. With the advancement of Internet of Things (IoT), wearable technologies, mobile and mixed reality, a more hybrid and connected experience and space can be designed and developed. Moreover, as the discipline of seamless learning merges the technological and human challenges faced by the emerging new technologies of the last decade, it is becoming clear that the ultimate learning environment will have to provide a smooth learner experience, with options to both consume and create content [3] in both formal and informal setting. A more sustained and seamless engagement is a key challenge that needs to be addressed in the design of such an environment.

3 Playful and Gameful Learning

Play is key to intrinsically expanding and broadening our embodied experience with our surroundings, fostering autonomy and freedom. It is an exploratory and experiential means for incrementally, iteratively and continuously updating our understanding and interpretation of the various concepts, objects, people, emotions and the mapping between these variables [4, 5]. It is a complex process that is difficult to decode and measure. We are however in the world where almost everything is measured and within the context of education, measures and assessments are key to ensuring that the learning process leads to the desired learning outcomes and some forms of certification.

With these perspectives, for play to be included in learning to increase motivation intrinsically, it will have to be more structured and "formal", adhering to the play-learn rules and associated measures. How do we design this playful and gameful experience without making it too restricting and to allow the feedback cycle to be as natural as possible so that it may add to the "play" experience? "*This shouldn't be construed as a claim that "everything is a game." Games are a particular manifestation of play, not its totality. They happen to be a good starting point for an investigation of play because the formality of their rules makes the machinery of play easier to observe and analyse*" [6]. Hence, games are a means by which play can be observed in a more objective way, which will lead to purposeful and meaningful engagement.

The increasing use of games in non-entertainment contexts, also known as Serious Games (SG) is transforming everyday lives and most importantly injecting more fun in everyday contexts [7]. The power of games to immerse and motivate [8, 9] and the capabilities of games to foster and facilitate cognitive gain, awareness, and behavioral change have encouraged more games of this nature to be developed within a research context as well as to be deployed in real application settings. There is also an increasing use of games techniques in non-game contexts known as Gamification [10], which demonstrated potential impact in improving engagement, nurturing attitude and behaviour, and facilitating learning in a wide range of subjects [11].

4 Pervasive Games and Gamification

The diminishing boundaries between physical and digital spaces provide great opportunities for game-based learning approaches (serious games and/or gamification) to be applied in everyday contexts. Game mechanics are becoming more pervasive as real and virtual interactions and events are merged within the context of game-play.

Advances in ubiquitous computing, mobile and location-based technologies open up opportunities for digitally-enabled learning to be facilitated in everyday spaces, increasing flexibility for learning experience to be made more engaging, contextualized and seamless. With game-based learning in mind, potentials include educational games taking place in the physical world, concurrently with the normal activities of learners' everyday lives, where virtual actions may be the trigger for physical actions in the real world and vice versa [12]. Ubiquity is expanded by context awareness, a term that "*describes the ability of the computer to sense and act upon information about its environment, such as location, time, temperature or user identity*" [13]. This information can be used to enable selective responses such as triggering events or retrieving and prompting information relevant to the task at hand. This affords virtualisation, which provides a more seamless means to link formal and informal learning approaches, and blend digital and physical learning mechanics. Example games adopting such a pervasive approach, which can be used as inspirations for a more playful and pervasive learning process include Zombies Run[1] - an adventure location-based mobile game that advocates running and Ingress[2] and PokemonGo – pervasive games that transform local landmarks into game objects in a viral and global gaming.

5 Exploring Pervasive and Gamified Learning via Beaconing

By further investigating how learners use the different spaces for learning, how to exploit learners' preferences for enhancing the use of digital platforms and the potential of gamification, pervasive gaming and context-aware technologies in enhancing a blended learning process, the expected benefits of blended spaces and contexts can be optimised.

The Beaconing project (beaconing.eu) funded by the European Commission Horizon 2020 programme investigates playful approaches for digitally enabling play-learn in everyday spaces fostering cross-subject learning. Figure 1 illustrates the pervasive learning concept that will be supported by the play-lesson plan.

---

1 https://www.zombiesrungame.com/.

2 https://www.ingress.com/.

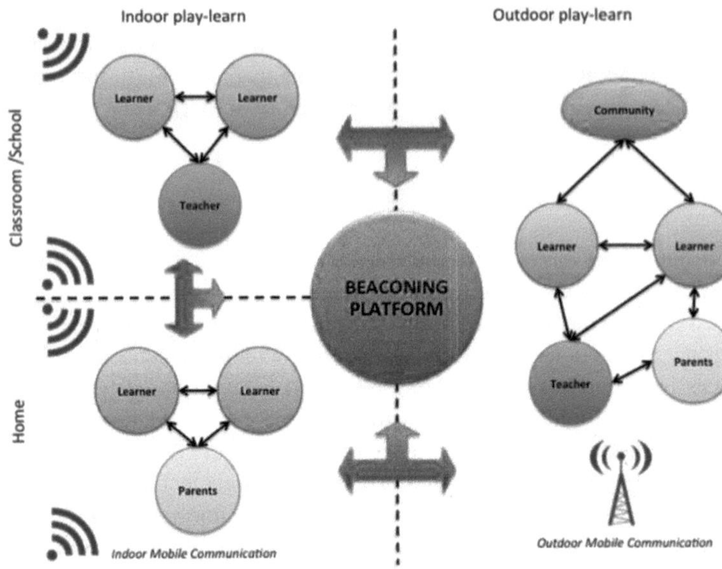

Fig. 1. Beaconing conceptual ecosystem

Learning with a classroom setting is expanded into the outdoor including personal spaces at home, which will provide support from the seamless transition from formal to informal contexts and vice versa. The key challenge for this approach is the feasibility of tracking meaningful measures and indicators for performance of informal learning activities. One of the mitigation strategies is to apply the Beaconing approach as part of the "homework" to complement the formative and summative assessment approach already implemented by the participating schools in Europe.

The holistic approach focuses on the pedagogy of Problem-Based Learning [14] in structuring learning and the relevant measures based on the mechanics of levelling up missions with associated quests. Figure 2 illustrates the taxonomy of a mission within the play-lesson plan. There will more than one mission per lesson plan, which will connect learning carried out in the different contexts and spaces.

The approach aims to increase flexibility for learners aligning with CEDEFOP's recommendations - *"the importance to Europe of a skilled and knowledgeable citizenry extends beyond formal education to learning acquired in non-formal or informal ways"*[3]. Beaconing will implement and evaluate the mechanism for proactive discovery and learning in large-scale pilots, offering real benefits for teaching, where they have the potential to enable active pedagogy through physical and contextual immersion of learners, "in situ" information while practicing within authentic context.

[3] http://www.cedefop.europa.eu/en/events-and-projects/projects/validation-non-formal-and-informal-learning.

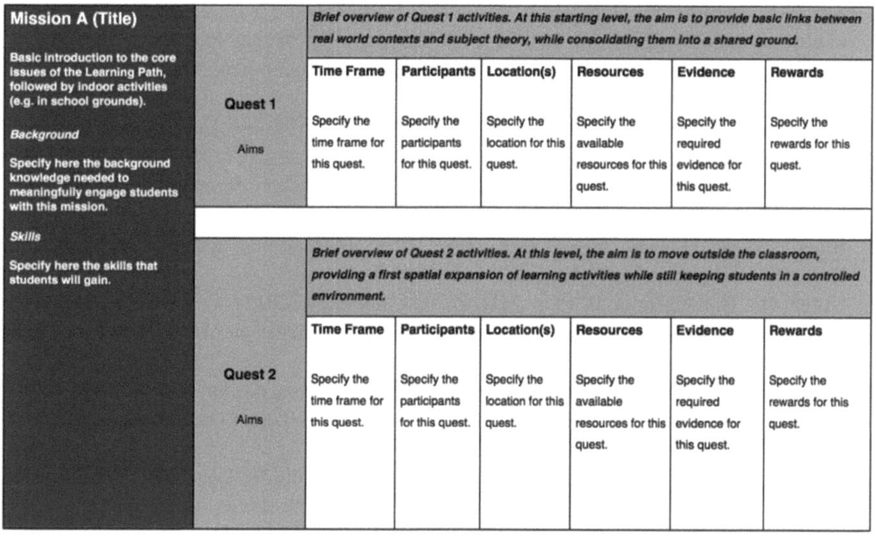

Fig. 2. Beaconing Play-Lesson Path Taxonomy

6 Conclusions

There are still studies and investigations that need to be carried out on the mapping between the autonomy of play, the formality of games, the desired serious outcomes and the individual needs of the target audience, which could transform ordinary activities into extraordinary experiences. Motivated by the need to merge formal/informal and digital/physical contexts and spaces, there is a potential impact that can be achieved through pervasive play-learning in everyday spaces. The hybrid-ness of space and contexts afforded by the advancement of technologies, such as the IoT will supersize the playful and gameful experience. Games and gamification are the instruments that can help to formalise and structure the experience to create context, narrative, process and assessment for the experience and the Beaconing project amongst other initiatives within the domain are investigating the potential to support anytime anywhere learning in real operational environments aiming to provide a blueprint and tools for pervasive learning to be facilitated in an engaging, seamless and sustainable manner.

Acknowledgement. This work has been co-funded by the EU under the H2020 Beaconing project, Grant Agreement nr. 687676.

References

1. Warburton, S.: Second life in higher education: assessing the potential for and the barriers to deploying virtual words in learning and teaching. Br. J. Educ. Technol. **40**(3), 414–426 (2009)

2. Arnab, S., Petridis, P., Dunwell, I., de Freitas, S.: Enhancing learning in distributed virtual worlds through touch: a browser-based architecture for haptic interaction. In: Ma, M., Oikonomou, A., Jain, L.C. (eds.) Serious Games and Edutainment Applications, pp. 149–167. Springer, London (2011). ISBN: 978-1-4471-2160-2
3. E-Learning Guild, Seamless Learning: Forget MOOCs, Mobile Learning, and Ubiquitous Access. Learning Solutions Magazine (2014)
4. Pramling Samuelsson, I., Johansson, E.: Play and learning—inseparable dimensions in preschool practice. Early Child Dev. Care **176**(1), 47–65 (2006)
5. Broadhead, P., Howard, J., Wood, E. (eds.): Play and Learning in the Early Years: From Research to Practice. Sage, Thousand Oaks (2010)
6. Upton, B.: The Aesthetic of Play. MIT Press, Cambridge (2015)
7. McGonigal, J.: Reality Is Broken: Why Games Make us Better and How They Can Change the World. Jonathan Cape, London (2011)
8. Rooney, P.: A theoretical framework for serious game design: exploring pedagogy, play and fidelity and their implications for the design process. Int. J. Game Based Learn. **2**(4), 41–60 (2012)
9. Arnab, S., Brown, K., Clarke, S., Dunwell, I., Lim, T., Suttie, N., Louchart, S., Hendrix, M., de Freitas, S.: The development approach of a pedagogically-driven serious game to support relationship and sex education (RSE) within a classroom setting. Comput. Educ. **69**, 15–30 (2013). Elsevier
10. Deterding, S., Khaled, R., Nacke, L., Dixon, D.: Gamification: toward a definition. Presented at the Computer Human Interaction, CHI 2011, Vancouver, British Columbia, Canada. ACM (2011)
11. Hamari, J., Koivisto, J., Sarsa, H.: Does gamification work? – A literature review of empirical studies on gamification. In: Proceedings of the 47th Hawaii International Conference on System Sciences, Hawaii, USA (2014)
12. Jantke, K.P., Spundflasch, S.: Understanding pervasive games for purposes of learning. In: 5th International Conference on Computer Supported Education, CSEDU 2013, pp. 696–701 (2013)
13. Schmidt, A.: Context-aware computing: context-awareness, context-aware user interfaces, and implicit interaction. In: Soegaard, M., Dam, R.F. (eds.) The Encyclopedia of Human-Computer Interaction, 2nd edn. The Interaction Design Foundation, Aarhus (2014)
14. Savin-Baden, M.: Facilitating Problem-Based Learning. OUP, Buckingham (2003)

Improving the Learning of Child Movements Through Games

Miguel Raposo[1], Raquel Barateiro[2], Susana Martins[2], Tiago Cardoso[1(✉)], Miguel Palha[2], and José Barata[1]

[1] Faculdade de Ciências e Tecnologias, Departamento de Engenharia Eletrotécnica e de Computadores, Universidade Nova de Lisboa, Monte da Caparica, Portugal
mc.raposo@campus.fct.unl.pt, {tomfc,jab}@uninova.pt
[2] Centro Diferenças – Centro de Desenvolvimento Infantil, Bela-Vista, Lisbon, Portugal
raquelmariabarateiro@gmail.com, susana.gmar@gmail.com, miguelpalha@diferencas.net

Abstract. A Developmental Coordination Disorder can be identified when children show motor skills either below the expected levels considered adequate to their physical age or the opportunities provided for their learning. This problem affects four to six percent of school-age children, meaning that, from a very early stage of their life, they have several difficulties to adapt to the daily needs. In order to reduce the impact caused by this disorder, a team of therapists from "*Centro DIFERENÇAS – Centro de Desenvolvimento Infantil*" collected a wide range of exercises that allow the stimulus of several motor areas, including both the Gross and Fine Motor Skills. However, the application of this therapeutics is restricted to regular appointments. Since the motor stimulus, in order to be effective, need continuous application, it was found to be necessary to have a tool that in a practical and affordable way, fulfill this need. Therefore, the proposal presented in this article describes the creation of a systematic collection of such exercises in a friendly user manner for the children to be able to exercise elsewhere.

Keywords: Developmental Coordination Disorder · Serious games · Kinect Sensor · Natural user interface

1 Introduction

A Developmental Coordination Disorder can be identified when children show motor skills either below the expected levels considered adequate to their physical age or the opportunities provided for their learning. It is estimated that the number of children affected by this disorder ranges from four to six percent of the children at school age. This disorder is one of the many areas that therapists of "*Centro DIFERENÇAS – Centro de Desenvolvimento Infantil*" focus on. The DCD requires regular stimulus, meaning the children must do regular exercises, despite many of these exercises are restricted to books that the children's parents do not have neither the access nor the time to search for them. In order to provide both the correct exercises and to continue

C. Vaz de Carvalho et al. (Eds.): SGAMES 2016, LNICST 176, pp. 15–22, 2017.
DOI: 10.1007/978-3-319-51055-2_3

the work done on the regular appointments, the therapists of *Centro DIFERENÇAS* collected a wide range of exercises from the books [1, 2], dividing them by area, category and age. This information was transferred to an application so it can be available to anyone in a practical and affordable way.

1.1 Developmental Coordination Disorder

The Developmental Coordination Disorder is a neurological disorder defined in the Diagnostic and Statistical Manual of Mental Disorder, Fifth Edition (DSM-5) [3]. Here were defined a set of parameters that have to be found in children in order to diagnose them with DCD. These parameters are:

- The learning and execution of coordinated motor skills show to be below the expected level for age, given opportunity for skill learning;
- Motor skill difficulties significantly interfere with activities of daily living and impact academic or school productivity and vocational activities, leisure and play;
- Onset is in the early developmental period;
- Motor skill difficulties cannot be better explained by intellectual delay, visual impairments or other neurological conditions that affect movement.

In the past 40 years, many treatments were developed, roughly divided into two categories: process-oriented and task-oriented treatments. The process-oriented treatments that focus on reducing the deficit of the body structure responsible for the motor skill problems still, this approach is not the recommended by the European Academy of Childhood Disabilities (EACD). The recommended approach is the task-oriented treatments that by defining a set of tasks that one child has difficulties with, divide them into a set of objectives that have to be accomplished and, according to the child's progress, adapt the difficulty of the exercises have better results [4].

1.2 Serious Games

Serious games are a set of software or hardware solutions that are designed to, with the use of games, teach their players. Two of serious games' areas are games for health and exergaming, being the first one related to the improvement of the health of a child and the second one related to games where the exercise is required to play them. Being the solution developed both a tool for the parents to guide them when doing the exercises with their sons and one game that needs movement to be played, these two categories are the ones that this solution can be put on. The application of serious games was studied in [4] with some promising results. Despite the effectiveness of serious games, the traditional approach of task-oriented process is more effective. Because these games cannot replace the physical or occupational therapy, the solution developed was divided in two to provide both the traditional task-oriented exercises and the practice of a game to improve the motor skills. Some serious games were previously developed by students of Faculdade de Ciências e Tecnologias with promising results, examples of them are: [5] where is described the implementation of a serious game to teach medical students to carry out neurological examinations and [6] where was constructed a tool to teach non-deaf people sign language.

2 State of the Art

Some games have been developed to provide solutions in this area. Examples of them are the "Uni_Paca_Girl" using the Kinems approach (the use of Kinect Sensors to empower children to reach their full potential) [7] and Kinect-o-Therapy [8].

The "Uni_Paca_Girl", later renamed to "Walks", was developed in 2013 and is similar to the "Pacman" game, requiring the movement of the users arm to move the character along the track avoiding both the margins and other obstacles.

The "Kinect-o-Therapy" was also developed in 2013 including four games: Shoulder Exercise, Balloon Pop, Path Follower and Play Along, aiming to develop four different areas of motor skills. The movements of the hand also control the navigation in this software.

Despite the most common hardware found at educational centers be the Wii console, the Kinect Sensor is easier to play with, this is due to the requirements of Wii (the need to use in one hand one controller with buttons and, at the same time, practice body movements). As many of DCD's children have hyperactivity disorder or attention deficit, they tend to cheat when using this type of hardware. As the Kinect Sensor is based only on body movements, solutions that use this sensor are expected to be better.

3 "Aprender os Movimentos" (Learning to Move)

The application developed was named "*Aprender os Movimentos*" (Learning to Move), divided into two complementary parts: one search motor that allows the access to the information gathered by the *Centro DIFERENÇAS* therapists and one game that aims to develop the eye-hand coordination, weight transfer, reflexes and locomotion, achieved with a game of catching multiple balls in different positions.

The main screen of *Aprender os Movimentos* application is shown in Fig. 1.

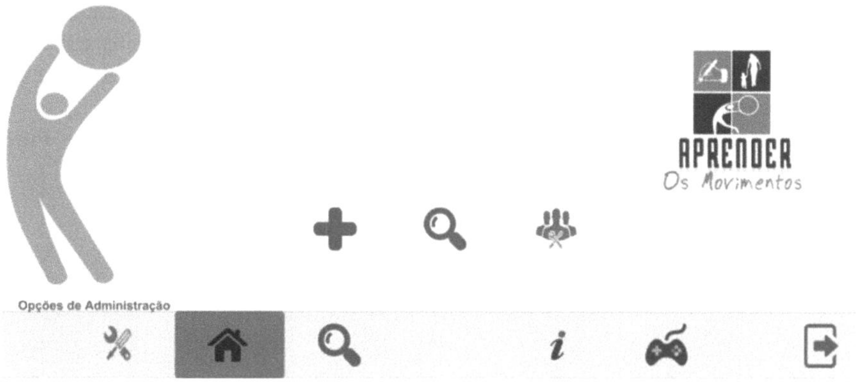

Fig. 1. Application main screen

As can be seen in the figure shown below, there are multiple options available to the user. The grey bar at the bottom displays all the options available to common users but the options at the middle of the screen are only for administrators. When the application is opened, it reads a unique number of the machine who runs it, consulting the file with all the user's data, the application automatically distinguishes from a common user and from an administrator. However, if the unique number wasn't found in the file, it is necessary to fill a new user page information.

As the first part of the application is an information database, it was required to develop a method to transfer the information in papers to a digital support. Analyzing the documents the therapists gathered it was possible to identify a set of fields that were common to all exercises. These fields were:

- **Area** – Identifying the area that the exercise will stimulate, it can be either Gross Motor Skills or Fine Motor Skills;
- **Category** – Divided in a set of sub-categories according to Gross Motor Skills and Fine Motor Skills. For Gross Motor Skills, the categories are: Reflexes, Weight Transfer, Locomotion and Reception and Propulsion of Objects; for Fine Motor Skills, the categories are: Grasp, Manipulate, Coordination Eye-Hand and Dexterity;
- **Age** – As not all exercises are adequate to any age, it was required to specify the age, in moths, that should be appropriate to each exercise;
- **Materials** – Identifying the material needed to do the exercise;
- **Description** – Presents generically what will the exercise be about;
- **Objective** – Specifies what are the objectives to be achieved by the exercise;
- **Image** – In some exercises, shows how some objects are supposed to be placed;
- **Strategies** – From one to eight, indicates step by step how the exercise is supposed to be done. As some strategies may require different images or videos, it is also allowed the association of one image and/or video to each strategy.

After filling all the required fields, they will be converted to an eXtensible Markup Language (XML) file.

It was also developed a search engine/browser that uses the area, the category and the age to search through the XML file. As the videos were recorded using either blue or orange shirts and background, it was essential to change the search bar to match this colors, as can be seen in Figs. 2 and 3.

As soon as all search fields are selected, the results are shown as seen in Fig. 4, including:

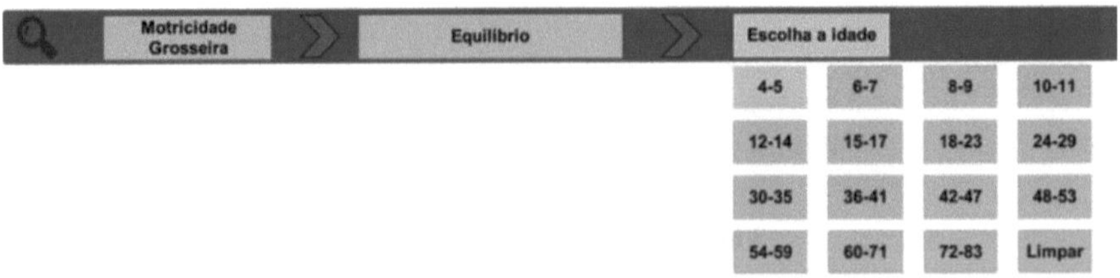

Fig. 2. Gross motor skills (Color figure online)

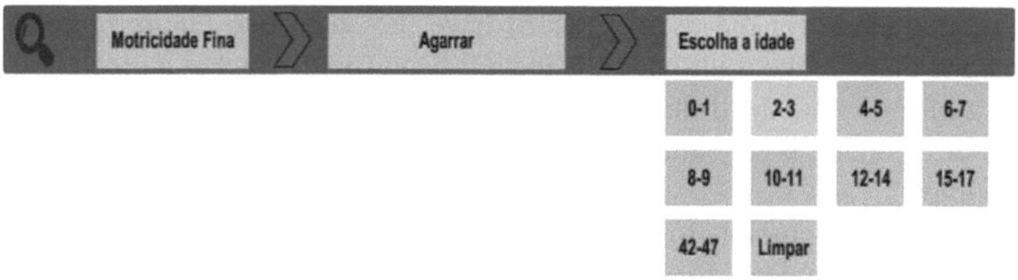

Fig. 3. Fine motor skills (Color figure online)

- The main objective to be achieved;
- The materials needed to practice the exercise;
- A set of sub-objectives to be fulfilled;
- Images or videos explaining the exercise steps.

To prevent the need of filling all the fields if some information changes, it was developed a screen, similar to the Fig. 4, that allows changing the field's information individually, saving automatically on the XML file.

The second part of "*Aprender os Movimentos*" (Learning to Move) application is the game "*Apanha-me se puderes*" (Catch me if you can). This game, as the presented in the state of the art chapter, uses one Kinect Sensor to track the user's body. Using a Software Development Kit (SDK), the user's joints are converted into 26 spherical objects. Being the objects the main resource of Unity3D, it is important to do this conversion otherwise, it would not be possible to attach colliders for collision detections, retrieving its special coordinates or change its graphical properties (colors, materials and so on).

"Apanha-me se puderes" is then a game that, with the use of two colored targets (green and blue) stimulates the shoulder abduction, lateral walking, jumps and cross-arm movements. This variety of movements goes further than the ones found in the state of the art applications however, follows the same thoughts. The spherical

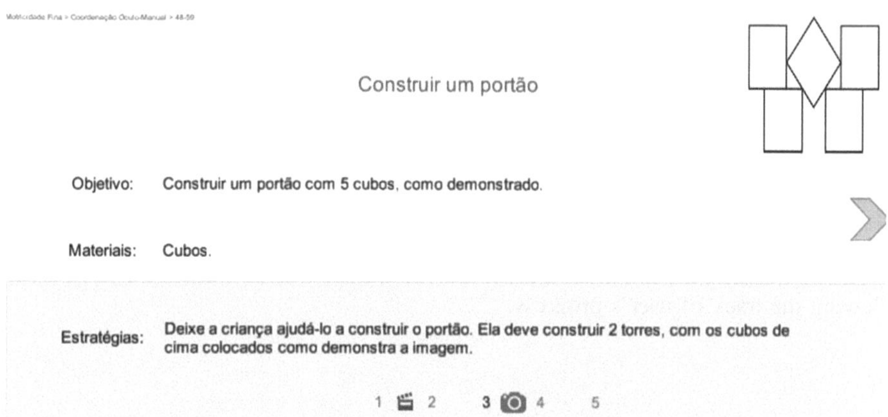

Fig. 4. Results of searching

objects of the hands (in the user skeleton) have the same two colors (green for the left-hand and blue for the right-hand). If the left-hand (blue) touches a green target, one life is lost, on the contrary, if the left hand touches a blue target, points are added. The objective of the game is to gather the most points possible in 3 min without losing all the three lives.

In the Fig. 5 it is possible to find both the avatar that the user controls (represented by the 26 spherical objects forming a skeleton) and one target (inside the number 1 area). The possible locations where the targets can be spawn are represented by the areas 1, 2, 3 and 4. These areas were found to be the ones that require some movement by the user to reach the targets, however these movements do not need to be highly difficult.

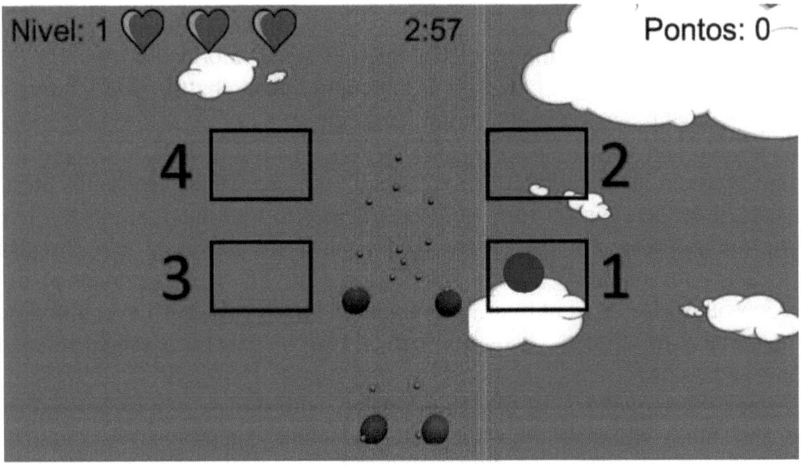

Fig. 5. Game environment (Color figure online)

The game is divided into five levels, each one more difficult than the previous. At Table 1 it is intended to demonstrate the behavior of the game. The “Blue target” and “Green target” fields represent the areas where the corresponding targets can spawn, the “Sequence” represents the sequence in which the targets will spawn if correctly hit, and the “Position” identifies if the target will spawn always at the same spot (Fixed) or if it can be random within the defined areas (Variable).

A user’s page was also developed, here each user of *Aprender os Movimentos* can see what exercises are supposed to be done according to the time planned. Each time the player plays the game, the application will save the data retrieved from the try allowing the track of user’s progress.

Table 1. Game behavior

Level	Blue target	Green target	Sequence	Position
1	1, 2	3, 4	1->2->3->4	Fixed
2	1, 2	3, 4	1->2->3->4	Variable
3[a]	1, 2	3, 4	1+3->2+4	Variable
4	1, 2, 3,4	1, 2, 3, 4	Random	Variable
5[b]	1, 2, 3, 4	1, 2, 3, 4	Random	Variable

[a]The + (plus) signal represents the targets spawn simultaneously.
[b]In this level, opposing to the 4th level, it is possible to spawn two targets at the same time.

4 Results

This research initiative took place within the Social Tech Booster (http://stb.uninova.pt) branch from the Robotics and Industrial Complex Systems (RICS) research group, trying to solve a concrete problem and pursuing the real deployment of the result, as illustrated in [9].

This application currently sums 284 different exercises saved in the XML file. The filling of this data file was divided by five assistants resulting in five separated files. After all files were completed, the information was grouped in a single file. During the implementation of the application, the structure of the file changed several times, however none of the information already saved was lost. This adaptability shows the possible scale-up of this application to whatever number of exercises needed to be included in it.

DCD's players due the time they need to be familiarized with the software and hardware did not yet test the game, however, it was presented to 20 non-DCD player's requesting critic opinions. The majority of these players confirm the utility of this game in the stimulation on motor skills. In addition, they suggest the implementation of rewards purchases with the points gathered and the implementation of new levels with higher difficulty objectives to stimulate other motor areas.

During the playtime of non-DCD player's it was possible to observe that they require a lot of movements to hit the targets but at the same time they really seem to enjoy the game proving the concept of serious gaming.

5 Conclusions

Serious games are a powerful tool that provides a fun way to learn new skills. The Developmental Coordination Disorder was proved an area where these games can be helpful despite the reduced existing solutions. Studies suggest that the best way of acquiring motor skills is to conciliate the traditional therapy with fun games however, the solutions that were found in the research done only focus in the game's area. This way, this article proposes one application that combines both the information available in the therapy centers and one fun game that stimulates several motor skills.

Despite the lack of results with DCD users, the non-DCD player's results proved to be promising.

References

1. Winders, P.C.: Gross Motor Skills in Children with Down Syndrome: A Guide for Parents and Professionals, 1st edn. Woodbine House (1997)
2. Bruni, M.: Fine Motor Skills for Children with Down Syndrome: A Guide for Parents and Professionals (Topics in Down Syndrome), 2nd edn. Woodbine House (2006)
3. APA, Diagnostic and Statistical Manual of Mental Disorder - DSM-V, 5th edn. American Psychiatric Association, Washington, DC (2013)
4. Ferguson, G.D., Jelsma, D., Jelsma, J., Smits-Engelsman, B.C.M.: The efficacy of two task-orientated interventions for children with developmental coordination disorder: neuromotor task training and nintendo wii fit training. Res. Dev. Disabil. **34**(9), 2449–2461 (2013)
5. Rybarczyk, Y., Carrasco, G., Cardoso, T., Pavão Martins, I.: A serious game for multimodal training of physician novices. In: ICERI 2013 Proceedings, pp. 4944–4949 (2013)
6. Gameiro, J., Cardoso, T., Rybarczyk, Y.: Kinect-Sign, Teaching sign language to 'listeners' through a game. Procedia Technol. **17**, 384–391 (2014)
7. Altanis, G., Boloudakis, M., Retalis, S., Nikou, N.: Children with motor impairments play a kinect learning game: first findings from a pilot case in an authentic classroom environment. Interact. Des. Archit. J. - IxD&A **19**, 91–104 (2013)
8. Roy, A.K., Member, S., Soni, Y., Dubey, S.: Enhancing effectiveness of motor rehabilitation using kinect motion sensing technology. In: 2013 IEEE Global Humanitarian Technology Conference: South Asia Satellite (GHTC-SAS), pp. 298–304 (2013)
9. Cardoso, T., Santos, V., Santos, C., Barata, J.: Games' "Social Tech Booster". Serious Games, Interaction, and Simulation, pp. 119–126 (2016)

ClueKing: Allowing Parents to Customize an Informal Learning Environment for Children

Vanessa Cesário[1(✉)], Valentina Nisi[1], and António Coelho[2]

[1] Madeira Interactive Technologies Institute, 9020-105 Funchal, Portugal
{vanessa.cesario,valentina.nisi}@m-iti.org
[2] INESC TEC/DEI, Faculty of Engineering, University of Porto, 4200-465 Porto, Portugal
acoelho@fe.up.pt

Abstract. This paper introduces ClueKing, a children's pervasive game which encompasses context-aware and parents mediation to create an informal learning environment. In this paper we review related theories of inquiry-based learning and parent involvement, the basic pedagogical model, and mobile learning and pervasive games as the technological framework. The basic concept of ClueKing defines an interactive environment where teachers define the learning goals and challenges and parents mediate their application on the home setting, the children schedule and how to promote their engagement. The system's architecture is also presented, as well as the workflows for the development of ClueKing. Since this is work in progress the paper concludes with the next steps and future work to be carried out.

Keywords: Mobile learning · Location-based games · Inquiry-based learning · Parents' mediation · Children

1 Introduction

In the twenty-first century we are literally surrounded by digital devices. Digital devices, such as mobile phones and tablets, are transforming the way children interact with multimedia content. Whether we are at home with our families and friends, at school or work, or on the move, most of our activities are mediated through technology, including often digital games. Blanchard and Cheska [1] hold that play is widely perceived not as the opposite of work, but as an accepted form of learning.

Everything today is interactive, even education is turning more interactive with the advent of mobile learning and games-based learning. A number of educators agree that the variety of popular game types that we are noticing today are "*untapped educational resource*" [2] that might "*give a glimpse of how we might create new and more powerful ways to learn*" [3].

For players and educators, the power and appeal of games comes from its capacity to generate intrinsic motivation in the players [4]. With this capacity to engage, playing

C. Vaz de Carvalho et al. (Eds.): SGAMES 2016, LNICST 176, pp. 23–30, 2017.
DOI: 10.1007/978-3-319-51055-2_4

becomes something absorbing, and hence much more memorable and meaningful to the player.

In such digitally rich space there is a unique opportunity to design and create new modes of supporting children in learning through pervasive games. However, it's hard to find a children's game where parents have an active role. Mediation can add several benefits and strengthen motivation in children's learning activities, where both children and parents could benefit from it [5]. Mediation is a crucial component to any digital experience that targets young children and has as a goal a specific learning outcome, it can play a substantial role in supporting children's learning in digital environments. The role of mediation in its various forms can benefit both children and the adults working with them [5]. In the next section we will outline the main areas that interplay at the basis of this concept. Afterwards we will describe both the initial concept and the system's architecture. We will conclude with future work and next steps.

2 Inquiry-Based Learning and Parent Involvement

Inquiry-based learning is a pervasive activity [6]. Such technique is intended to engage and motivate the learners by immersing them into authentic situational contexts in order to allow them to practice skills prior to mastery [7]. Song [8] suggests that the use of mobile devices can create seamless inquiry-based learning environments, consisting of six activities: explore, engage, explain, observe, reflect and share. In inquiry-based learning the teachers in school have a supportive role in these tasks, as described in the problem-based learning pedagogy. We argue that parents can take up a complementary role at home. Since parents often help their children executing their home works at home, we envisage the scope for an application that facilitates this process by engaging children in a gaming experience that encompass specific contents appropriately tailored for each one, and adaptable to distinct places and times. With this approach, children might be immersed in a learning environment that benefits the children's learning process either at school with teachers or at home with parents. Moreover, improving inquiry-learning is very important throughout life as it supports a lifelong learning attitude [9].

Parental influences on children's early cognitive development and parental involvement in children's education have been widely explored. Parents have a significant impact on how children spend their time during early years. According to some researchers in the area [10, 11] parents shape the environments that establish the scene for children's time-use, they have the power to determine the type and number of activities that children are involved in [12, 13] and the toys they play with [10, 14]. Such research shows that parents tend to choose games that have a wide variety of activities and content over games that do not allow customization between the content itself.

A study by Hoover-Dempsey et al. [15] have explored parental involvement in their child's homework and have identified two main categories of practice: (1) enhancement practices which included monitoring children's learning and engaging in the homework process; and (2) basic practices which encompassed setting a time-table for homework completion and interacting with children's teachers. According with this study, parental involvement in homework was seen as a positive influence on children's academic achievements through role modelling, reinforcement and instruction. We are envisioning a similar positive influence on the child through mediation in digital games by empowering parents to customize the inquiry-based learning activities for their child.

3 Mobile Learning and Pervasive Games

Overtime, mobile learning applications have evolved from the use of mobile devices as simple players to publish multimedia resources to more sophisticated learning applications which support the learning process in a complex way. Due to the increase of mobile devices and consequently mobile application revolution, a large diversity of learning applications has been developed, although a lot of these with a simplistic pedagogical framework. This might be one of the reasons why mobile learning is considered like other technically driven innovations that have come and gone in the past, as being a hype [16].

Mobile devices offer many different opportunities to detect the user's location, and especially how contextual information can be provided in the context of developing pervasive games and learning activities. The main technology used in outdoor settings to detect user's location is the GNSS (Global Navigation Satellite System) technology. Although the GPS (Global Positioning System) is the most common system, most recent devices have additional support to GNSS, Galileo or BeiDou, which increases the range and precision of the positioning. Nowadays, even the geolocation API, which can be used to track the user's position [17], is supported by HTML 5. Although the detection of user's location has improved over the years, the GNSS technology is only suitable to be used outdoors, and its accuracy can be problematic if required to be under a few meters precision.

Since GNSS can only be used outdoors, other technologies such RFID, QR codes and Bluetooth are used for indoor learning settings [18]. Through tag-based solutions such as RFID or QR codes we can easily identify the exact location of the learning object to present information to the user. When using QR codes the tags generated are physical objects printed in paper. And the content creator needs to take the QR codes to the destination beforehand, which might be complicated if the locations are far away. In the same way, Bluetooth technologies (such as beacons) need to be placed as QR codes are, the difference between them is that with QR codes the user needs to find the mark and capture it, while with beacons the user doesn't need to find any physical beacon, but the beacon itself, through Bluetooth finds the users and unlocks information for them as the user approaches the device. On the other hand, QR codes are cheap to produce and easy to print [19].

There are some mobile learning platforms which supports location-based learning content for outdoor, such as *QuesTinSitu* [18] and *Treasure-HIT* [20] and for outdoor and indoor learning alike, such as *Wandering* [21] and *Mobilogue* [19]. Learning authoring tools enable teachers to use a map to assign questions to a location by clicking on the desired location, although for this to be possible, it is necessary that someone physically explores those locations to retrieve content in order to shape the questions that will be answered by students [18]. These are usually simple questions that requires the user to engage and interact with the environment in order to select the correctly answer [19]. The author of the learning content assignments can define a route that players have to follow, or this one can be automatically generated by the system with certain preconditions like calculating the route based on the shortest path, also the route can also be different for each player, based on the author's definition [20]. We have learned and adopted many of the lessons learned from the above systems in order to design our location-based learning game environment which will be described in the next section.

4 ClueKing Concept and System Description

ClueKing is a pervasive game which creates an informal learning environment customized and mediated by parents and teachers. Children are engaged on a sequence of learning activities under the inquiry-learning framework, where they are able to explore, engage, observe and reflect, advance their knowledge and improve their inquiry-based skills [8].

We propose a "parents + learning + location + play" quadruple, as the underlying framework for children to engage in the informal learning environment and to generate intrinsic motivation for the learning activities and to advance their knowledge.

The ClueKing concept relies on a location-based digital treasure hunt where parents are engaged in creating a setting for the challenges developed by the teachers in the form of questions and levels of difficulty. The questions or challenges will be distributed around the pervasive space and the game will be played with the child's or parent's mobile device. The child will move from one place to another as he/she successfully answers questions and the next challenge location is revealed. The parents together with the teachers if so desired, can set a specific final prize to be anything relevant to each child.

These inquiry-based skills mentioned above will be improved by various locations in the game. Each location consists of a challenge that the child would have to accomplish in order to progress further into the game. These challenges will be specifically tailored by the parents to that particular setting where the child is playing the game. For instance, if the child has the clue to go where the eggs are located in the house (fridge), they go to that specific place and will unlock that specific challenge (the unlock process will be triggered by a beacon which will be automatically read, or by reading a QR code). In this case, the challenge unlocked will be the one related to the fridge. For other subjects, like Mathematics, a suitable question for this case could be "If mom bought 7 eggs in addition to the ones in the fridge, how many eggs we will have in the fridge now?". For the answer the children will need to count how many eggs are in the fridge and do the calculation of adding 7 more. This example could be applied to other subjects and locations. It is a matter of imagination from parents, and from their awareness of what type of subject the child needs to focus more on.

4.1 The System's Architecture

Teachers and parents are allowed to customize the ClueKing game through a web based interface. Teachers should be the creators of the inquiry learning challenges (Fig. 1) and parents should customize it to the home setting and the children's preferences (Fig. 2).

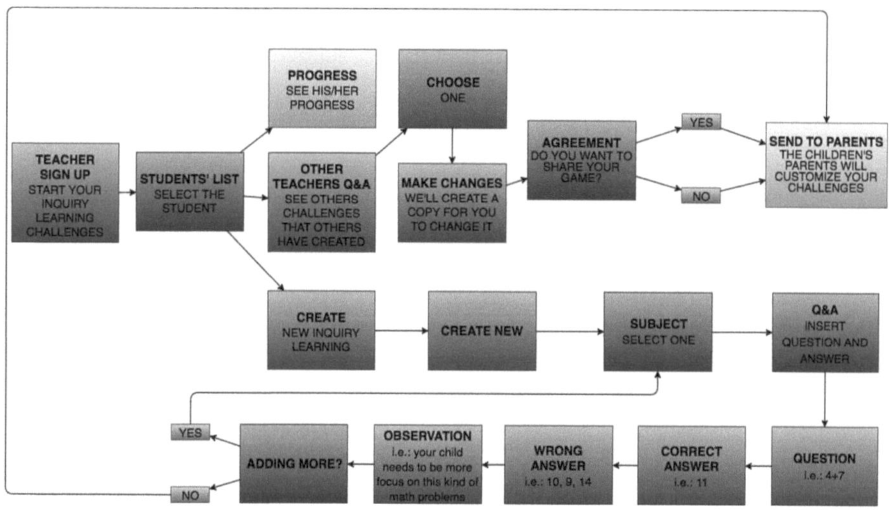

Fig. 1. Teacher's role in the web server of the ClueKing location-based game system with an example of a numbers' challenge.

Teachers have the role to create challenges in specific subjects (e.g. words, numbers, colors…) and to send it to children's parents. They are already able to see other challenges that other teachers have created and they can also see the progress of their students when they have finished a game.

In other hand, parents can select the teacher's challenges and can choose an indoor environment, for which they can use QR codes or beacons to trigger the position of the player after, or an outdoor setting, using the GNSS technology. After these steps parents are prompted to choose the type of game for that challenge that the teacher has created (e.g. puzzle, question, tasks…). Parents are also able to create games according with teacher's notes, and they are aware that those games will be seen by them.

When parents are interacting with ClueKing for the first time (via web), they will know that the triggers are assigned by utilizing QR codes or beacons for the indoor environments. In case they select the beacons, they will need to pair each beacon with the service (via web). Afterwards they are required to choose which beacon they will be using and just have to place the right beacon in the right location. If they don't have beacons, they can easily customize the game with the QR codes, by printing it.

Once the game is finalized they can download a PDF with all information of the game that they have created, the printable QR codes to place in the game setting, or the

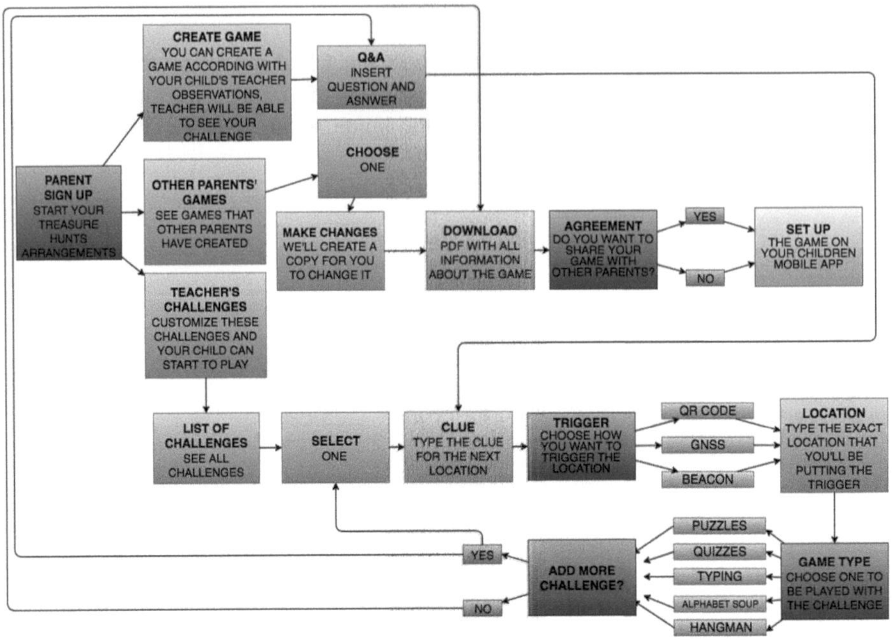

Fig. 2. Parent's role in the web server of the ClueKing location-based game system.

code of the beacon for each position. Afterwards they have the option to make the game public or private. If they make a game public, it will be available to other parents of the same children's class. Other users (parents) will be able to see and customize its locations along with their challenges.

Because of the spatial variation of the home setting, the tagging combinations might differ from family to family. ClueKing offers two approaches: when beacons are used in a game, a shared game in the beginning will ask the parents to select their previously paired beacons. So, if a parent will be using a game that is from another parent, they will need to select their own beacons in order to complete the creation of the game. Due to the diversity of contents in a single shared game, parents are able to customize not only the above mentioned features but also the subjects and types of the game. In the example above about the fridge and the eggs, a parent might want to use the same approach to a different learning challenge previously created by the teacher.

Parents configure the game in the mobile app by typing a code that the PDF has generated, then the rest of the game is to be played by the children (Fig. 3). They read and listen the first clue to reach the first location and unlock the next clue. When they reach the location they are either instructed to capture the QR Code or the content is automatically unlocked by the beacon or GNSS. Afterwards children are required to engage with the challenge that appears on the screen in order to get the next clue and reach the next location. This repeats until they get to the final location and solve the game to win the prize.

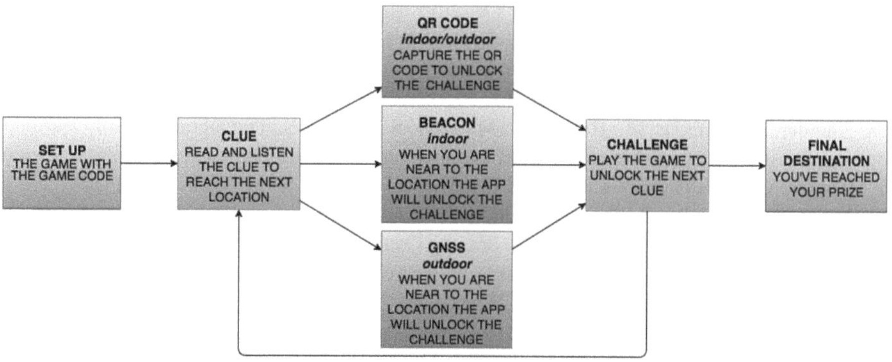

Fig. 3. Children's mobile app of ClueKing location-based game system.

5 Conclusions and Future Work

In this paper we have presented the theoretical background and preliminary design of ClueKing, a pervasive game intended to support parents' involvement in mobile based learning for children. Our application relies on inquiry-based learning theory in order to extend the learning opportunities of children outside the classroom as well as stimulating intrinsic motivation in learning and acquiring new knowledge. Through our system, parents are allowed to customize the game, its challenges and its final prize. In this way, parents take an active role in the ClueKing informal learning environment and can foster children's motivation to learn by playing. The children's inquiry-based learning activities will occur in each milestone through those challenges that parents have previously customized for them to play.

Our next steps involve the development of the pervasive game and the web-based, where parents can set up the game. The complete ClueKing solution will mediate parents, teachers and children interactions. Once a working prototype is ready we will proceed to cognitive walkthroughs, heuristic evaluation and user tests to inform the refinements of the next cycle of development.

Acknowledgments. The research leading to this work has received funding from ARDITI (Agência Regional para o Desenvolvimento da Investigação, Tecnologia e Inovação), under grant No. 002458/2015/132 and from the European Union's Horizon 2020 – The EU Framework Programme for Research and Innovation 2014–2020, under grant agreement No. 687676.

References

1. Blanchard, J.S., Cheska, A.: The Anthropology of Sport: An Introduction. Bergin and Garvey, Massachusetts (1985)
2. FutureLab, Using computer games in the classroom (2009). http://futurelab.org.uk/resources/documents/project_reports/becta/Games_and_Learning_survey_analysis.pdf

3. Shaffer, D., Squire, K., Halveron, R., Gee, J.P.: Video games and the future of learning. Phi Delta Kappan **87**, 104–111 (2005)
4. Malone, T.: What makes things fun to learn? heuristics for designing instructional computer games. In: Proceedings of SIGSMALL 1980. ACM (1980)
5. Kamdar, D., Silandar, M., Hupert, N., Moorthy, S., Gerard, S.: Digital media, early learning, and the impact of mediation on child learning outcomes. In: Games + Learning + Society Conference, Madison, Wisconsin (2015)
6. Isaacs, S., Farber, M., Millstone, J., Dikkers, S.: An inside look at getting and using games in classrooms. In: Games + Learning + Society Conference, Madison, Wisconsin (2015)
7. Domingos, E., Lee, J.: The evolution of scenario-based learning. In: Games + Learning + Society Conference, Madison, Wisconsin (2015)
8. Song, Y.: "Bring your own device (BYOD)" for seamless science inquiry in a primary school. Comput. Educ. **74**, 50–60 (2014)
9. Crompton, H.: A historical overview of mobile learning: toward learner-centered education. In: Berge, Z.L., Muilenburg, L.Y. (eds.) Handbook of mobile learning, pp. 3–14. Routledge, Florence (2013)
10. Caldera, Y., Huston, A., O'Brien, M.: Social interactions and play patterns of parents and toddlers with feminine, masculine, and neutral toys. Child Dev. **60**, 70–76 (1989)
11. Dearden, L., Sibieta, L., Sylva, K.: The socio-economic gradient in early childhood outcomes: evidence from the millennium cohort study. Longitudinal Life Course Stud. **2**, 19–40 (2011)
12. Baxter, J., Hays, A.: How four year-olds spend their days: insights into the caring contexts of young children. Fam. Matters **76**, 34–43 (2007)
13. Baxter, J.: An Exploration of the Timing and Nature of Parental Time With 4–5 Year Olds Using Australian Children's Time Use Data. Australian Institute of Family Studies, Melbourne (2010)
14. Freeman, N.: Preschoolers' perceptions of gender appropriate toys and their parents' beliefs about genderized behaviours: miscommunication, mixed messages, or hidden truths? Early Child. Educ. J. **34**, 357–366 (2007)
15. Hoover-Dempsey, K., Battiato, A., Walker, J., Reed, R., DeJong, J., Jones, K.: Parental involvement in homework. Educ. Psychol. **36**, 195–209 (2001)
16. Falloon, G.: Young students using iPads: app design and content influences on their learning pathways. Comput. Educ. **68**, 505–521 (2013)
17. Dive Into HTML5 (2013). http://diveintohtml5.info/geolocation.html
18. Santos, P., Hernández-Leo, D., Blat, J.: To be or not to be in situ outdoors, and other implications for design and implementation, in geolocated mobile learning. Pervasive Mob. Comput. **14**, 17–30 (2014)
19. Giemza, A., Ulrich, H.: Mobilogue – a tool for creating and conducting mobile supported field trips. In: QScience Proceedings of 12th World Conference on Mobile and Contextual Learning (2013)
20. Kohen-Vacs, D., Ronen, M., Cohen, S.: Mobile treasure hunt games for outdoor learning. IEEE Bull. Tech. Committee Learn. Technol. **14**, 24–26 (2012)
21. Barak, M., Ziv, S.: Wandering: a web-based platform for the creation of location-based interactive learning objects. Comput. Educ. **62**, 159–170 (2013)

The Importance of Socio-Emotional Agency in Applied Games for Social Learning

Rui Prada(✉)

INESC-ID and Instituto Superior Técnico, Universidade de Lisboa, Avenida Professor Cavaco Silva, Taguspark - Edifício IST, 2744-016 Porto Salvo, Portugal
rui.prada@tecnico.ulisboa.pt

Abstract. Games have a great potential as learning tools, in particular, because they provide means for players to safely explore and fail, and because they promote personal emotional experiences. To be successful, games must present a good coverage and fidelity of the interaction experience regarding the target learning goals. In the case of learning of social skills, which is one prominent area of application of games, the use of AI characters with socio-emotional agency has great potential value. These characters may increase the range of social situations that players can explore (coverage). However, in order to achieve that the AI characters need to be able to present good social behaviour (fidelity). Although, several examples of computational models to achieve this can be found, developing these models remains a challenging research question.

1 Applied Games and Learning

Games have been used for other purposes beyond entertainment for several years. For example, as tools to engage people in crowdsourcing tasks, e.g. ESP Game [1], for citizen science [2], e.g. Foldit [3], to motivate people to do more physical exercise, e.g. Exergames [4], to create awareness of some subjects, e.g. Darfur is Dying [5], and for training and learning, e.g. CellCraft[1], DragonBox[2], Treme-Treme[3] [6].

The use of games for learning is sustained in the strong connection between play and learning, noted in child development studies [7], an idea that was already discussed in the seminal work of John Locke and Jean-Jacques Rousseau in the XVII and XVIII centuries. In turn, learning has been regarded as an important activity in games for promoting fun. Following the Natural Funativity theory [8], which presents fun as a reward for learning, a game that has nothing to teach to a player will become boring and will, therefore, be abandoned.

The work of Clark Abt [9], in 1970, fostered the idea of having games directly presented as tools for learning. He coined the term *serious games* as games that have "an explicit and carefully thought-out educational purpose and are not intended to be

[1] http://www.carolina.com/teacher-resources/Interactive/online-game-cell-structure-cellcraft-biology/tr11062.tr.

[2] http://dragonbox.com/.

[3] http://treme-treme.pt/.

C. Vaz de Carvalho et al. (Eds.): SGAMES 2016, LNICST 176, pp. 31–35, 2017.
DOI: 10.1007/978-3-319-51055-2_5

played primarily for amusement". Abt argued for the development of new games taking learning goals as their main concern. Since then, serious games have grown as a research field and the term has evolved (commonly, referred now as applied games or games with purpose) to incorporate other serious applications besides education. Education and training are still, nevertheless, regarded as one of the application fields with most potential.

2 Why Applied Games Work for Learning

There are two main reasons why (good) applied games work as learning tools. First, because they enable practice, or, more importantly, because they support proactive exploration and failure. While playing, learners are motivated to explore the range of options presented in the game in the search for specific outcomes. Intended outcomes are not easily achieved, which means that players fail in the process until they achieve a good outcome. Games are good at supporting players recovering from those failures, because they do not imply major consequences in real-life. This means that players can safely fail. They do not fear failure too much and are, therefore, encouraged to explore the different options that the game offers and, for that reason, gain understanding of what works better for achieving different outcomes. The other main reason is, because games support the creation of personal emotional experiences, which have great impact in learning [10]. For example, note that you remember better the details of a city or country that you visited compared to the ones that you read about. This is due to the autobiographic emotional memories that were formed during your travel experience. One can also build emotional memories by reading a book, however, the immersive nature of games and the fact that they give the control (and responsibility) of actions to the player is prone to deliver a stronger emotional experience. And the brain remembers better things that are more emotionally relevant [11]. Additionally, players have individual learning experiences while playing games as they explore options in the game in different ways.

Despite the learning potential of applied games, one can only learn about what the gameplay space affords. In other words, the learning experience is only achieved within the exploration space of the options presented by a game. For example, imagine learning how to play *8 ball pool* through a digital game. A top down 2D game would support well learning the *8 ball pool* rules, and some strategy and tactics, such as, position play. But, it would be limited for learning the execution of the shots, since the gameplay options regarding the angle and the force of the cue would be limited. To support better learning of the execution of shorts, the game would need to simulate the variables involved in the real world action in a better way. This implies an immersive 3D view, but also, and more importantly, direct controls over the cue using a first person perspective. Moreover, given the physical nature of the task, having haptic feedback on the cue would be important as well.

Note that despite the clear differences of the two games, we cannot claim that one would be better than the other. It depends on the target learning goals. In fact, having levels of detail in different areas of the learning domain in a game (or in game modes within a game) is important to support different focus in learning.

The effectiveness of an applied learning game depends on the *coverage* and *fidelity* of the game interaction space given the specific target learning goals. *Coverage* means that the game enables the player to explore options within all the dimensions that are relevant for the learning goals (e.g. the cue angle and force for learning how to perform shots in 8 ball pool), and *fidelity* means that the options available in each dimension are believable in the sense that the player can relate them to the real world action that he is trying to learn (e.g. the manipulation of the angle of the cue in the game is similar, in degrees of freedom and granularity, to the one performed with a real cue).

3 The Case of Learning Social Skills

One of the prominent areas for applied games is learning of social skills [12]. To be effective in this case, the interaction space of the game needs to support exploration and failure of social actions. I argue that the use of AI characters with social emotional agency is crucial to achieve this. On one hand, AI characters increase the size of the social interaction space (increasing coverage) by supporting the generation of social behaviour based on the player interaction that does not need to be fully scripted beforehand. Thus, supporting a wider range of social situations for the player to explore. But, on the other hand, the AI characters need to be socially intelligent and believable to support the fidelity of the learning experience.

To develop AI characters with good social intelligence and believable behaviour is quite a challenging research problem. It implies developing characters that: act socially (i.e. taking others in consideration), according to social context, with socio-emotional states, and having social needs and social goals. Additionally, these characters need three major type of concerns: to understand others (e.g. developing Theory of Mind), to understand the social reality (e.g. social categories, moral values, norms) and to be able to adapt to different situations, including, learning how to deal with new situations. To deal with all this we need to develop computational models that address many different aspects of social behaviour, such as, group dynamics [13], social power [14], cultural behaviour [15], social importance [16], social relationships [17], interaction dynamics [18], social identity [19], personality [20] and social practices [21]. However, although we can find models with good results for particular aspects of social behaviour, it is not common to find models that are able to deal with many of the aspects at the same time. Hence, to integrate a comprehensive set of social behaviour capabilities in a unique model remains a challenge.

Acknowledgements. The work presented here was supported by national funds through Fundação para a Ciência e a Tecnologia (FCT) with reference UID/CEC/50021/2013 and by the research project RAGE (Realising an Applied Gaming Eco-System) funded by the EU under the H2020-ICT-2014-1 programme with grant agreement no 644187.

References

1. Von Ahn, L., Dabbish, L.: Labeling images with a computer game. In: Proceedings of the SIGCHI Conference on Human Factors in Computing Systems, pp. 319–326. ACM (2004)
2. Khatib, F., Cooper, S., Tyka, M.D., Xu, K., Makedon, I., Popović, Z., Baker, D., Players, F.: Algorithm discovery by protein folding game players. Proc. Nat. Acad. Sci. **108**(47), 18949–18953 (2011)
3. Cohn, J.P.: Citizen science: can volunteers do real research? Bioscience **58**(3), 192–197 (2008)
4. Göbel, S., Hardy, S., Wendel, V., Mehm, F., Steinmetz, R.: Serious games for health: personalized exergames. In: Proceedings of the 18th ACM International Conference on Multimedia, pp. 1663–1666. ACM (2010)
5. Brown, J.G.: Teaching about genocide in a new millennium. Soc. Educ. **71**(1), 21 (2007)
6. Barreto, P., Prada, R., Santos, P.A., Ferreira, M.A., O'Neill, H., Oliveira, C.S.: Treme-treme - a serious game to teach children earthquake preparedness. In: Proceedings of Videojogos 2014 - Sétima Conferência de Ciências e Artes dos Videojogos, Barcelos, Portugal. Digital Games Lab, IPCA, November 2014
7. Vygotsky, L.S.: Mind in Society: The Development of Higher Mental Functions. Harvard University Press, Cambridge (1978)
8. Koster, R.: Theory of Fun for Game Design. O'Reilly Media, Sebastopol (2013)
9. Abt, C.: Serious Games. University Press of America, New York (1987)
10. Kolb, D.A.: Experiential Learning: Experience as the Source of Learning and Development. FT Press, Upper Saddle River (2014)
11. Nelson, K.: The psychological and social origins of autobiographical memory. Psychol. Sci. **4**, 7–14 (1993)
12. Pereira, G., Brisson, A., Prada, R., Paiva, A., Bellotti, F., Kravcik, M., Klamma, R.: Serious games for personal and social learning & ethics: status and trends. Procedia Comput. Sci. **15**, 53–65 (2012)
13. Prada, R., Paiva, A.: Teaming up human with synthetic characters. Artif. Intell. **173**(1), 80–103 (2009). Elsevier
14. Pereira, G., Prada, R., Santos, P.A.: Conceptualizing social power for agents. In: Aylett, R., Krenn, B., Pelachaud, C., Shimodaira, H. (eds.) IVA 2013. LNCS, vol. 8108, pp. 313–324. Springer, Heidelberg (2013)
15. Mascarenhas, S., Dias, J., Prada, R., Paiva, A.: A dimensional model for cultural behaviour in virtual agents. Appl. Artif. Intell. **24**(6), 552–574 (2010). Taylor & Francis
16. Mascarenhas, S., Degens, N., Paiva, A., Prada, R., Hofstede, G.J., Beulens, A., Aylett, R.: Modeling culture in intelligent virtual agents: from theory to implementation. Auton. Agents Multi-Agent Syst. **30**, 1–32 (2015). Springer
17. Leite, I., Pereira, A., Mascarenhas, S., Martinho, C., Prada, R., Paiva, A.: The influence of empathy in human-robot relations. Int. J. Hum Comput Stud. **71**(3), 250–260 (2013). Elsevier
18. Pereira, A., Prada, R., Paiva, A.: Improving social presence in human-agent interaction. In: Proceedings of CHI 2014 - 32nd Annual ACM Conference on Human Factors in Computing Systems, pp. 1449–1458, Toronto, Canada. ACM (2014)
19. Dimas, J., Lopes, P., Prada, R.: One for all, all for one: agents with social identities. In: Proceedings of CogSci 2013 - 35th Annual Meeting of the Cognitive Science Society, pp. 2195–2200, Berlin, Germany. CSS (2013)

20. Prada, R., Ma, S., Nunes, M.A.: Personality in social group dynamics. In: Proceedings of International Conference on Computational Science and Engineering, vol. 4, pp. 607–612. IEEE (2009)
21. Dignum, F., Dignum, V., Prada, R., Jonker, C.M.: A conceptual architecture for social deliberation in multi-agent organizations: a position paper. Int. J. Multiagent Grid Syst. **11**(3), 147–166 (2015). IOS Press

Learning Analytics Model in a Casual Serious Game for Computer Programming Learning

Adilson Vahldick(✉), António José Mendes, and Maria José Marcelino

Department of Informatic Engineering, CISUC, University of Coimbra, Coimbra, Portugal
adilson.vahldick@udesc.br, {toze,zemar}@dei.uc.pt

Abstract. Games have been used by teachers as a support tool to engage students in learning tasks. As they often record student's performance as learning progresses, it interesting and useful to discuss how that information can be used to assess learning and to improve the learning experience. For instance, teachers can use that information to give personalized attention in classes. In computer programming learning, games can provide an alternative way to introduce concepts and, mainly, to practice them. This paper proposes a model to identify the students' progress considering their performance in programming tasks. The model is demonstrated by an implementation in a casual computer programming serious game.

Keywords: Novice programmers · Learning analytics · Fuzzy systems

1 Introduction

Initial programming learning is known to be complex for many students. Games have been proposed to help students in their initial learning stages, namely to increase their motivation and engagement with the learning process [1]. Two approaches have been used: creating and playing games. In the first approach students are asked to develop small games in order to apply the programming concepts [2]. In the second approach the students play games to reinforce and practice concepts and programming skills [3]. The main idea is to motivate students to the learning activities, shortening the time between theory and practice, and bringing together abstract concepts and concrete activities.

Digital educational environments generate vast amounts of track data that could be used for the development of learning theories and applications [4]. Learning Analytics (LA) rely on data generated by the user's interaction with these environments. LA approach applied in educational games is an alternative to more traditional forms to evaluate learning [5] and it avoids to brake the game-flow experience risking to lose student's interest [6]. We only found in literature one study with LA applied in programming learning games [7]. It proposed a framework with six axes. A mathematical model, relating each axis to a variable, was created to implement this framework. The game rates the student considering each variable and normalizes the data based on a teacher defined ideal behaviour.

C. Vaz de Carvalho et al. (Eds.): SGAMES 2016, LNICST 176, pp. 36–44, 2017.
DOI: 10.1007/978-3-319-51055-2_6

In this paper, we propose a LA model applied in computer programming games focused in the student's performance, rating them automatically based on the performance of their classmates. The model was designed as a Fuzzy Logic Controller (FLC). Fuzzy Logic is closer to human thinking and natural language than other artificial intelligence approaches [8]. The system is modelled using linguistic terms and thus it is easy to represent human knowledge [9].

Casual games usually have smooth learning curves and their assignments are often short [10]. These aspects should also be considered in the design of serious games reducing the time needed to learn the game features and mechanics, and freeing more time to learn [11]. We developed a casual serious game for initial computer programming learning, called NoBug's Snack Bar, using a Blocks-Based Programming (BBP) approach. In BBP the program is constructed through assembling functional blocks [12]. The LA model was tested in this game.

Section 2 presents the design principles followed and the architecture of the FLC to design and implement the LA model. Section 3 describes briefly the developed game and Sect. 4 explains the proposed model. Section 5 demonstrates its implementation and the data gathered by this model. The final section concludes the paper.

2 Fuzzy Logic Controller and Design

The essential part of a FLC is a set of linguistic control strategies based on expert knowledge mapped into an automatic control strategy [9]. A basic configuration of a FLC is depicted by a block diagram such as that shown in Fig. 1.

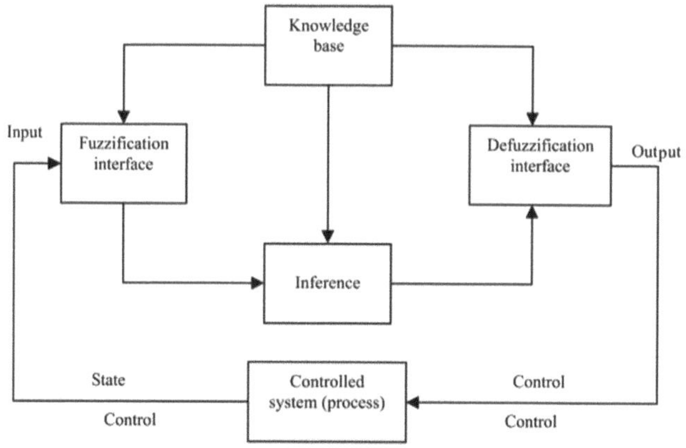

Fig. 1. Configuration of a FLC [9]

The controlled system represents a process that is regulated through a control action. The fuzzification interface is responsible for converting the input data (current state of the controlled system) into suitable linguistic values (fuzzy sets). The knowledge base module contains knowledge about all the input and output fuzzy partitions. The inference module simulates the human decision-making procedure based on fuzzy concepts, inferring fuzzy control actions to employ fuzzy implications and linguistic rules. The defuzzification interface converts the range of output values into the corresponding universe of discourse.

The design procedure of a FCL is divided in several steps as follows [8, 9]: 1-identification of the variables (states and controls); 2-normalization and partition of the variables space; 3-determination of the shapes of the fuzzy sets and their membership functions; 4-construction of the fuzzy rule base; 5-definition of the inference method; 6-determination of the defuzzification strategy.

There are many Fuzzy Logic software packages, as the MATLAB Fuzzy Toolbox and jFuzzyLogic [13]. jFuzzyLogic is an open source library written in Java that supports a Fuzzy Control Language (FCL) defined in the IEC-1131 specification. This specification defines the syntax and semantic of the FCL's components. jFuzzyLogic provides an API that interprets and executes a FCL program. It is also possible to define some or all members of a FLC through Java programming.

3 NoBug's SnackBar

NoBug's Snack Bar game mechanics are inspired in time management games. The player controls an attendant of a snack bar. Customers require some combination of foods and drinks, and the attendant must go to places where they are prepared, fetch them and serve them. The mission ends when the player meets all requests.

Figure 2 shows the game's interface. The animation area (on the left) shows the mission situation and shows the attendant behavior controlled by the player solution. The central area allows the construction of the mission solution. The player can run or debug her/his code. If she/he debugs, then the game shows the list of variables (at the right side of the figure) and runs one block at a time after each click of the debug button.

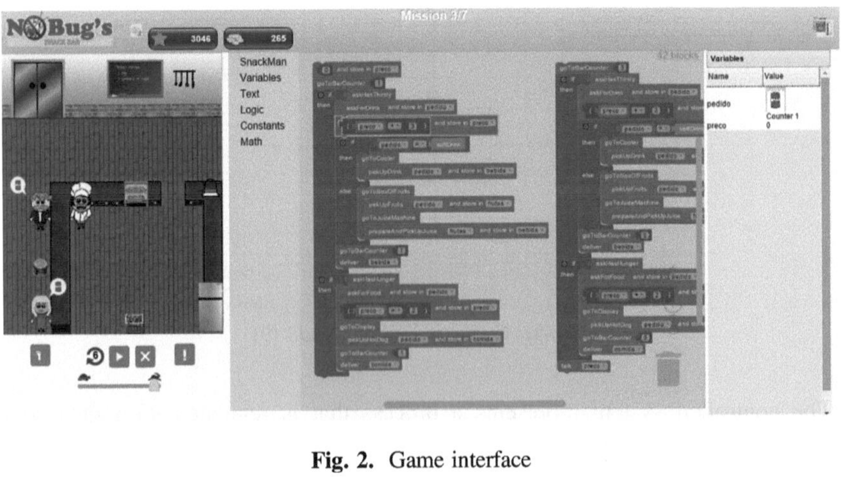

Fig. 2. Game interface

The game covers the initial topics usually included in introductory computer programming courses. It is divided in five levels with 55 missions: 1-Sequence actions (10 missions); 2-Variable manipulation (8 missions); 3-Conditionals (13 missions); 4-Loops (14 missions) and 5-Functions and arrays (10 missions). The first four missions in level one serve only to familiarize the student with basic interface of the game. That is the reason why we will not include them in our statistics in this paper.

4 LA Model in Computer Programming Learning Games

Following the FLC design procedure described in Sect. 2, our initial concerns were the definition of state and control variables, their partition in fuzzy subsets and the assignment of a membership function for each of them. The input variables of the proposed model are the missions' level and the time spent to solve them:

- **Mission:** classify the mission as introductory, development or mastery level.
- **Time Spent (TS):** is the accumulated time spent by the student to solve the last three missions. In our first experiments, we used the total time spent in the missions. However, after some tests, we verified that once a student had a bad performance in any previous mission, this was propagated for a very long time. Then we constrained it to the last three missions. This variable is partitioned into five subsets: *very fast, fast, normal, slow* and *very slow*. The subsets *very fast* and *very slow* are trapezoidal asymmetrical membership functions and the other three are trapezoidal symmetrical. The universe of discourse range varies according to students' experience. The students' performance in the game depends on several factors, such as the teaching methodology (learning content, assignments, etc.) and the previous programming knowledge or literacy (according to the region or country where the game is being used). To have a general model it is necessary to consider these divergences. We created a *Time Normalization* module to deal with these issues. This module assigns the membership function parameters dynamically, before it fuzzifies the input variables, performing 5 steps (Fig. 3). In the first step, the module retrieves from the game database the time spent in the previous three missions of each student using the Eq. 1:

$$TS_{(i,m)} = \frac{T_{(i,m-1)} + T_{(i,m-2)} + T_{(i,m-3)}}{3}. \qquad (1)$$

where i denotes the student identification, $i = 1$ denotes the current player which the system is computing for, m denotes the current mission, $T_{(x,\ y)}$ denotes the time spent on mission y by student x, and $TS_{(i,\ m)}$ denotes the average time spent on the three missions before the mth mission of student i. Thus, $TS(i, m)$ is the crisp value of the input variable TS. The second step identifies and removes students ($i >= 2$) with average time spent that are at least moderate outliers. The third step aims to create five clusters, one for each subset, of average times using the process of hierarchical cluster analysis (HCA) with the complete-linkage method [14]. The fourth step identifies the lowest (l)

and the highest (*g*) values on each cluster (*c1, c2, c3, c4, c5*) where *c1* has the lowest average time values and *c5* the highest values. The final step defines each membership function parameters (*veryfast, fast, normal, slow* and *veryslow*) as described in Eqs. 2, 3, 4, 5 and 6:

$$u_{veryfast}(x) = trape\left(x, 0, 0, c1(g), c2(l) + \frac{c2(g) - c2(l)}{2}\right). \quad (2)$$

$$u_{fast}(x) = trape(x, c1(g), c2(l), c2(g), c3(l)). \quad (3)$$

$$u_{normal}(x) = trape(x, c2(g), c3(l), c3(g), c4(l)). \quad (4)$$

$$u_{slow}(x) = trape(x, c3(g), c4(l), c4(g), c5(l)). \quad (5)$$

$$u_{veryslow}(x) = trape\left(x, c4(l) + \frac{c4(g) - c4(l)}{2}, c5(l), c5(g), c5(g)\right) \quad (6)$$

where $c_n(g)$ denotes the greatest value of cluster *n*, $c_n(l)$ denotes the lowest value of cluster *n*, and *x* denotes the parameter that is converted to a membership degree ($u_{membership}(x)$).

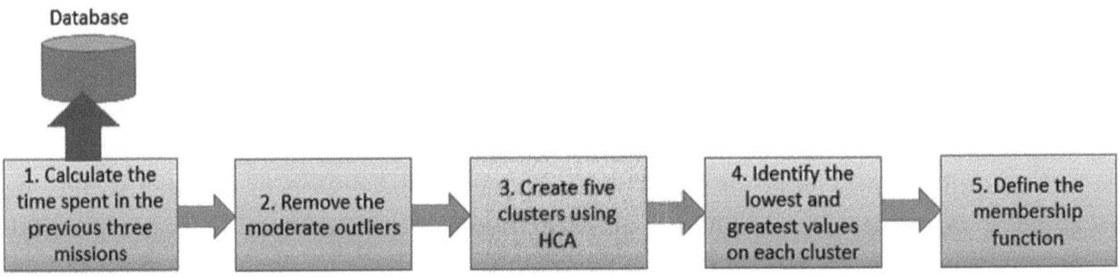

Fig. 3. Time Normalization module

The output variable is the *knowledge level* of the student. This variable is partitioned into three subsets (*bad, good* and *excellent*) and their membership function are triangles as defined in Table 1.

Table 1. Membership functions of the output variable *knowledge level*

Subsets	Membership functions
Bad	*trian (0, 0, 11)*
Good	*trian (10, 14, 18)*
Excellent	*trian (17, 20, 20)*

The next step of the FLC design is to define the inference method and form the rule base. The Mamdani inference method was adopted because it does not have nonlinear dynamic equations. The system rates a student according to the time she/he spends to solve the missions. Table 2 summarizes the rule-base, the relation between the two input variables and the output variable. When the player takes a long time to finish a mission, the model assumes that she/he has *bad* knowledge. On the other hand, the model rates the player as *excellent* when she/he finishes the mission *very fast*. In the other rules, the student classification varies according to the mission level. As the introductory missions presents new concepts and do not present challenges, it is expected that the player finishes them quickly. Yet the mastering missions are harder and full of constraints, really challenging the player.

Table 2. Fuzzy rule-base.

Mission	Time spent				
	Very slow	*Slow*	*Normal*	*Fast*	*Very fast*
Introductory	Bad	Bad	Bad	Good	Excellent
Development	Bad	Bad	Good	Good	Excellent
Mastering	Bad	Good	Good	Good	Excellent

Centre of Gravity is defined as the defuzzification method. Figure 4 shows the components relation of the proposed LA model. The ellipses are the input variables. The Time Normalization module accesses the database of the game and the current mission to define which is the time spent by the student and updates the knowledge base. The diamond designates the output variable.

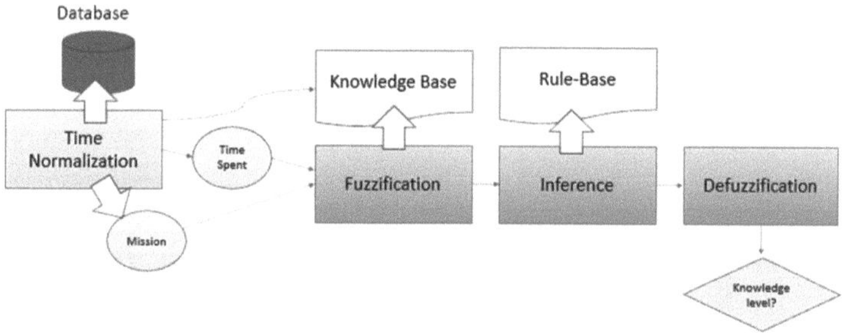

Fig. 4. LA Architecture

5 Implementation and Discussion

The proposed model was instantiated as a FLC in Java with jFuzzyLogic. The code below exemplifies the fuzzy rule-base by FCL. Nine rules were created to cover all the cells in Table 2. The variables definition was suppressed in the code because they were explained in the previous section.

LA model defined by IEC-FCL

```
FUNCTION_BLOCK nobugs_usecode
...
RULEBLOCK OnlyThis
  AND : MIN; OR  : MAX; ACT : MIN; ACCU : MAX;

  RULE 1 : IF TimeSpent IS verySlow THEN
               KnowledgeLevel IS bad;
  RULE 2 : IF TimeSpent IS fast THEN
               KnowledgeLevel IS good;
  RULE 3 : IF TimeSpent IS veryFast THEN
               KnowledgeLevel IS excellent;
  RULE 4 : IF Mission IS introductory AND
           TimeSpent IS slow THEN KnowledgeLevel IS bad;
  RULE 5 : IF Mission IS introductory AND
           TimeSpent  IS  normal  THEN  KnowledgeLevel  IS
bad;
  RULE 6 : IF Mission IS development AND
           TimeSpent IS slow THEN KnowledgeLevel IS bad;
  RULE 7 : IF Mission IS development AND
          TimeSpent  IS  normal  THEN  KnowledgeLevel  IS
good;
  RULE 8 : IF Mission IS mastering AND TimeSpent IS slow
                THEN KnowledgeLevel IS good;
  RULE  9  :  IF  Mission  IS  mastering  AND  TimeSpent  IS
normal
                THEN KnowledgeLevel IS normal;

END_RULEBLOCK
END_FUNCTION_BLOCK
```

We tested our game with 52 students. Figure 5 shows the results obtained in the first 15 missions, divided in introductory (1–7), development (8–11) and mastery (12–15).

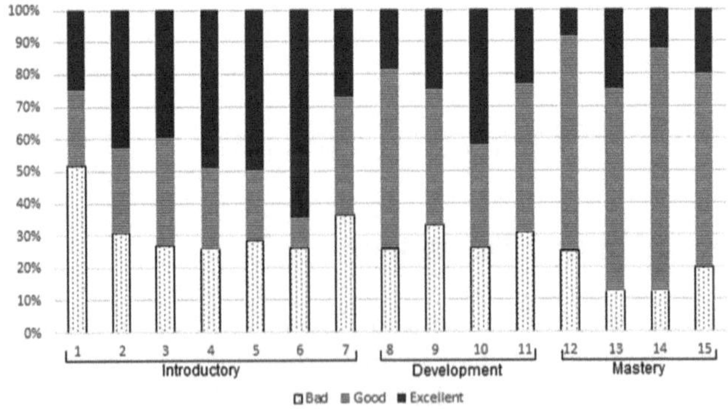

Fig. 5. Distribution of the students' knowledge classification

On average 30% of students are badly classified in introductory missions. This rate could alert the teacher or the game designers to review the missions. However, it is also observable that many students perform very well in the same missions. As the quantity of bad performing students is stable in introductory missions, maybe the teacher should address individually those students. As the students advance in the game, less of them are classified as excellent. This also happens frequently in the classroom: the very well performing students are a small part of the class.

6 Conclusions

Serious games are played in computer programming classes to motivate students overcome the initial natural barriers. However, to maximize the adoption of games in educational settings, it is important that teachers could track the overall progress of the students. In this paper, we presented a LA model based essentially on the time spent by the student to finish each mission. The model classifies the student (as bad, good or excellent) taking into consideration each mission level. We tested the model during a fist experiment. We found out that initially most students were classified as bad or excellent. However, as students advance in the game, they had a more similar performance and more students are classified as good. Although more experiments are necessary to evolve and validate the model, we believe this information can be used by teachers to adapt their lessons giving special attention to less performing students.

Acknowledgments. AV acknowledges the doctoral scholarship supported by CNPq/CAPES – Programa Ciência sem Fronteiras – CsF (6392-13-0) and authorized retirement by UDESC (688/13). We also want to thank the students that played the game and their teachers that allowed us to try it with them.

References

1. Vahldick, A., Mendes A.J., Marcelino, M.J.: A review of games designed to improve introductory computer programming competencies. In: 44th Annual Frontiers in Education Conference, Madrid, Spain, pp 781–787 (2014)
2. Bayliss, J.D., Strout, S.: Games as a "flavor" of CS1. In: 37th SIGCSE Technical. Symposium on Computer Science Education, Houston, Texas, pp. 500–504 (2006)
3. Barnes T., Powell E., Chaffin A., et al.: Game2Learn: building CS1 learning games for retention. In: 12th SIGCSE Conference on Innovation and Technology in Computer Science Education, Dundee, Scotland, pp. 121–125 (2007)
4. Greller, W., Drachsler, H.: Translating learning into numbers: a generic framework for learning analytics. Educ. Technol. Soc. **15**, 42–57 (2012)
5. Shute, V.J., Ke, F.: Games, learning, and assessment. In: Ifenthaler, D., Eseryel, D., Ge, X. (eds.) Assessment in Game-Based Learning. Foundations, Innovations, and Perspectives, pp. 43–58. Springer, New York (2012)
6. Chen, J.: Flow in games (and everything else). Commun. ACM **50**, 31 (2007)

7. Malliarakis, C., Satratzemi, M., Xinogalos, S.: Integrating learning analytics in an educational MMORPG for computer programming. In: 14th International Conference on Advanced Learning Technologies, ICALT 2014, pp. 233–237 (2014)
8. Jantzen, J.: Foundations of Fuzzy Control. Wiley, Chichester (2007)
9. Lee, K.H.: First Course on Fuzzy Theory and Applications. Springer, Heidelberg (2005)
10. Juul, J.: A Casual Revolution: Reinventing Video Games and Their Players. MIT Press, Cambridge (2010)
11. Landers, R.N., Callan, R.C.: Casual social games as serious games: The psychology of gamification in undergraduate education and employee training. In: Ma, M., Oikonomou, A., Jain, L.C. (eds.) Serious Games Edutainment Applications, pp. 399–423. Springer, London (2011)
12. Nor S., Mohamad H., Patel A., et al.: Block-based programming approach: Challenges and benefits. In: International Conference on Electrical Engineering and Informatics, Bandung, Indonesia, pp. 4–8 (2011)
13. Cingolani P., Alcalá-Fdez J.: jFuzzyLogic: a robust and flexible fuzzy-logic inference system language implementation. In: IEEE World Congress on Computational Intelligence, Brisbane, pp. 1090–1097 (2012)
14. Johnson, S.C.: Hierarchical clustering schemes. Psychometrika **32**, 241–254 (1967)

GLAID: Designing a Game Learning Analytics Model to Analyze the Learning Process in Users with Intellectual Disabilities

Ana R. Cano[1(✉)], Baltasar Fernández-Manjón[1], and Álvaro J. García-Tejedor[2]

[1] Universidad Complutense de Madrid, Madrid, Spain
anarcano@ucm.es, balta@fdi.ucm.es
[2] Universidad Francisco de Vitoria, Madrid, Spain
a.gtejedor@ceiec.es

Abstract. Educational Games are increasingly popular in teaching as they have proven to be effective learning tools. Educational videogames are beneficial for all kind of students but we think they are especially suited for users with intellectual disabilities due to the opportunity of tailoring the content to their in-game performance. Adapting the game experience to the cognitive and learning abilities to this type of students also make videogames a powerful source of learning data. In this paper we introduce the GLAID (Game Learning Analytics for Intellectual Disabilities) Model, a theoretical adaptation of a more general analytics framework. It describes how to collect, process and analyze videogame interaction data in order to provide an overview of the user learning experience, from an individualized assessment to a collective perspective. But to obtain these goals it is necessary to take into account the restrictions and special needs of users with intellectual disabilities both in the learning design and in translating them into game mechanics and the corresponding observables that will be collected for the subsequent data analysis. We conclude with a discussion and considerations about the model and future steps to follow in our investigation.

Keywords: Serious games · Intellectual Disabilities · Game Learning Analytics · Analytics maturity framework · Educational games · Down syndrome · Autism spectrum disorders

1 Introduction

The impact of new technologies on education is changing the way teaching is occurring in the classroom as technology can ease a more active approach of the students in their own learning process. Videogames are increasingly used in education because of their capacity to engage the user, making the learning experience a more dynamic activity where the student needs to make decisions and learn from their effects. Educational videogames are attractive and engaging to students. Usually, videogames are designed to adapt the game experience to different users, offering different levels of difficulty or tailoring the content to the in-game performance [1].

C. Vaz de Carvalho et al. (Eds.): SGAMES 2016, LNICST 176, pp. 45–52, 2017.
DOI: 10.1007/978-3-319-51055-2_7

But videogames can also be used as research and/or measurement tool [2], giving educators the opportunity of collecting information about the user's behavior and interactions within the game. A game, due to its highly interactive nature, can generate larger amounts of data than other tools [3]. When using an educational videogame, it is possible to record all the interactions of the player during the game session in order to track the evolution of the student and use that data to better understand or to improve the learning process. The processing and analysis of all that interaction data and transform it into valuable information for the student's assessment is the target that we pursue with the application of our model. The emerging field that address these aspects is called Learning Analytics (LA), defined as "the measurement, collection, analysis and report data about learners and their context, for purposes of understanding and optimizing learning and the environments in which it occurs" [4].

The application of LA in educational videogames is called Game Learning Analytics (GLA) and combines the educational goals of LA with the tools and technologies from Game Analytics [5]. GLA is specifically conceived to facilitate the process of analyzing significant variables or observables (like playing time, level changes or goals achieved) to better understand how users learn and to provide a better assessment.

All these GLA processes of automatic collection and analysis of interaction data become even more important when the students are people with special needs. For instance, intellectual disabilities cause several communication problems [6] that can prevent educators to understand the way students are processing the information and the effectiveness of their learning experience. This makes very difficult to use standard game evaluations that are usually based on pre-post forms that users fill before and after playing the game.

In this article we introduce the GLAID Model as a variation of the classical Analytics Maturity Framework defined by the Big Data industry [7]. This model is intended to describe the different stages of data that educators and game designers can analyze from students with intellectual disabilities when they are playing a learning video game. The last section of the article discusses recommendations and next steps to follow this line of research.

2 The Importance of Game Design While Working with Users with Intellectual Disabilities: Restrictions, Requirements and Game and Learning Design

Users with intellectual disabilities have problems not only interacting with the game but also communicating the difficulties found while they are playing. As a result, we cannot fully rely on their testimony when we are evaluating their learning experience within the game.

Some of these communication problems can be troubles in ordering thoughts and language in a 'logical' layout; problems learning to listen and taking turns in conversations; difficulties using communication in an interactive sense or problems relating objects and actions to spoken or written words [8]. LA can help to address this issue by evaluating the adequacy of the learning experience to this kind of users through an indirect way: a data-driven analysis instead of a subjective responses analysis.

Creating an adequate learning videogame suitable for users with intellectual disabilities requires to have in mind all the player special needs that can affect the game mechanics. Defining the user characteristics and cognitive restrictions and translating them into formal user requirements is a pre-requisite to build an inclusive game design. That information would be used in the learning design and in the identification of information about the learning process that will be collected and analyzed. Therefore, a good design is essential to obtain meaningful data for a reliable assessment.

User features, either cognitive, psychological or motor, determine the learning methods to design the mechanics of the game (like the possibility of select the difficulty level adapted to each user or the use of a dynamic pop-up aid) and the interpretation of the collected interaction information.

Some of the user's restrictions and characteristics that designers should consider during the development of a learning game, specifically for players with intellectual disabilities, divided by psychological areas can be [9–11]: (Table 1)

Once we know what is distinctive in this type of users, the second step is to translate these characteristics into formal user requirements. Having specific cognitive accessibility guidelines, like the ones that appear in the standard WCAG 2.0 [12] or in the GAG [13], can be used to streamline the design process.

Table 1. User characteristics related to intelligence, memory and perception, personality and motor skills

Intelligence, Memory and Perception
- Visual perception and visual retention better than hearing
- Procedural memory good enough for playing
- Short Memory limitation. Limitation in the number of instructions/numbers that they can handle at the same time (3 sequential instructions and 3–6 digits)
- Difficulty sustaining attention during long periods of time
- Mild intellectual deficiency
- Problems of understanding the information
- Difficulty in the process of abstraction, conceptualization, generalization and learning transfer
Personality
- Limited initiative
- Persistence of behavior and resistance to change
- Few response capacity and reaction to the environment
- Poor social and collaboration skills (depending on the disability)
Biological and Motor Skills
- Listening and sight problems
- Heart diseases
- Clumsiness in motor skills (gross and fine)
- Poor coordination

The application of the standards and a deep knowledge of the idiosyncrasy of the user and can minimize the number of backward changes in an agile videogame development.

3 The Game Learning Analytics for Intellectual Disabilities Model

Once known the user unique characteristics and how this affects the translation of the learning design into game mechanics, next step would be working on creating an effective game design suitable for the users. The development should also include the traces of information needed for the students' assessment inside the code.

Since there are not reference guides to include GLA in videogames for players with intellectual disabilities, we adapted a classical analytics framework used in the business industry [7] to create our own model. We called it Game Learning Analytics for Intellectual Disabilities (GLAID) Model. This model describes what type of data would be useful to collect, group and analyze to provide an overview of the learning experience of each user from an individualized assessment to a collective perspective. The last step of the model is the prediction of the potential behavior of new players within the game and the evolution of the learning progress of existing users, attending to the learning experience, based on other users' historical data.

In this section we describe each step of the model and its correlation with each phase of the analytics framework. (Figure 1).

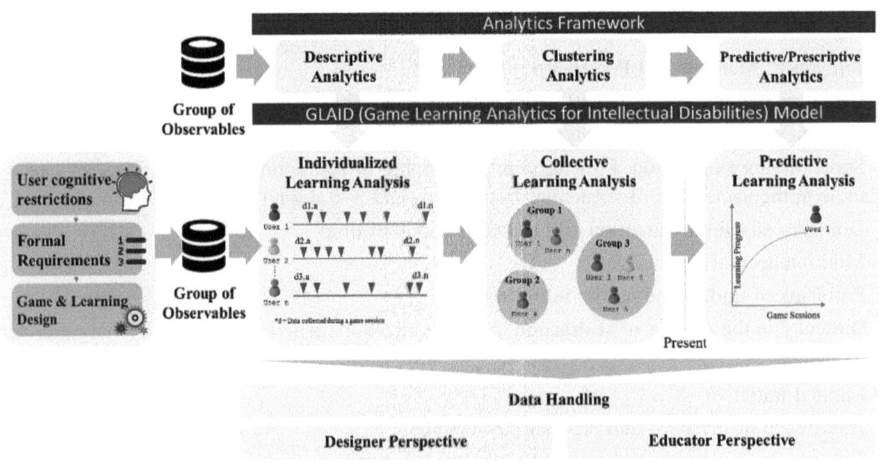

Fig. 1. Analytics maturity stages of the GLAID

3.1 Individualized Learning Analysis

The first step of the GLAID Model is the *Individualized Learning Analysis.* This phase corresponds with the *Descriptive Analytics* stage. The goal in this phase is to describe and analyze historical learning data from the student's perspective.

In this phase, educators and game designers collect all the interactions of the user within the game to analyze which data are/are not relevant for future assessment. The real challenge of this stage is taking into account all the users' special requirements, the learning design and the game design to select the signals or game observables (i.e. variables) that can give useful information about the user's learning behavior. Once the variables are identified, educators can describe the trends of each student for a personalized assessment. The better the design is adapted to the cognitive features of the user, the easier the assessment can be settled.

Typical data to collect and analyze in this stage can be:

- **Timestamps**. Generating a trace with data about when the user starts, ends, quits the game or stays inactive [14] provide relevant information about the level of engagement of the player, the effectiveness of the game design and the evolution of the learning process.
- **Level changes**. Videogames are structured by levels, screens, missions or chapters. Tracing each level status during a certain period of time can help educators and researchers to figure out if the student is understanding the purpose of the game and, as a result, if the learning experience is being successful.
- **Achievements vs Fails**. Tracing the evolution of the ratio achievements/fails during several consecutive game sessions is a good indicator about how the user's learning experience is progressing.
- **User interactions**. Any user interaction like number of clicks, *heatmaps*, number of times that the help button is pressed, time between clicks, number of attempts completing a task, etc. can be potentially useful for the assessment, giving a more comprehensive overview about the behavior of the student inside the game.

Data handling, visualization and interpretation is described below, in its own separate section.

3.2 Collective Learning Analysis

The next level of maturity in GLAID is the *Collective Learning Analysis* where the researcher and educator could identify causes of trends and learning outcomes of a group of users. In this stage, a collection of reports and statistics are generated from the perspective of a class, a group, or even more granular, a certain type of disability. As an example, we can obtain relevant information about the level of understanding of users with Autism Spectrum Disorder (ASD) tracing data and patterns throughout their common conducts inside the game.

The purpose of the clustering analysis is to diagnose learning outlines in different segments to obtain conclusions about how the learning process of different users with a common pattern has occurred. The game designer can obtain information about the adequacy of the game's mechanics to certain types of disabilities or groups of users (i.e. players with Down Syndrome between 10 to 15 years old that play twice a week obtain better results that those with ASD in the same range of age and playing three times a week). It can also be used to test the efficacy of some of the decisions made on the learning design.

Clustering methods or any other machine learning techniques can be applied in this stage to uncover patterns in the data that provide additional unknown information from the previous stage of the model.

3.3 Predictive/Prescriptive Learning Analysis

The *Predictive Learning Analysis* is the third and last phase of the model. It embodies a group of statistical techniques and analyzes current and historical data (obtained in the descriptive analysis and clustering analysis/machine learning phase) to make predictions about future learning outcomes [15]. To make accurate predictions it is necessary to collect data from a large population of users (which could be problematic in this case due to the specificities of the target users).

3.4 Data Handling

The information described above can be automatically collected and displayed in reports, but data visualization would differ depending on the recipient of the report and its final purpose.

Ideally, educators and researchers should be able to get insight about how the user has been playing within the game at a glance of the report, without directly observe the user playing. The analysis of the data collected can be done through two different perspectives:

1. **Game Designer's perspective**. The game designer is interested in collecting and analyzing all the states that the user can reach at any moment within a game session. The purpose of this analysis is to determine if the gameplay and mechanics designed are properly adapted to the user and effective for their cognitive, psychological and motor capabilities.
2. **Educator's perspective**. The educator is focused on each user learning experience and this report should provide the relevant data about it. Videogames can be considered as a new learning tool that offer useful information that may not be collected using traditional methodologies, like the exact number of failures/achievement in each learning session. Ideally this report should inform the educator if the user is learning or struggling with the game or at least help them to identify users that may need some extra support.

4 Conclusions and Future Work

Our paper proposes a model called GLAID (Game Learning Analytics for Intellectual Disabilities) that aims to incorporate different levels of data treatment into a learning game development for users with intellectual disabilities, like Down syndrome, mild cognitive impairments or Autism Spectrum Disorders.

Although the model proposed is theoretical and should apply to any development, some considerations about it deserve discussion: The game engine used for the development should allow collecting the observables to analyze the learning process. We are currently working on the development of a GLA module for Unity3D engine as part of the H2020 RAGE project that can address this issue and can work as an example to replicate for other game engines. Once this module is working, the application of the GLAID model to the data handling will be easier. But this still requires that the learning design and game mechanics should be specifically designed for the gamers that are going to use the videogame as a learning tool. As long as there is a wide range of cognitive conditions, it is not possible to fully standardize the game design process but the application of this framework step by step should provide feedback depending on the commonalities and divergences found in the target audience. The help of experts (not only psychologists, social workers or specialized teachers but also game and interactions designers) is essential to obtain a truly valuable learning game. The application of our model is focused on users with intellectual impairments, which struggle with several communication problems making the process of obtaining feedback of the player more complex and less reliable.

Next step in our investigation will be the evaluation of the GLAID model using a case study, a 3D adventure game currently under development called *Downtown: A subway Adventure.* The game exploits playful aspects to improve the learning process of young people with Down syndrome and other impairments to increase their autonomy using the public transportation system. We are currently finishing the game and selecting the variables and data that researchers and educators will need to evaluate the effectiveness of the game design and the user learning experience. Once the development is finished, users will test the game, data will be collected and analyzed and future conclusions and lessons learned about the model will be released.

Acknowledgements. The e-UCM research group has been partially funded by Regional Government of Madrid (eMadrid S2013/ICE-2715), by the Ministry of Education (TIN2013-46149-C2-1-R) and by the European Commission (RAGE H2020-ICT-2014-1-644187, BEACONING H2020-ICT-2015-687676). The CEIEC Institute has been partially funded by the Francisco de Vitoria University (UFV-2015-05).

References

1. Annetta, L., Minogue, J., Holmes, S., Cheng, M.: Investigating the impact of video games on high school students' engagement and learning about genetics. Comput. Educ. **53**, 74–85 (2009)

2. Griffiths, M.: The educational benefits of videogames. Educ. Health **20**(3), 47–51 (2002)
3. Campbell, D.: Xbox Data is XXL. In: Strata Conference 2013, Santa Clara, California, 28 February 2013. https://www.youtube.com/watch?v=ZLKf1AhLQ30&feature=youtu.be. Accessed 10 Mar 2016
4. Long, P., Siemenes, G.: Penetrating the fog: analytics in learning and education. In: 1st International Conference on Learning Analytics and Knowledge, Banff, Alberta, Canada (2011)
5. Freire, M., Serrano-Laguna, A., Manero, B., Martínez-Ortiz, I., Moreno-Ger, P., Fernández-Manjón, B.: Game learning analytics. In: Learning Analytics for Serious Games (2015)
6. Roberts, J., Price, J., Malkin, C.: Language and communication development in down syndrome. Ment. Retard. Dev. Disabil. Res. Rev. Spec. Issue: Lang. Commun. **13**(1), 26–35 (2007)
7. Gartner, Introduction to the Gartner Maturity Model for Web Analytics, 03 July 2008. https://www.gartner.com/doc/713210/introduction-gartner-maturity-model-web. Accessed 03 Mar 2016
8. Australian Government. Department of Families, Housing, Community Services and Indigenous Affairs, "Intellectual disabilities, communication and learning", 20 January 2009. http://resources.fahcsia.gov.au/consumertrainingsupportproducts/employers/intellectual_disability/sec3.htm. Accessed 11 Mar 2016
9. Arranz, P.: Niños y jóvenes con Síndrome de Down, Egido Editorial (2002)
10. Troncoso, M., Jesús, F.: Síndrome de Down: Avances en acción familiar, Santander: Fundación Síndrome de Down de Cantabria (1988)
11. Chapman, R., Hesketh, L.: Behavioral phenotype of individuals with Down Syndrome. Ment. Retard. Dev. Disabil. Res. Rev. **6**(2), 84–95 (1999)
12. W3C World Wide Web Consortium, "WCAG 2.0." http://www.w3.org/TR/WCAG20/. Accessed 09 Mar 2016
13. Ablegamers Foundation, "Game Accessibililty Guidelines," 2012–2015. http://gameaccessibilityguidelines.com/. Accessed 09 Mar 2016
14. Serrano-Laguna, A., Torrente, J., Moreno-Ger, P., Fernández-Manjón, B.: Tracing a little for big improvements: application of learning anañytics and videogames for student assessment. Procedia Comput. Sci. **15**, 203–209 (2012)
15. Nyce, C.: Predictive Analytics White Paper, American Institute for Chartered Property Casualty Underwriters/Insurance Institute of America (2007)

Automatic Extraction of Gameplay Design Expertise: An Approach Based on Semantic Annotation

Kaouther Raies[1,4(✉)], Maha Khemaja[2,4], and Yemna Mejbri[3,4]

[1] Faculty of Economic Sciences and Management of Sfax, Sfax, Tunisia
kaoutherraies@yahoo.fr
[2] The Higher Institute of Applied Sciences and Technology of Sousse, Sousse, Tunisia
maha_khemaja@yahoo.fr
[3] National School of Computer Sciences of Tunisia, Mannouba, Tunisia
mejbriyemna@yahoo.fr
[4] Prince Research Group, ISITCom, University of Sousse, GP1 Hammam Sousse, 4011 Sousse, Tunisia

Abstract. A Game Based Learning System (GBLS) constitutes an interesting learning environment. However, many problems are facing the general adoption of learning approaches based on this system. For instance, complexity of GBLS design process and problems of integrating learning outcomes with fun aspects constitute the major challenges. Therefore, novice game designer have not only to acquire specific skills and expertise but also to acquire them in an efficient and active pedagogical manner. For that aim, extraction and representation of knowledge related to GBLSs design become necessary to render possible accessibility and transfer of that knowledge to novice actors and further to meet aforementioned challenges. In this context the use of learning ontology techniques based on semantic annotation of gameplay description seems promising as it facilitates knowledge extraction, elicitation process, and grants more formal knowledge representation which allows answering to growing needs of sharing data within and across organizations and actors.

Keywords: GBLS · Gameplay · Automatic knowledge extraction · Ontology learning

1 Introduction

Despite the numerous Internet monitoring tools and content management systems to acquire Experts' knowledge, Knowledge collecting process is still performed manually. Generally, this gathering process leads to the construction of knowledge sheets that sum up all the information (theoretical and technical competencies), which make difficult the knowledge accessibility, representation and sharing.

To tackle this issue, several research studies have shown the importance of integrating various tools to enhance knowledge discovery and extraction [1].

C. Vaz de Carvalho et al. (Eds.): SGAMES 2016, LNICST 176, pp. 53–63, 2017.
DOI: 10.1007/978-3-319-51055-2_8

In this paper, we aim to extract GBLS gameplay design knowledge and make them accessible to novice GBLS designer. For that purpose, we use automatic knowledge extraction based on semantic annotation. This allows to: (i) Exploit the considerable increase of freely available data about gameplay design, (ii) Acquire and present knowledge in a machine-readable and machine-interpretable format, (iii) Answer to the growing need of making this knowledge accessible and (iv) to foster opportunities of sharing data within and across organizations and actors participating in GBLSs design processes.

This proposal follows the following steps: problem identification and motivation, definition of the objectives for a solution, design and development, demonstration and validation.

This paper is organized as follows: In Sect. 2 we describe the problem's statement and major difficulties to overcome; in Sect. 3 we present works related to expertise and knowledge extraction approaches, automatic knowledge extraction methods as well as works having dealt with eventual tentative of extracting GBLS gameplay design knowledge; in Sect. 4 we detail the approach of Automatic Extraction of GBLS Gameplay Design Expertise by presenting fundamental steps of extraction process. In Sect. 5 we conclude and outline our future works.

2 Problem Statement

GBLSs are considered as a branch of serious games that deal with applications that have defined learning outcomes [2].

Actors participating in this process still suffer from many challenges that span all over the design and development cycle. Problems of integrating enough educational outcomes without sacrificing the fun characteristics and problems inherent to the complexity of each step in a GBLS design process are already well entrenched and critical which require relevant expertise to be resolved.

According to [3], designing serious games where fun qualities and serious aspects are integrated and respected requires specific skills and expertise in terms of theoretical and technical knowledge background.

Unfortunately, novice game designers who do not have technical and theoretical competency inspired from both educational and video games systems cannot successfully create GBLS.

For that aim, we shall have an appropriate environment allowing the participating actor to curry out his/her tasks efficiently either alone or collaboratively. The overall system should be enough flexible and able to cope with business domain changes or IT changes. The same system must provide to novice actors relevant assistance accordingly to their skills, tasks and context in order to achieve their jobs effectively. Figure 1 presents fundamental components of our future system which is based on two major components. The first one is relative to gameplay design process; it presents steps to follow by the game designer [4]. The second one contains four models (gameplay model, game designer model, error model and pedagogical model). The gameplay model presents the set of knowledge to be required, actions to be performed and rules to be respected by the game designer. The game designer model presents skills and context of the current actor which can determine the type of system intervention. The error model, presents the set of game designer errors, which are classified in categories. The Pedagogical model determines the teaching methods as well as the way in which the intervention can take place (alert notification, assistance messages, a detailed explanation …..).

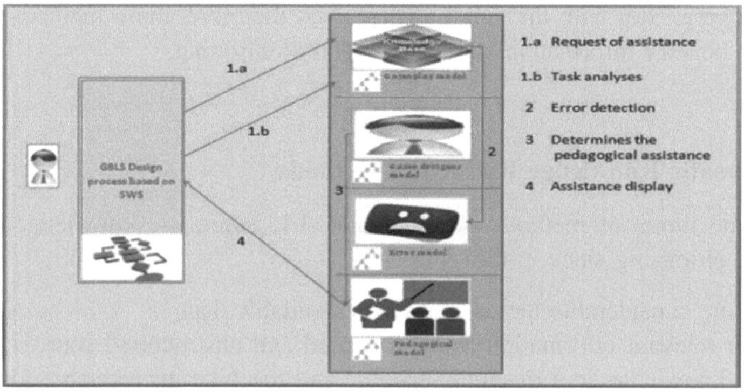

Fig. 1. Architecture of the GBLS design platform

In this paper we focus on the development of the gameplay model through the extraction and representation of knowledge related to GBLSs design and especially that of gameplay design.

3 Related Work

Over the last decade, due to the considerable increase of freely available data, the extraction of relevant information from structured and unstructured content has encouraged researchers in acquiring expertise knowledge.

In this section, we will present expertise knowledge extraction approaches as well as automatic knowledge extraction methods. Alternatively, we will describe eventual attempts among knowledge extraction applied to GBLS design and we attempt to highlight their respective limitations.

3.1 Knowledge Acquisition Methods

According to [5], there are five methods that can be used to extract expertise knowledge from human experts. These are respectively method of familiar tasks, method of structured and unstructured interviews, method of constrained processing task and method of tough cases. These methods require a detailed analysis of expert's tasks, tactics and strategies.

The shortcomings of these methods are that they:

- Provide imperfect results if they are applied separately.
- Provide data in non standardized format which requires further analyses and transcription.
- Are based on a single expert which can result a single line of reasoning that makes it difficult to evoke in depth discussions of the domain. Moreover, not all expert knowledge resides with the single expert. And therefore, these methods might not actually be very informative about the expert's reasoning.

3.2 Automatic Knowledge Extraction Methods

To overcome limits of methods cited in Sect. 3.1, automatic knowledge extraction seems very promising since it allows to:

- Exploit the considerable increase of freely available data.
- Discover relevant information from structured and unstructured sources.
- Acquire knowledge in a machine-readable and machine-interpretable format.

In this context, the use of learning ontology techniques can facilitate not only knowledge extraction and elicitation processes, but also grants more formal knowledge representation which allows to answer to the growing need of sharing data within and across organizations and actors.

Learning Ontology, also called ontology population and enrichment, is the task of extending an existing ontology with additional objects as instances, concepts and semantic relations. This task is considered as a knowledge acquisition task [6]. The process of constructing, enriching and populating ontologies is considered as resource demanding and time-consuming. Thus, the automated or semi-automated construction, enrichment and population of ontologies are highly desired.

In [7] authors propose an incremental process to populate ontology, including 4 steps:

- Ontology-based Semantic Annotation: The instances of the domain ontology are used to semantically annotate a domain-specific corpus in an automatic way. In this step disambiguation techniques are used exploiting knowledge captured in the domain ontology.
- Knowledge Discovery: An information extraction module is used in this step to locate new ontological instances. The module is trained, using machine learning methods, on the annotated corpus of the previous step.
- Knowledge Refinement: A compression-based clustering algorithm is used in this step for identifying lexicographic variants for each instance supporting the ontology enrichment.
- Validation and Insertion: A domain expert validates the candidate instances that have been added to the ontology.

This process demands human intervention to validate and insert extracted entities, which constitutes a very time consuming and error prone task.

In [8], authors decompose the ontology learning process into six steps. Starting by identifying terms (objects), then defining synonyms terms, thereafter selecting concepts and finally establishing relations and acquiring rules.

This process neglects an important task related to redundancy detection, which constitutes the major defect of this approach.

Authors in [6] consider that the ontology learning process involves population, enrichment, and inconsistency resolution steps. Indeed, an initial ontology is used to analyze and extract information from a corpus. The extracted information is used to populate and enrich the ontology. This process continues until no more information can be extracted from the corpus. In every cycle the consistency of the ontology is checked and redundancy problems are detected.

3.3 Knowledge Extraction Methods Applied to GBLS Design

Authors in [3] present an overall classification system for Serious Games. The intention of this classification is to guide people through the vast field of Serious Games by providing them with a general overview. For that aim, authors present a G/P/S model (Gameplay/Purpose/Scope model) that propose a classification based on gameplay, purpose and scope criteria of the game.

Authors have built a collaborative online database. This database assembles the classification information about 550 Serious Games. The G/P/S model it is not able to provide detailed information concerning serious games design knowledge which constitutes its main limitation.

In similar approaches, [9–11] propose classification systems to index games according to the "markets" that use them (i.e. the kind of people who play them).

Proposed solutions are not able to provide detailed information concerning Serious Games. It can only differentiate between games according to a limit number of criteria (target audience, purpose, …). These limits restrict the general use of this system to respond to GBLS designer's requirements. Additionally, they are based on the applications of Serious Games rather than on the games Design process.

To conclude, we did not find any research work that aims to extract automatically GBLSs design knowledge, and present that knowledge through a precise and semantic model. At the best of our knowledge, there are no works based on semantic web technologies to automatically extract information specific to GBLS from texts and to give a structured organization to such knowledge.

In order to reap the full benefits of automatic knowledge extraction techniques, we opt to use learning ontology techniques.

In the present paper, we will focus on the enrichment and the population of the GBLS gameplay ontology developed in [12] to:

- Entail the semantic description of the concepts related to GBLS gameplay design process.
- Present the set of experts' knowledge about gameplay design.
- Specify the knowledge about tasks to be performed when designing GBLS.
- Present the set of knowledge that the novice game designers have to acquire.

4 Automatic Extraction of GBLS Gameplay Design Expertise

4.1 GBLS Gameplay Design Expertise

Helping beginners to acquire a new set of competencies related to GBLS gameplay design consists on acquiring a set of fundamental competencies responded on both, the game designer profile and the game design job. Figure 2 presents GBLS game designer competencies model.

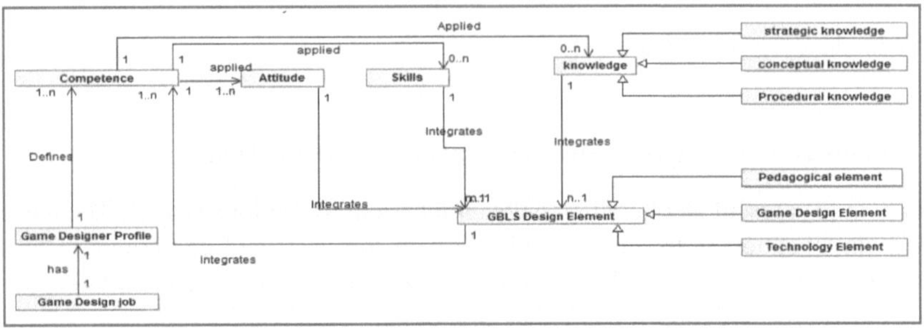

Fig. 2. GBLS designer competencies

These competencies are applied on three axes:

The first axe includes attitudes: which present the work methods, they determine not only the sequence of steps to follow but also capability of adapting their approach to the project problems, the communication and coordination with the GBLS design team. The second axe concerns skills related to manipulating new technologies as the GBLS design constitutes a permanent evolution field. The final axe concerns Knowledge that includes three main types [13] as conceptual knowledge, procedural knowledge and strategic knowledge.

Conceptual knowledge: presents different static knowledge about facts and concepts related to GBLS gameplay design. This type of knowledge is presented in Fig. 3. Procedural knowledge: includes the set of operations that can be applied on concepts to make transition from one problem state to another. The final type of knowledge concerns the capability that enables game designer to combine its procedural and conceptual knowledge with change adaptation. It can be seen as a general plan of actions in which the sequence of solutions activities is laid down. It concerns knowing how to organize and interpret the information given.

The Automatic Extraction of Gameplay Design Expertise focuses on collecting conceptual knowledge of GBLS gameplay design presented in Fig. 3.

Indeed, as the GBLS gameplay design was presented through ontology [12], enrichment and population of this ontology with information extracted from various sources in automatic is a pertinent solution. It's giving the opportunity to exploit web resources of gameplay that contains necessary knowledge to be acquired.

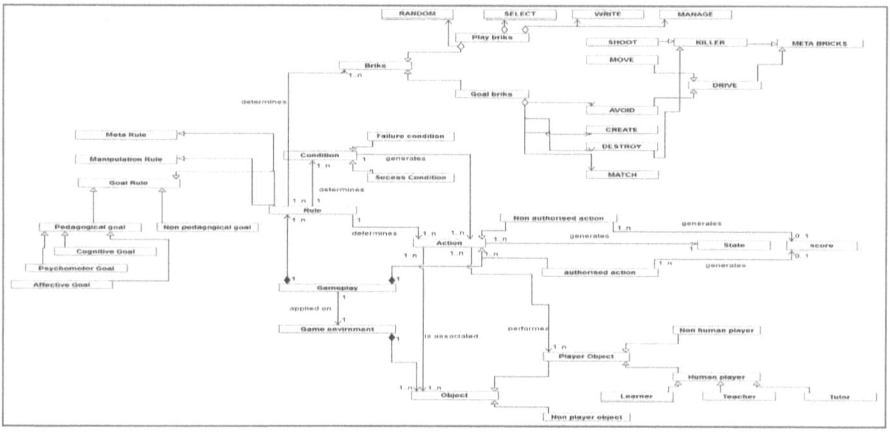

Fig. 3. GBLS gameplay model: conceptual knowledge

4.2 GBLS Gameplay Ontology Population and Enrichment

The attraction of using a semantic technology, to address the problem of gameplay modeling, lies in its potential to associate a semantic network of knowledge related to gameplay description.

These descriptions can then be exploited to add new instances, concepts, relations and rules to the gameplay ontology, providing the developer with new ways and knowledge to design GBLS gameplay.

Two fundamental tasks are addressed to obtain the aforementioned goals, the semantic annotation and the Ontology Learning.

In fact, gameplay descriptions come from multiple resources such as those presented in game instructions, descriptions, and presentation or in GDDs (Game Design Documents).

For this end, four tasks can be identified. The first task concerns initial ontology building. The second task is related to the addition of new instances of concepts/relations into the initial ontology to produce the populated ontology, usually by locating the corresponding object/terms and synonyms in the corpus. The third task is the consistency resolution; it is the responsible for remedying problems introduced by population and enrichment to obtain the consistent ontology. After that, the obtained ontology is exported as RDF file and finally, performance evaluation can be calculated.

Figure 4 depicts a typical Ontology Learning process that we will describe in details in the following sections.

Corpus construction The corpus is composed of GBLS gameplay descriptions collected from many resources as game instructions presented in social network e.g. facebook, Game Design Documents….

For that aim, we select GBLS designed in different periods to limit the impact of technological change on the results that may be obtained. Also, we choose GBLS with single players and GBLS with graphical outputs. Figure 5 presents GBLS description corpus.

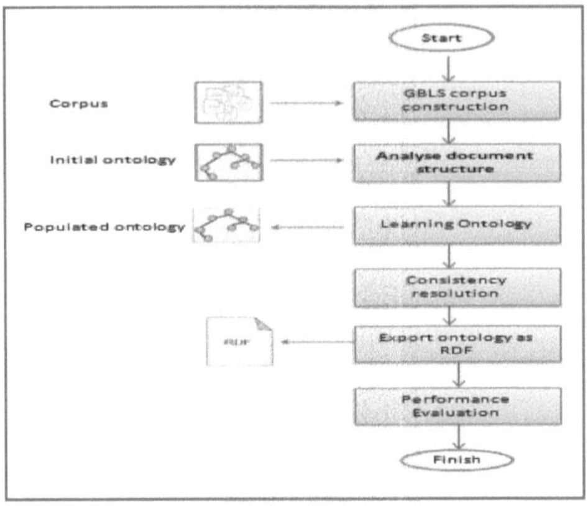

Fig. 4. Ontology learning process

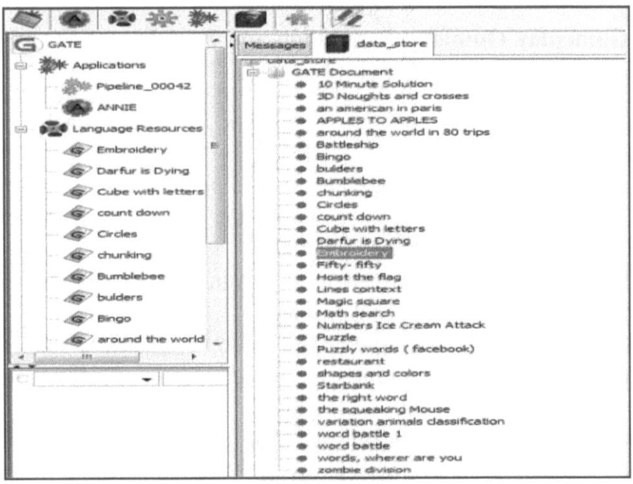

Fig. 5. GBLS Gameplay corpus

Initial gameplay ontology The formal representation of concepts, relationships and instances are described in ontology named initial ontology. Many methodologies are used to design ontology (i.e., [14–16]). All of them consider basically the following steps: definition of the ontology purpose, conceptualization, formalization, and validation. The GBLS gameplay ontology is built according to steps aforementioned; it is presented in our previous work [12]. Figure 6 depicts the initial GBLS gameplay ontology.

Ontology population Ontology population requires (i) an initial ontology that will be populated by inserting concepts and relations, and (ii) an instance extraction engine. For this end we use the information extraction toolkit GATE [17] which performs named entity recognition, syntactic and semantic analysis [18].

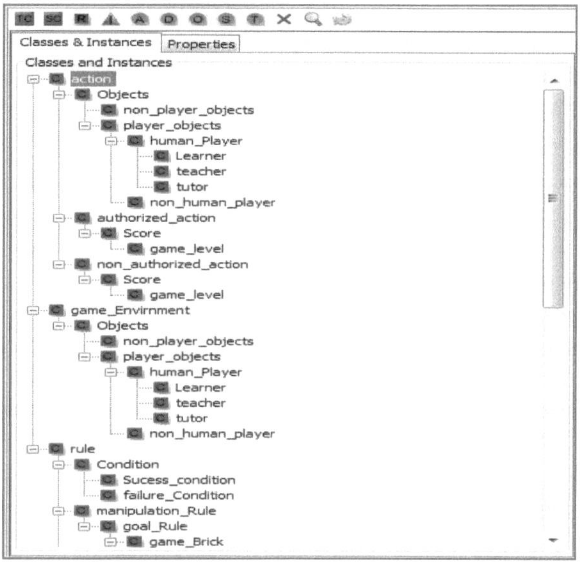

Fig. 6. Extract of Gameplay initial ontology

The extracted concepts and relations are used to populate the GBLS gameplay ontology. The result is an annotated corpus.

The structure of ontology does not change throw ontology population, the concept hierarchy and relations are not modified. What changes is the set of instances of concepts and relations in the domain. The annotated corpuses as well as the ontology population are depicted in Fig. 7.

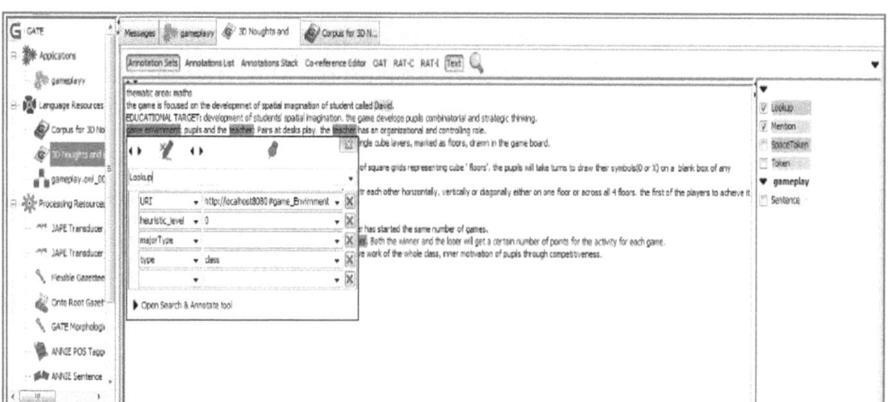

Fig. 7. Example of annotated corpus using the gameplay ontology

Inconsistency resolution This key process constitutes aims to maintain the consistency of the ontology and to eliminate redundancies. Consistency maintenance and redundancy elimination are both automated processes. The first one can be performed with the help of WSMO [19], while redundancy elimination is performed by adding word net plugin in GATE toolkit.

Performance Evaluation Information extraction adopts the typical evaluation measures for text classification tasks being recall and precision, their combination into the Fmeasure, and accuracy. The effectiveness of automatic assignment of the semantic classes is directly computed by comparing the results of the automatic assignment with the manual assignments by an expert [20].

Recall (R) is the proportion of class members that the system assigns to the class. Precision (P) is the proportion of members assigned to the class that really are class members. Fallout (Fal) computes the proportion of incorrect class members given the number of incorrect class members that the system could generate. Ideally, recall and precision are close to 1 and fallout is close to 0. Figure 8 presents the document statistics as the Recall, Precision and Fallout.

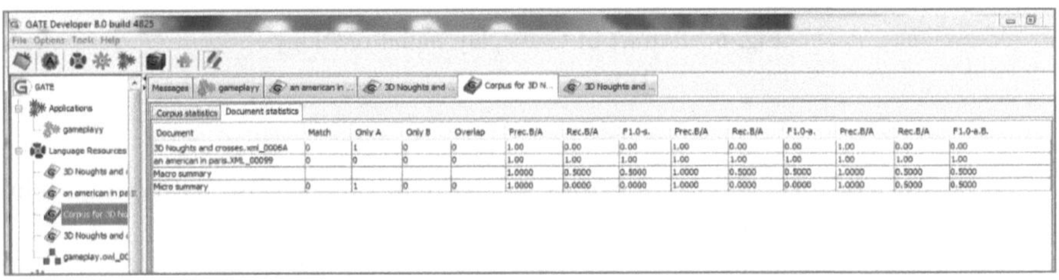

Fig. 8. Performance evaluation of the annotated document

5 Conclusion and Future Work

The principal aim of the work presented in this paper is to define GBLS gameplay knowledge. The idea is to help novice game designer by giving them the opportunity to access, acquire, exploit and share expertise knowledge to produce more attractive and efficient GBLSs.

Our future work will consist on integrating the obtained ontology to the GBLS design frame work that will assist novice game designer through an assistance system where the populated ontology constitutes its expert domain model.

References

1. Giroux, P., Brunessaux, S., Brunessaux, S., Doucy, J., Dupont, G., Grilheres, B., Mombrun, Y., Saval, A.: Weblab: an integration infrastructure to ease the development of multimedia processing applications. In: ICSSEA (2008)

2. Corti, K.: Games Based Learning. A Serious Business Application. PIXELearning Limited (2006)
3. Djaouti, D.: Game Design: Considérations théoriques et techniques sur la création de jeux vidéo à vocation utilitaire, Doctoral dissertation, Toulouse 3 (2011)
4. Raies, K., Khemaja, M., Brahem, R.: Towards game based learning design process based on semantic service oriented architecture (SSOA). In: Proceedings of the 7th European Conference on Games-Based Learning, Porto, pp. 698–705 (2013)
5. Hoffman, R.: The problem of extracting the knowledge of experts fkom the perspective of experimental psychology. AI Mag. **8**(2), 53–67 (1987)
6. Petasis, G., Karkaletsis, V., Paliouras, G., Krithara, A., Zavitsanos, E.: Ontology population and enrichment: state of the art. In: Paliouras, G., Spyropoulos, C.D., Tsatsaronis, G. (eds.) Knowledge-Driven Multimedia Information Extraction and Ontology Evolution. LNCS (LNAI), vol. 6050, pp. 134–166. Springer, Heidelberg (2011). doi:10.1007/978-3-642-20795-2_6
7. Valarakos, A.G., Paliouras, G., Karkaletsis, V., Vouros, G.A.: A name-matching algorithm for supporting ontology enrichment. In: Vouros, G.A., Panayiotopoulos, T. (eds.) SETN 2004. LNCS (LNAI), vol. 3025, pp. 381–389. Springer, Heidelberg (2004)
8. Buitelaar, P., Cimiano, P., Magnini, B.: Ontology Learning from Text: Methods, Evaluation and Applications. IOS Press, Amsterdam (2005). ISBN: 1-58603-523-1
9. Chen, S., Michael, D.: Serious Games: Games That Educate, Train and Inform. Thomson Course Technology, USA (2005)
10. Zyda, M.: From visual simulation to virtual reality to games. Computer **38**(9), 25–32 (2005)
11. Alvarez, J., Michaud, L.: Serious Games: Advergaming, edugaming, training and more. IDATE, France (2008)
12. Raies, K., Rebhi, K., Khemeja, M.: Towards ontology of gameplay: application to game based learning systems. In: Deuxième Journée AIM Systèmes d'Information & Serious Games, AIM SG 2014, Paris, France, pp. 26–37 (2014)
13. Paquette, G.: Modélisation des connaissances et des compétences Un langage graphique pour concevoir et apprendre (2002). ISBN: 978-2-7605-1163-7
14. Grüninger, M., Fox, M.S.: Methodology for the design and evaluation of ontologies, Technical report, University of Toronto, Canada (1995)
15. Lopez, M.F., Gomez-perez, A., Sierra, J.: Building a chemical ontology using methontology and the ontology design environment. IEEE Intell. Syst. Appl. **14**(1), 37–45 (1999)
16. Noy, N.F., McGuinness, D.L.: Ontology Development 101: A Guide to Creating Your First Ontology, Stanford Knowledge Systems Laboratory Technical report KSL-01-05 and Stanford Medical Informatics Technical Report SMI 0880 (2001)
17. General Architecture for text engineering, GATE.ac.uk - index.html
18. Cunningham, H., Maynard, D., Bontcheva, K.: Gate: an architecture for development of robust HLT applications. In: Proceedings of ACL (2002)
19. Dimitrov, M., Simov, A., Momtchev, V., Konstantinov, M.: WSMO studio – a semantic web services modelling environment for WSMO. In: Franconi, E., Kifer, M., May, W. (eds.) ESWC 2007. LNCS, vol. 4519, pp. 749–758. Springer, Heidelberg (2007)
20. Marie-Francine, M.: Information Extraction: Algorithms and Prospects in a Retrieval Context. Springer, Netherlands (2006)

Designing Game Strategies: An Analysis from Knowledge Management in Software Development Contexts

Jose L. Jurado[1(✉)], Cesar A. Collazos[2], Francisco L. Gutierrez[3], and Luis M. Paredes[1]

[1] San Buenaventura University, Avenida 10 de Mayo, La Umbria, Cali, Colombia
{jljurado,lmerchan}@usbcali.edu.co

[2] Cauca University, Carrera 2 A No 3N-111, Sede Tulcan, Popayán, Colombia
ccollazo@unicauca.edu.co

[3] ETS Ingenieria Informatica y de Telecomunicaciones, Granada University, Granada, Spain
fgutierr@ugr.es

Abstract. This document describes a model for the design of game strategies. This proposal is based on related works in the field of gamification and its applications. The proposed model is composed of three components: A game environment process, a game environment and a component for measurement and evaluation. This proposition seeks to offer a methodological tool for the design of game strategies in the field of gamification, applied to knowledge management. This document makes an analysis between gamification and knowledge management, with the goal of determining motivation's relationship with properties such as participation, collaboration and contribution, in the implementation of knowledge management processes, particularly in academic software development scenarios. The aforementioned properties are used for the evaluation of three validation scenarios.

Keywords: Gamification · Knowledge management · Organizational process · Motivational process

1 Introduction

In the field of organizational processes, knowledge is a vital element, which provides the bases for all kinds of entrepreneurial decisions, in aspects such as: infrastructure, processes, and roles, among others, taken from [1]. Considering the importance of knowledge at an organizational level, and particularly considering software engineering as a field of interest, knowledge management KM has been determined as a discipline that offers effective methods and methodologies for software process improvement, as cited by [2, 3]. Considering the definition of [4] about KM in software processes, which defined as an effective alternative for providing the organization with processes for the creation, modification and sharing of their knowledge assets, facilitating their internal relationships, for an optimal development of their software products.

C. Vaz de Carvalho et al. (Eds.): SGAMES 2016, LNICST 176, pp. 64–73, 2017.
DOI: 10.1007/978-3-319-51055-2_9

The aforementioned allows us to support considerations like those exposed in [7], where a variety of challenges in the implementation of KM, associated with software development processes, have been analyzed. Some of the identified problems consist in: mishandling of priorities when aligning KM with organizational needs; indiscriminate and disorganized storage of organizational information; lack of understanding when individually implementing KM processes; low participation in the creation of new knowledge assets; issues in the development of knowledge assets in a collaborative way; lack of diversification and retention of lessons learned during development projects; lack of interest by the development team, when it comes to knowledge contribution; among many others, exposed in [4].

Taking the aforementioned problems into consideration, along with works such as [5, 6], where another set of problems associated to the implementation of knowledge management is listed; we identify, among many of the factors that affect human capital and its involvement with KM processes, the concept of motivation. Considering that motivation influences people's behavior, their performance, drive to continue, work satisfaction, and even life satisfaction, according to [5]. We take the concept of motivation, in order to analyze its impact in the mitigation of problems associated to KM. Gamification is known for its efficient motivation enhancing techniques, both in groups and individually, which generate benefits such as knowledge retention, increased productivity, improved project delivery times, improved usage of budgets and reduced absenteeism. The aforementioned benefits are considered to be within the context of software engineering, according to [6]. For this reason, the analysis presented in this document is focused in proposing a method that allows for the design of game strategies, which support problem solving, in the context of software development organizations which implement knowledge management activities.

This document is structured as follows: Sect. 2 depicts an analysis of the use and impact of gamification in knowledge management processes, particularly in software development contexts. The next section presents a description of the proposed method, as well as its components. Additionally a section is presented, in which a set of properties related to the evaluation of KM processes is proposed. Properties such as participation, collaboration and contribution, are analyzed from the perspective of gamification, considering the application mechanics for each aspect. Finally, conclusions are presented, as well as a preview of future works.

2 Gamification and Knowledge Management in Software Development

The relationship between gamification and knowledge management is a field of study still in development, therefore, finding common elements and conditions between these approaches, requires a methodological process. Initially, a literature review was made, in which we identified works that related KM propositions within software development contexts. Interesting works were found, which allow us to identify propositions on methodologies, applications and approaches of KM associated to software development processes. For example the model proposed in [7] where the authors describe eight KM procedures (identification, creation, acquisition, storage, application, sharing, protection and evaluation), in software development contexts. Products associated with these processes are also identified, and it is interesting to see the relationships between products and some of the less favorable conditions found in their application, as it discussed in [14].

Works such as [4, 5] describe common activities associated with common problems found in KM. The results of the literature review were analyzed with referential works, such as [7], where a very extensive review of KM processes, in software contexts, is made. This analysis allowed us to conclude the relationship between software development processes and the different approaches of knowledge management. Also, it allowed us to identify frequent conditions that could generate problems associated to the development of KM in software engineering processes. These conditions highlight the importance of estimating the impact of properties such as *participation*, *collaboration*, and *contribution*, during the execution of KM procedures; therefore, it will be important to analyze these 3 properties, as well as their evaluation, in the context of gamification.

Considering the described relationship between KM and software development, which was established in the previous paragraph, the results of this analysis allowed us to identify a set of issues associated to the interaction of development groups when it comes to the application of knowledge management processes. Particularly, we have identified a common factor mentioned in each of the related works: *motivation*. Therefore, several definitions and interpretations have been considered, regarding the importance of a proper management of motivation in organizational processes. Some of these are taken from [4], where motivation is considered to be an influential factor in human capital, which requires continuous motivation in order to function properly. Another definition to consider is suggested in [8], where it is stated that lack of motivation can derive in a considerable amount of problems, which are not foreign to knowledge management processes, and particularly not to software development organizations. Therefore, all these works share considerations where they suggest the use of agile alternatives that are captivating to the users, regarding strategies that help mitigate problems related to motivation.

Considering the previous analysis and the relationship between motivation and KM processes, some of the problems identified are: A direct relationship between low motivation within the development team, with a potential decline in knowledge sharing and transferring, with other members of the organization, taken from [6]; Low motivation in new members of the development team makes the acquisition of tacit knowledge more difficult, which needs to be expressed as explicit in their developments and future projects, exposed in [5]; Lack of will by the employees to share knowledge is the main obstacle in knowledge transfer into organization, taken from [3]. All related works in this analysis suggest that organizations require both technological and methodological tools, which support the motivation to identify, create, share, transfer and use knowledge, suggesting gamification as a method to achieve intrinsic motivation and obtain a massive extrinsic motivation that generates specific benefits for the organization, exposed in [11].

Taking all of the above into consideration, we have made an initial analysis based on motivation and the use of alternatives such as gamification, which can be taken from its definition in [4], as a potential tool for the improvement of various aspects within the software industry. Also, works such as [12] suggest a set of benefits related to the implementation of gamification in software process improvement; these consist in the improvement of: communication between roles, feeling of advancement, competition, altruism, commitment and participation. Considering what's been exposed in this section, along with works like [8, 9], where they share the initiative of developing game strategies, as propositions for the improvement of motivational management in work groups; and considering the work of [12], where they propose a process to guide the design of applications that use Gamification; the current work looks to propose a method based on gamification principles that allow us to design agile strategies for the improvement of knowledge management processes. It is also necessary to propose a set of evaluation properties (collaboration, participation and contribution), that allows us to estimate, measure and control problems associated to knowledge management. These topics will be exposed in later sections.

3 Proposed Model for the Design of Game Strategies

The proposed model considers the work of [12] as a fundamental concept, amplifying the initial proposition with game elements that allow us to cyclically measure and evaluate the mechanics and dynamics of designed game elements. In this sense, this method is composed of three phases: A game environment analysis procedure; the game environment, and the measurement and evaluation. Figure 1 shows a conceptual representation of this method, and the three components of each phase. Next, we describe the three phases and their respective components.

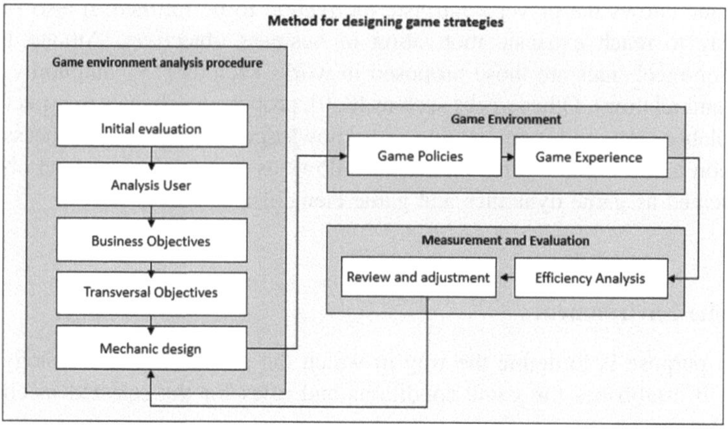

Fig. 1. Conceptual model for the design of game strategies.

3.1 Game Environment Analysis Procedure

This is composed of 5 steps, which are as follows

1. *Initial evaluation:* Allows for the definition of a set of problems, identified within the organizational interactions. This component suggests considering information such as affected population, estimated time to finish the strategy, involved technologies, artifacts (documents and such).
2. *User analysis:* Users are considered as players according to [13]. The result of this phase will be a characterization of players based on their game experience, this approach is based on works such as [11], where players are analyzed according to their interactions and play style. This phase suggests an analysis among experts and the organization, in order to define the types of players that will be involved in the game strategy.
3. *Business objectives:* Business objectives are of interest to the high management. They establish the organization's extrinsic motivations according to [12]. Goals to be reached with the implementation of the game strategy are defined. The business objective must be measurable and verifiable. This allows for the investments of time and money to be returned.
4. *Transversal objectives:* These establish the initial conditions for the execution of the business objectives. They're specific goals of the player's interest. Transversal objectives allow us to define a way to estimate and measure a player's intrinsic motivation in their game experience. It is suggested to establish short, medium and long term goals, in order to be developed by the player.
5. *Mechanic design:* A mechanic in gamification, according to [13], is the design and configuration of different game elements, grouped for a common goal. A game mechanic allows the player's intrinsic motivation to be fulfilled; it also represents the way to reach extrinsic motivation in business objectives. Among the most common mechanics are those proposed in works such as [13] (autonomy, competence and relation). Other works such as [8, 9], propose mechanics in aspects related to collaboration and participation, in knowledge management processes. The selection and design of game mechanics allows us to model transversal objectives, represented as game dynamics and game elements.

3.2 Game Environment

The main purpose is to define the way in which the proposed game strategy will be executed. It establishes the game conditions and rules for the selected mechanics. It includes 3 aspects:

1. *Game policies:* A game policy determines the rules and conditions of the game strategy according to [12]. Game policies are designed with the purpose of generating and sustaining entertainment over time, as well as motivating the player during their game experience. This way, game policies define conditions and restrictions for the manipulation and configuration of the game dynamics, and the way these are used during the game experience. In this component, the player's

levels of experience and adaptability are analyzed and adjusted accordingly with the game strategy. Levels such as: onboarding, habit-building and mastery, mentioned in several works such as [11], have been considered, where activity cycles, as described by [10] are proposed as well.

2. *Game experience:* This component allows us to establish the way game mechanics and dynamics affect the player's perception. Game experience evolves over time, during the use of the gamified application, which utilizes all of the proposed game mechanics. On the other hand, experiences such as the improvement of game knowledge, ability and skill, are experienced by the player.

3.3 Measurement and Evaluation

1. *Efficiency analysis:* It is proposed to use metrics, based on gamification principles such as the propositions in [9], where they define metrics with a specific purpose in knowledge management processes. These metrics use elements defined in the game mechanic, and they establish proper indicators, in order to measure the advancement of transversal objectives.
2. *Review and adjustment:* Reviewing is a task that allows us to analyze if transversal objectives have been fulfilled. In the opposite case, the designed mechanic is adjusted. The review compares data obtained by indicators, with the purpose of the transversal objectives. If at least one transversal objective doesn't fulfill its purpose, the process must return to the mechanic design, in order to make an adjustment, either in the selected elements for the game mechanic, or the selection of the mechanic.

4 Evaluation Properties Associated with Knowledge Management

The purpose of this section is to present 3 properties (collaboration, participation and contribution), which have been considered for the evaluation of game strategies. Particularly, the proposal is focused on knowledge management processes. These properties have been taken from recommendations and contributions by works such as [8, 9], where they expose the need of considering variables related to collaboration and participation, in a qualitative and quantitative measurement of motivation. On the other hand, the contribution aspect exposed in [6, 10], is adopted as another variable to consider for the evaluation of motivation in KM processes. The proposed definition for the 3 evaluation approaches is as follows.

4.1 Collaboration

This aspect allows us to analyze, estimate and measure effective interactions between the work group and the processes associated with KM. An interaction is measured by conditions in which an activity or set of activities is carried collaboratively [15].

4.2 Participation

Estimating the effective participation of a work group in KM, allows for the analysis of situations related to motivation and commitment in an organization [14].

4.3 Contribution

It isn't enough to determine the quality and quantity of participants in a KM process. This aspect has the goal quantifying the degree of contribution from each participation and its relationship with the work team, which is vital for determining profiles, roles, responsibilities and competences, which are specific for an organization [15].

The relationship between evaluation properties and game mechanics is established based on the theory of game elements by self-determination, proposed by [12]. This theory produces an association between game mechanics and the 3 dynamics of the self-determination theory (autonomy, competence and relation). The proposition of these properties establishes a relationship between each game mechanic and elements based on gamification principles, taken from [13]. This way, Table 1 shows a summary of the association between evaluation properties and a set of game mechanics. In order to evaluate the effectiveness of the proposed properties, we intend to measure the dynamics that take place within the game environment, in order to estimate the level of encouragement for these properties. Considering the elements that have been proposed for such dynamics, and their use by the players, the increase/decrease of participation, collaboration, and contribution rates, can be measured in knowledge management projects.

Table 1. Association of evaluation properties with game mechanics and game elements.

Properties	Dynamics	Proposed elements
Participation	Autonomy	Profiles, avatars, macros, configurable interfaces, alternative activities, privacy control and notification control
	Relation	Groups, social networks and teams
	Competence	Badges and leaderboards
Collaboration	Relation	Groups, messages, blogs, teams, friending, connection to social networks and chats.
	Autonomy	Avatars, profiles and virtual trade.
	Competence	Positive feedback and reputation points
Contribution	Competence	Positive feedback, optimal challenge, progressive information, intuitive controls, points, reputation points, badges, levels and leaderboards.
	Autonomy	Profiles and avatars.
	Relation	Group tasks

5 Validation of the Proposed Method

The method proposed in this document has been used to validate properties of collaboration, participation and contribution. The selected scenarios are a group of five companies located in the southern region of Colombia, among a potential of 250. All of the companies that participated in the experimentation are dedicated to software development. The validation was developed throughout a period of 3 months, in which every experimentation was carried during real projects. Results have been satisfying, regarding mitigation and management of the impact of problems associated to knowledge management, in software development processes. Quantifiable data, analysis and details of the implemented case studies will be exposed in extended versions

Table 2. Data sheet of the experiments conducted using the proposed method.

Case study	Evaluated properties	Implemented dynamics	Results' analysis
Description: 2 scenarios with similar application conditions were defined. In the first case, a repository (wiki) was used for the publication of good practices. In the second case, the proposed method was applied, and a support application was developed. **Implemented software:** Web application that promotes the voluntary publication of good software development practices, within a software development company. The designed strategy offers bonuses (points), and awards (badges), when employees post good software development practices, both individually and in groups. **Required time:** 3 months **Participants:** 45 employees	Participation	3 types of badge are defined (professional, junior and amateur). Each badge provides points. These points are bonuses for the quality of the practices. There is also a leaderboard, which validates the best scores within the established categories.	**Scenario 1:** 5 out of 45 employees posted new practices. 11% participation. **Scenario 2:** 40 out of 45 employees posted new practices. 88.9% participation. Effective participation reached 75%. Out of 40 active participants, 30 obtained professional badges, 8 obtained junior, and only 2 remained as amateur.
	Collaboration	There are 2 special badges (senior and master), which are obtained by the employees with the highest score in the professional category, who must also post good practices, developed by a team with tasks and roles.	**Scenario 1:** 4 out of 45 employees engaged in teamwork, in order to post new collaborative practices. 8.9% participation. **Scenario 2:** 28 out of 45 employees developed new practices, which were posted. 62.2% collaboration. Effective collaboration reached 89.2%. Out of the 28 participants who developed collaborative practices, 25 obtained senior badges, whereas 3 got master badges.

of this document. An example of the experiments conducted with the group of selected companies, is summarized in Table 2. This table shows one case study that implemented the method proposed in this document. The data sheet show the properties evaluated, the dynamics implemented and the results obtained.

6 Conclusions and Future Work

Knowledge management, due to its complexity when it comes to comprehension and implementation, invites the proposition of alternatives that help generate more agile, motivating and flexible comprehension spaces. An alternative to consider is gamification, due to its emerging field of study and flexibility of application, as well as its easy adaptability to a variety of contexts. In this case, we found that gamification is an agile and viable alternative for the mitigation of problems associated to motivation in knowledge management processes, in software development contexts.

The method presented in this document, is a proposition designed based on the contributions made in several works, which propose processes in the design of game strategies, and proper usage of game mechanics. The key differences with other articles consist in the proposition of: Designing game strategies that part from a specific problem, in order to design measurable and controlled objectives during the execution of the strategy. Offering ways to measure a game strategy and control complex variables such as: reach and impact of the business objective. Another distinctive element is counting with an exclusive component, for the estimation and evaluation of the game mechanic.

Several propositions and studies support the interests of the current work; in which the applicability and efficiency of using gamification in several contexts, with a particular interest in KM, are praised. We make special emphasis in the advantage of game mechanics and the correct application of their elements, in the management and mitigation of problems related to motivation in KM. This work praises gamification characteristics for the evaluation of processes and activities such as autonomy, relation and competence, and their relationship with properties such as participation, collaboration and contribution.

The evaluation properties describes in this document can be applied not only in knowledge management contexts. Its initial analysis allowed us to define a method of application, although it doesn't imply they can't be used and analyzed in different contexts. Right now, the project is developing new validation prototypes, which will be applied in academic contexts and will be used, in order to analyze problems associated to motivation and commitment within specific groups.

References

1. Bjørnson, F.O., Dingsor, T.: Knowledge management in software engineering: a systematic review of studied concepts, findings and research methods used. Inf. Softw. Technol. **50**, 1055–1068 (2008)
2. Herranz, E., Palacios, R.C., Seco, A.A.: Towards a new approach to supporting top managers in SPI organizational change management. In: International Conference on Project Management Procedia Technology, vol. 9, pp. 129–138 (2013)
3. Capote, J., LLanten, C., Pardo, C., Collazos, C.: Knowledge management in a software process improvement program in micro, small, and medium –sized enterprises: KMSPI model. Revista de Ingeniería, No 50, pp. 205–216 (2009)
4. Helen, S., Nathan, B., Sarah, B., Tracy, H., Hugh, R.: Models of motivation in software engineering. Inf. Softw. Technol. **51**(1), 219–233 (2009)
5. Galvis, E., Sanchez, J.M.: A critical review of knowledge management in software process reference model. J. Inf. Syst. Technol. Manag. **10**(2), 323–338 (2013)
6. Schacht, S., Maedche, A.: Project knowledge management while simply playing! gaming mechanics in project knowledge management systems. In: Reiners, T., Wood, L.C. (eds.) Gamification in Education and Business, pp. 593–614. Springer, Switzerland (2015)
7. Galvis, E.A., Sanchez, J.M., Gonzalez, M.P.: Towards a reference model for knowledge management processes for software-developing organizations: validation by experts. AD-minister, EAFIT **26**, 41–72 (2015)
8. Yip, M.W., Hong, A.H., Chai Lau, D.H.: Employee participation: success factor of knowledge management. Int. J. Inf. Educ. Technol. **2**(3), 262–264 (2012)
9. Knutas, A., Ikonen, J., Nikula, U., Porras, J.: Increasing collaborative communications in a programming course with gamification: a case study. In: Proceedings of the 15th International Conference on Computer Systems and Technologies, CompSysTech 2014, pp. 370–377. ACM (2014)
10. Osipov, I.V., Nikulchev, E., Volinsky, A.A., Prasikova, A.Y.: Study of gamification effectiveness in online e-learning systems. Int. J. Adv. Comput. Sci. Appl. **6**(2), 71–77 (2015)
11. Werbach, K., Hunter, D.: For the Win: How Game Thinking Can Revolutionize Your Business. Wharton Digital Press, Philadelphia (2012)
12. Francisco, A., Gutiérrez, F.L., Isla, J.L., González, J.L.: Gamification: analysis and application. In: Penichet, V.M.R., Peñalver, A., Gallud, J.A. (eds.) New Trends in Interaction, Virtual Reality and Modeling, pp. 113–126. Springer, London (2013). Chap 8
13. Seaborn, K., Fels, D.I.: Gamification in theory and action: a survey. Int. J. Hum Comput Stud. **72**(3), 14–31 (2015)
14. Jurado, J., Fernandez, A., Collazos, C.: Applying gamification in the context of knowledge management. In: i-KNOW 2015 Proceedings of the 15th International Conference on Knowledge Technologies and Data-driven Business. ACM (2015)
15. Collazos, C., Toledo, P., Gonzalez, C.: Design and analysis of collaborative interactions in social educational videogames. Comput. Hum. Behav. **31**, 602–611 (2014)

Neurocognitive Stimulation Game: Serious Game for Neurocognitive Stimulation and Assessment

João Costa[1(✉)], Jorge Neto[1], Ricardo Alves[2], Paula Escudeiro[1,2], and Nuno Escudeiro[1,3]

[1] Instituto Superior de Engenharia do Porto, Porto, Portugal
{1110783,1110156,pmo,nfe}@isep.ipp.pt
[2] Games Interaction and Learning Technologies - GILT, Porto, Portugal
ricalves03@gmail.com
[3] Laboratory of Artificial Intelligence and Decision Support, INESC TEC, Porto, Portugal

Abstract. The ageing process is naturally accompanied by changes in people's cognitive processes. The European population ageing is a challenge for the European social policy and for the mental health professionals. New technologies can play an important role in the neurocognitive stimulation area as they possess characteristics that might reduce the anxiety levels of patients participating in neurocognitive stimulation or assessment programs. In particular, serious games provide a setting that can be explored to improve the easy access to neurocognitive stimulation and assessment, regardless of place and time, at a lower cost then traditional approaches. This paper presents a serious game aiming to analyse neurocognitive deficits and stimulate the players' deficitary neurocognitive processes. This game is built on top of sound neurocognitive psychotherapy for adults, mainly addressing the cognitive processes of attention and memory. The game will simulate real world scenarios, allowing a better generalization process due to ecological validity.

Keywords: Active ageing · Neurocognitive deficits · Neurocognitive stimulation · Assessment · Serious games · Unity · DDA

1 Introduction

With the increasing number of the elderly in our population, it is possible to verify the consequent increase of the cognitive decline incidence. Neurocognitive stimulation has been a highly approached research area for the past years, as it offers new opportunities for people with cognitive impairments. Several neurocognitive stimulation programs are implemented in medical context, with the aim of slowing down cognitive decline [1] and, therefore, improving the life quality of the patients. However, these programs

J. Costa, J. Neto, R. Alves contributed equally to this work.

C. Vaz de Carvalho et al. (Eds.): SGAMES 2016, LNICST 176, pp. 74–81, 2017.
DOI: 10.1007/978-3-319-51055-2_10

have some limitations that might compromise the desired impact on the individual's quotidian. These limitations involve, for example, the lack of ecological validity and patients' low motivation, due to the high emotional pressure they feel on following these neurocognitive stimulation programs and assessments [3]. Ecological validity can be seen as a transitional phenomenon, which analyses the current behavior, within specific environments related to the real world, by using discrete and reliable research methods [2].

The use of serious games is turning into a remarkable resource, as it offers computerized alternatives to neurocognitive stimulation and assessment programs. By focusing our efforts on reducing the impact of the above-mentioned limitations, i.e., reinforcing the need for ecological validity and adapt the tasks' difficulty levels, there is a high probability that the results obtained from a serious game's neurocognitive stimulation program can show positive results [4, 5].

Although the few projects that use serious games try to solve these problems, none of them covers efficiently the core aspects, such as ecological validity, that we address. Current approaches usually focus on only computerizing the assessments and do not always consider the content of the program itself. In addition, there is no special attention given to the users' interaction.

Our methodology consists on developing a serious game, called SynapseToLife, which focus on the neurocognitive stimulation of the players, by making them perform several tasks, immersed in well-known scenarios, thus strengthening ecological validity. More importantly, the serious game will create a group of familiar daily life scenarios (e.g. kitchen) to the user, in order to allow an easier transfer of the stimulated cognitive abilities into the users' quotidian, given the ecological validity variable that we aim to approach [3, 6].

2 Problem Description

With the increasing number of the elderly and the consequent incidence of cognitive decline associated, it becomes important to invest in mental health, to minimize the social and economic impacts of this phenomenon, promoting active ageing.

Since the neurocognitive deficits may be present about 20 years before the clinical diagnosis on dementias, such as the Alzheimer disease [7], it is necessary to develop more effective and motivating strategies of monitoring and stimulating people's cognitive abilities, allowing them to follow an healthier life style [8]. SynapseToLife will be able to perform an early intervention, which is of major importance in order to slow down possible pre-clinical manifestations of neurocognitive [9] deficits, which, consequently, will contribute for public health's cost reduction [10].

2.1 State of the Art

Serious games allow the monitoring and presentation of stimulus, capable of motivating the user [11] and which show a greater accessibility [12], presenting positive results [13].

The use of serious games has been increasingly referenced as an important resource for psychological assessment and intervention [14]. Showing positive results in multiple domains, such as prevention [15], rehabilitation [14], neurocognitive stimulation [16], assessment [17] and monitoring neurocognitive changes [18], leading to beneficial changes, when it comes to brain plasticity [19], changing the brain's structure [20] and facilitating the impact of neurocognitive stimulation on everyday functioning [6]. However, the use of serious games, with older people, is still in an early phase [21] and there is little information when it comes to the impact of these programs on the users' quotidian activities and on their quality life [22].

There are several available games in the market, which aim neurocognitive stimulation [23, 24]. These, however, are not specifically developed to target a certain population and, in most cases, are not supported by robust studies on ecological validity. Although there are empirical evidences of neurocognitive improvements, several games do not evaluate the impact of a serious game in patients' daily life and do not offer content, which benefits the generalization process of, trained tasks, to their daily reality.

3 Proposed Solution

In this work, we propose to develop the ACT-Age platform, which includes the serious game SynapseToLife, aiming to promote neurocognitive stimulation and assessment. The serious game will enable an easier transfer of the neurocognitive stimulation results to users' quotidian activities, by simulating real life scenarios and users' interactions with them. This will be supported by the ecological validity concept, previously outlined, and which will play a significant role when it comes to reduce the users' anxiety levels, consequently enhancing their motivation, while being cognitively stimulated, and increasing the efficiency of the neurocognitive stimulation's results.

Throughout the game, tasks, adapted from the neurocognitive stimulation programs traditionally implemented, will be presented to the users along with a calculated difficulty level. The purpose of the game's tasks, is to simulate real life situations where users need to evoke their cognitive processes. A dynamic difficulty adjustment (DDA) component will also be an essential tool to develop, as it is a powerful expert control system, capable of studying and interpreting users' performances, throughout the game, and adapting (controlling) the game and tasks' difficulty according to the users' cognitive capabilities, directly assisting each one of them.

3.1 Main Components

SynapseToLife is organized in four different scenarios, where each will simulate real world situations, as the user will need to go through them, while performing the intended stimulation tasks. By structuring the game flow in mini games, adapted to real life situations or problems, users will hardly percept they are performing stimulation tasks and will only worry about having fun by completing these random tasks.

Another important component to be developed is the DDA system, as it is crucial when it comes to adapt the mini games' difficulty to the user's cognitive ability. Its job involves analyzing the player's performance and assure that he or she keeps relaxed and in a concentrated state of mind, by constantly presenting challenges and rewarding them accordingly (game flow). Shortly, the DDA allows the automatic readjustment of the game's difficulty, based on the player's performance results. These results, along with all users' interactions while playing the game, will be recorded in a centralized server. Later on, the expert will analyze these same results, by accessing this server. These actions are transformed into useful and careful information and, more specifically, in data that the expert needs in order to study the player's performance, such as the number of right answers, the number of attempts, the response times or the cognitive processes approached (e.g. memory).

Lastly, and before the game starts, a diagnostic test will be presented to the user with the aim of setting a baseline, enabling posterior comparisons and analyzing the evolution of the players' cognitive status. This way, it is possible to understand if neurocognitive stimulation occurred and if the game itself presents all the tools needed to perform this stimulation.

3.2 Game Structure

Figure 1 presents the relationship between the business concept (cognitive stimulation) and the project development. With this scheme, it becomes easier to visualize the interaction between the user and the expert.

Players will need to complete the mini games and a diagnostic test, which will be better approached further on. The final results are reported to the expert, to perform the diagnosis. Both the IT staff and the expert will provide assistance to the players, in case they have doubts related to the activities they will need to perform. In Fig. 2, it is possible to understand, more specifically, the game flow, which consists on the game's life cycle.

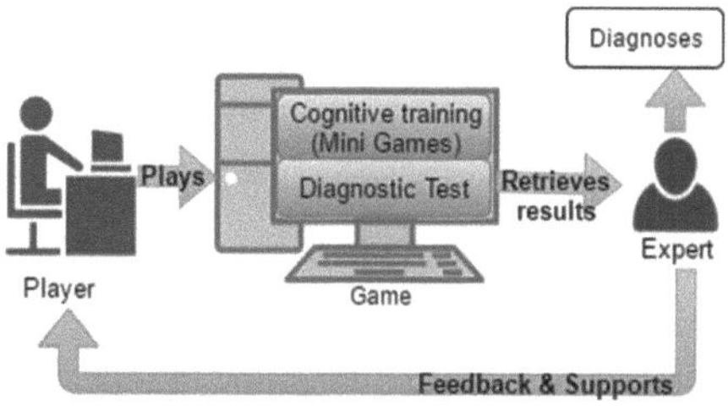

Fig. 1. Architectural model.

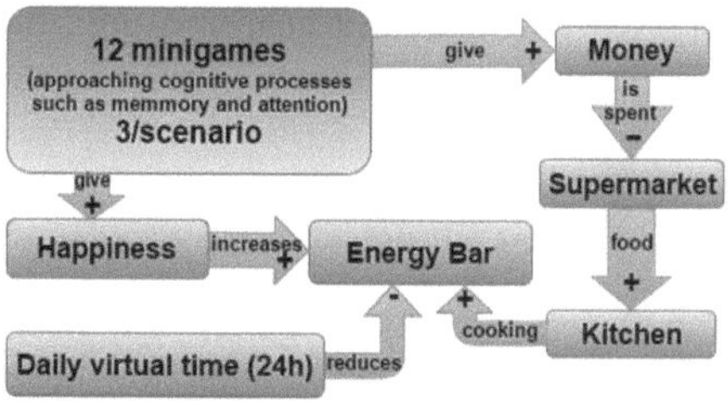

Fig. 2. Game flow

3.3 Game Scenarios

All scenarios, presented in Fig. 3, will be developed in 3D, by using the Unity3D platform. The tridimensional model was chosen due to the ecological validity factor. The more detail the game presents, the more the players become concentrated and the easier it is for them to understand the logic behind the tasks they perform throughout the game, which mainly focus on certain cognitive processes, like memory and attention. Each scenario is responsible for asking the completion of tasks related to that specific scenario. For example, in the Kitchen scenario, the player only performs kitchen related tasks, such as cooking, promoting stimuli on specific cognitive processes. The same applies to the other scenarios and this is the base of ecological validity, i.e., answer questions or performing tasks that are inserted in a given context and that can actually happen in a real life situation (Fig. 4).

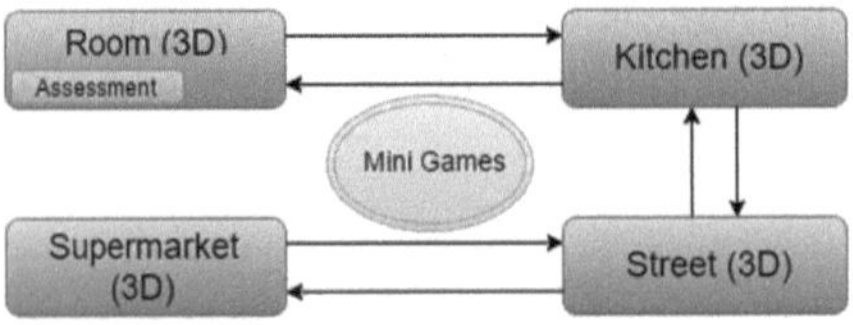

Fig. 3. Game scenarios.

Fig. 4. Scenario example.

4 Expected Outcomes

After the project development phase, the users and the serious game will be both evaluated, in different ways. The game must be able to retrieve, from the users' interaction with the game, information needed for the expert, in order for him to draw his conclusions. The serious game will also need to be able to analyze the players' responses throughout the game, since the tasks' difficulty levels must be adapted according to the user needs and since it is essential for us to study these same responses and observe their interaction. During this assessment phase, users' responses will be assessed and carefully analyzed, i.e., the extracted and quantified results, from the neurocognitive stimulation program performed, will be studied.

4.1 Output Model

The players' actions are directly connected to their performance, i.e., there is a set of features that help us understand how the user performance during the game or how this same user is dealing with it. The variables (e.g. right answers) together, form this output model so that the expert can analyze the players' cognitive ability in the best way possible. The output model, in turn, will be allocated in the available server.

However, the game has an error-free structure, which means that the player will not advance to the next phase without understanding what he or she did wrong and without knowing how can the current problem must be solved. This way, the neurocognitive stimulation has more impact on the player, as the probability of him solving an equal problem, in the future, increases.

4.2 Assessment Plan

The assessment will be based on a study with a quasi-experimental design, where an independent variable (cognitive training) is manipulated, verifying its effect on dependent variables (e.g. attention). Taking this into account, and shortly, the assessment process consists in the following steps:

- Interview and select the most suitable participants for the experiment, using the previously defined restrictions.
- Compare the pre-assessment results with the post-assessment results, analyzing all data obtained from the game and the neurocognitive assessment;
- Post-Post assess the participants after a few weeks or months, in order to confirm if there was retention of the cognitive skills acquired.

After the project development, six weeks will be reserved for this final assessment process, conducted by the expert and supported by the IT staff, in order to give a scientific answer to the work accomplished.

4.3 Main Contributions

Overall, the outcomes expected are based on the cognitive assessment itself, i.e., the game should present better results when compared with classic neurocognitive stimulation programs. The project ought to also show improvements on the interaction between the user and the computer, as efforts will be made related to this situation. Furthermore, it is essential making the system able to be sensitive to the players' interaction with the game's environment (e.g. verify if the tasks are having the correct reactions) and adapt its difficulty accordingly. We also expect to confirm that our serious game has ecological validity, since it has a preponderant role in the project's main purpose.

5 Conclusions

The serious game proposed in this work aims to overcome the limitations of current solutions addressing active ageing. It is based on a set of scenarios simulating familiar environments and everyday activities of an individual's daily life. This allows stimulating users' cognitive abilities and transferring the stimulation results to the tasks normally performed during their quotidian. The user interaction with the game, while playing it for stimulation, will be monitored and recorded in a cognitive model to allow guiding the effective stimulation towards deficitary cognitive processes. This model will also allow the neuropsychological profile monitoring and an effective intervention with ecological impact. We expect this serious game to become a robust tool being able to study, interpret and stimulate users' neurocognitive processes.

We aim to provide our future players a welcoming environment, by carefully analyzing which content is necessary to insert inside the game, in order to promote ecological validity, which is our main focus during the development phase, and by developing a tutorial which will help the player to get acquainted to the gameplay. Moreover, the DDA component must be able to analyze every situation possible and every user interaction throughout the game. It is also necessary to consider the interaction itself.

Thus, we seek to develop a solid serious game, in a technological and scientific point of view, which will promote the development of the knowledge necessary for the implementation of this technology in new markets with potential growth, aiming several domains, such as health, well-being, ageing and social inclusion. This project also seeks to give answers to questions based on the implementation, experimentation challenges, quality control in application domains and impact on users' quality life. These scientific evidences will allow a safer investment from the digital games' industry professionals in developing the "serious" market of games. Another important activity intends to disclose the project and its results.

References

1. Glisky, E.: Changes in cognitive function in human aging. In: Riddle, D.R. (ed.) Brain Aging: Models, Methods, and Mechanisms. CRC Press, Boca Raton (2007)
2. Rizzo, A., Kim, G.J.: A SWOT analysis of the field of VR rehabilitation and therapy. Presence Teleoper. Virtual Environ. **14**, 119–146 (2005). doi:10.1162/1054746053967094
3. Segal, R., Bhatia, M., Drapeau, M.: Therapist's perception of benefits and costs of using virtual reality treatments. Cyberpsychology Behav. Soc. Networking **14**(1–2), 29–34 (2011)
4. Fissler, P., Kolassa, I.T., Schrader, C.: Educational games for brain health: revealing their unexplored potential through a neurocognitive approach. Front. Psychol. **6**, 1056 (2015). doi:10.3389/fpsyg.2015.01056
5. Powers, K., Brooks, P., Aldrich, N., Palladino, M., Alfieri, L.: Effects of video-game play on information processing: a meta-analytic investigation. Psychon. Bull. Rev. **20**, 1055–1079 (2013). doi:10.3758/s13423-013-0418-z
6. Spector, A., Orrell, M., Woods, B.: Cognitive stimulation to improve cognitive functioning in people with dementia. Int. J. Geriatr. Psychiatry **25**(12), 1253–1258 (2010)
7. Rajan, K., Wilson, R., Weuve, J.: Cognitive impairment 18 years before clinical diagnosis of Alzheimer disease dementia. Neurology published online 24 June 2015. doi:10.1212/WNL.0000000000001774
8. Mcguire, A.M., Anderson, D.J., Fulbrook, P.: Perceived barriers to healthy lifestyle activities in midlife and older Australian women with type 2 diabetes. Collegian (2013). doi:10.1016/j.colegn.2013.07.001
9. American Psychiatric Association: Diagnostic and statistical manual of mental disorders, 5th edn. American Psychiatric Publishing, Arlington (2013)
10. Direção-Geral da Saúde: Portugal Saúde Mental – 2013. Programa Nacional para a Saúde Mental. Obtido em 7 de 2 de 2015, de Direcção-Geral da Saúde (2013). http://www.dgs.pt/publicacoes

11. Manera, V., Petit, P., Derreumaux, A., Orvieto, E., et al.: 'Kitchen and cooking', a serious game for mild cognitive impairment and Alzheimer's disease: a pilot study. Frontiers Aging Neurosci. **7**, 24 (2015). doi:10.3389/fnagi.2015.00024
12. Krebs, P., Prochaska, J.O., Rossi, J.S.: A meta-analysis of computer-tailored interventions for health behavior change. Prev. Med. **51**, 214–221 (2010)
13. Connolly, T., Boyle, E., MacArthur, E., et al.: A systematic literature review of empirical evidence on computer games and serious games. Comput. Educ. **59**(2), 661–686 (2012). doi:10.1016/j.compedu.2012.03.004
14. Robert, P.H., König, A., Amieva, H., et al.: Recommendations for the use of serious games in people with Alzheimer's disease, related disorders and frailty. Frontiers Aging Neurosci. **6**, 54 (2014). doi:10.3389/fnagi.2014.00054
15. Wiemeyer, J., Kliem, A.: Serious games in prevention and rehabilitation – a new panacea for elderly people? Eur. Rev. Aging Phys. Act. **9**, 41–50 (2012). doi:10.1007/s11556-011-0093-x
16. Nouchi, R., Taki, Y., Takeuchi, H., Hashizume, H., Akitsuki, Y., et al.: Brain training game improves executive functions and processing speed in the elderly: a randomized controlled trial. PLoS ONE **7**(1), e29676 (2012). doi:10.1371/journal.pone.0029676
17. Anguera, J.A., Boccanfuso, J., Rintoul, J.L., Al-Hashimi, O., et al.: Video game training enhances cognitive control in older adults. Nature **501**, 97–102 (2013). doi:10.1038/nature12486
18. Tarnana, I., Papagiannopoulos, S., Kazis, D., Wiederhold, M., Widerhold, B., Tsolak, M.: Reliability of a novel serious game using dual-task gait profiles to early characterize aMCI. Front. Aging Neurosci. **7**(50), 1–15 (2015). doi:10.3389/fnagi.2015.00050
19. Lövdén, M., Bäckman, L., Lindenberger, U., Schaefer, S., Schmiedek, F.: A theoretical framework for the study of adult cognitive plasticity. Psychol. Bull. **136**, 659–676 (2010). doi:10.1037/a0020080
20. Kühn, S., Gallinat, J.: Amount of lifetime video gaming is positively associated with entorhinal, hippocampal and occipital volume. Mol. Psychiatry **19**, 842–847 (2014). doi:10.1038/mp.2013.100
21. Tarnanas, I., Tsolaki, M., Nef, T., et al.: Can a novel computerized cognitive screening test provide additional information for early detection of Alzheimer's disease? Alzheimers Dement. **10**, 790–798 (2014). doi:10.1016/j.jalz.2014.01.002
22. Kazmi, S., Ugail, H., Valerie, L., Palmer, I.: Interactive digital serious games for the assessment, rehabilitation, and prediction of dementia. Int. J. Comput. Games Technol. **2014**, 1–11 (2014). doi:10.1155/2014/701565. Article ID 701565
23. McCallum, S., Boletsis, C.: Dementia games: a literature review of dementia-related serious games. In: Ma, M., Oliveira, M.F., Petersen, S., Hauge, J.B. (eds.) SGDA 2013. LNCS, vol. 8101, pp. 15–27. Springer, Heidelberg (2013). doi:10.1007/978-3-642-40790-1_2
24. Arambarri, J., Torre, I., Coronado, M., Álvarez, I.: Investigating the potential market of a serious game for training of alzheimer's caregivers in a Northern Spain region. Int. J. Serious Games **1**(4), 75–79 (2014). doi:10.17083/ijsg.v1i4.36. ISSN: 2384-8766

The Perspectives of Older People on Digital Gaming: Interactions with Console and Tablet-Based Games

Suriati Khartini Jali[1(✉)] and Sylvester Arnab[2]

[1] Serious Games Institute, Coventry University Technology Park, Coventry University, Coventry CV1 2TL, UK
jalis@coventry.ac.uk
[2] Disruptive Media Learning Lab, Frederick Lanchester Library, Coventry University, Coventry CV1 2TL, UK
s.arnab@coventry.ac.uk

Abstract. The paper aims to investigate the correlation between the challenges associated with older people, their existing engagement with digital gaming, the andragogical perspectives and existing game design attributes. A pilot study was performed with 14 participants aged 55 and above. Data was collected from their interactions with and experiences of digital gaming. Questionnaires and group discussions were performed to collect feedback and perspectives on the experience. Preliminary results demonstrated that older people's initial perspectives and perceptions towards digital gaming and gameplay were influenced by perceived or assumed difficulties, relevance and benefits. Furthermore, the participants' perspectives and attitudes changed once they have broken the confidence barrier associated to engaging with new technologies and experienced the enjoyment from the social aspects of the engagement. They have also demonstrated renewed interest in digital games, and understanding of the potential of using digital games for achieving serious purposes, such as promoting a healthy lifestyle.

Keywords: Older people · Andragogy · Digital game · Interaction · Experience

1 Introduction

Digital game technology usage and its capabilities have attracted educators and researchers worldwide to address specific interest for certain targeted group of users. Historically, the design of most games used for both entertainment and serious purposes however focuses on general player population, and mostly the younger population currently engaging with digital gaming. In recent years, a game-based approach is being widely used and accepted to cater and address the needs (educational, health, social interaction, etc.) of various target groups, including the older people.

The application of games is becoming a popular medium in promoting healthy lifestyle and improving the quality of life especially for older people; for instance fostering social connectedness through social interaction, physical activity and cognitive exercises that can be afforded by digital game technology. It is essential that users or

C. Vaz de Carvalho et al. (Eds.): SGAMES 2016, LNICST 176, pp. 82–90, 2017.
DOI: 10.1007/978-3-319-51055-2_11

players are captivated and engaged by the game before any serious purposes/activities can be imposed.

Besides that, most models or framework for designing and developing games were particularly developed for general type of games (commercial games) and aiming for younger users in mind. A small number of research proposed game design for older people, however none of them developed specifically for the use of older people that correlates the attributes of game technology and considerations; such as andragogy perspectives and challenges faced by this target groups.

The paper aims to investigate the correlation between the challenges associated with older people, their existing engagement with digital gaming, the andragogical perspectives and existing game design attributes.

2 Related Work

In early 80s, the usages of video games towards older people have been conducted. Among the early study is by Weisman, where the author introduced the video games to institutionalised older people [1]. Based on his studies, Weisman asserts that game should have different levels of difficulties to support individual preferences and sensomotor abilities. In addressing visual and auditory impairment, he suggested the use of large font, well-defined visual symbols and clear auditory feedback.

Similarly, Whitcomb and Ijsselsteijn et al. [2, 3] also propose several game designs and recommend appropriate user interface for older people which emphasises on impairments in visual and auditory perception and a loss of sensomotor skill. Extension on above approach has been done by [4] where the author recommends the design of appropriate cognitive challenges, a simple user interface and ability to provide feedback. There are a number of game designs specifically focusing on older people; which mainly focusing on accessibility [5] and player performance [6]. Due to challenges faced and lack of technological experience, usability is a key issue with the older population compared to the younger population.

With respect to game design for older people, studies showed that older people have specific gaming needs and preferences. It is also observed that their abilities differ from younger people [7–11]. De Schutter and Abeele [12] propose that the game design should consider topics that are related to older peoples' real life experiences, foster connectedness and nurture one's self and others. Gerling et al. [13] echoes De Schutter and Abeele's view by suggesting user experience and sufficient information needs to be examined and provided to capture adequate interaction between players and the games. Studies by [14] however indicates that involvement by older people themselves throughout the design process is important to obtain valuable information in meeting their needs (the transactions of the ageing process that relate to their likes and dislikes). These studies indicate the importance of the andragogical aspects when it comes to designing and developing games, specifically for older people.

Andragogy can be defined as the art and science of 'helping' adults learning. This is based on the assumption of the two different learner groups, adult and children [15]. It shows that the way adults learn or perceive thing is different from children. Therefore, to promote learning for an adult will require a different approach, through adopting the andragogical perspectives.

3 Methodology

This research involved multiple series of focus groups which comprised of; (1) the use of questionnaires, (2) game-play session for hands-on activities; and (3) group discussion for collecting feedback from the hands-on session. Games on two platforms including Xbox 360 console (*Kinect Sport: Bowling, Skiing*) and Android tablet (*Bowling, Car Racing*) were chosen for this research study. Xbox 360 console and Android tablet platforms selected for this study because they offer natural user interface (NUI) and intuitive, to ease the interaction between the participant and technologies in completely natural ways [16]. Each game was selected with regard to various skill and ability offered; and to trigger different reactions from the participants.

3.1 Participants

In total, 14 older people participated in the study (5 males, 9 females), aged 55 and above (55–60 (21.4%), 61–65 (28.6%), 66–70 (42.9%), Over 75 (7.1%)). The average age of participants was 65.04 (MEDIAN: 61–65) with more than 50% of participants were retired.

3.2 Recruitment

Target participants were recruited from various organisations, groups and forums, for instance *Research Support Volunteer Programme (RSVP), The Cheylesmore Good Neighbours* and *Neighbourhood University - Coventry Healthy Walks.* In total, 6 different organisations and groups were participated in the study.

The intended participants consist of independently living older people, who were physically and mentally healthy. The participants for this study were recruited using a combination of convenience and snowball sampling methods. The recruitment of participants was formed by approaching pre-existing groups, forums and organisations located in Coventry. Several other participants were referral from their friends. Institutional ethics approval was obtained for this study and participation was on voluntary basis confirmed by a signed consent.

3.3 Measures

This study employed a mixed approach. Results from the findings will help to inform user's interaction and experience in playing digital game. The following quantitative and qualitative measures were used in this study: (1) a questionnaire regarding participant's demographic background, user's acceptance towards technology and game experiences; and (2) the informal observations of participants during game-play and (3) group discussion.

3.4 Procedure and Data Analysis

In this study, only four focus groups were carried out with a total of 14 participants (n = 14). Each group consists of 2 to 4 people. The sessions took about 90 min each. Figure 1 shows the structure of focus group used in this study.

Firstly, there was *Introductory Session* where the participants were given a brief description on the main purpose of study, i.e. to investigate user's interactions and experience toward digital games.

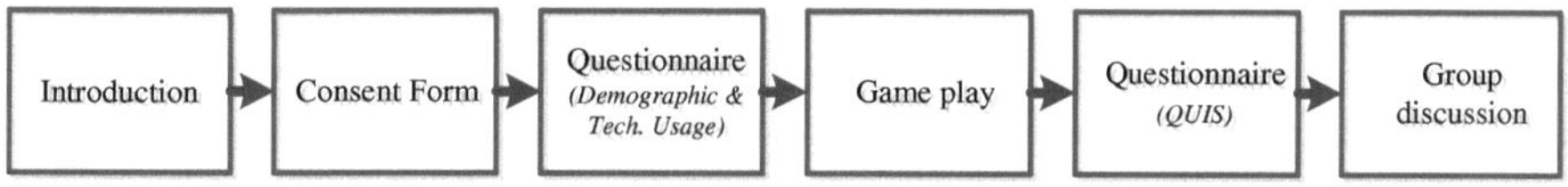

Fig. 1. Focus group flow chart

Later, *Questionnaire* was disseminated to gather participants' information, technology usage, game experiences and game interfaces. The questionnaire was a modified version of QUIS (Questionnaire for User Interaction Satisfaction) developed by The University of Maryland Human-Computer Interaction Lab (n.d.).

In *Game-play* session, participants were introduced and asked to take part in playing 3 games (i.e. *bowling, skiing, car racing*) on different platforms; console (Xbox 360) and tablet (Android operating system). This gameplay was conducted to gather participants' feedback, especially on their perceptions of game experience.

Finally, we conducted semi-structured interview in a *Group discussion* setting. The open-ended questions were asked aim to obtain participants' opinions about their game interactions and experiences and this offered in-depths information and understanding to researcher on participant's experiences.

All focus group sessions were recorded and transcribed. Participants feedback were analysed quantitatively and qualitatively. Quantitative data analysis was performed using IBM SPSS 22.0. Descriptive statistics was used to examine demographics data. *Mann–Whitney U test* was used to comparing scores of two platforms. The qualitative data was analysed mainly using Content Analysis (CA) to identify common codes and categorised them into themes. The findings were presented based on the relationship and commonality basis.

4 Results and Discussion

4.1 Participants' Background

All participants asserted that they own a personal computer and are familiar with using smartphones or tablets. They have used these technologies for many purposes such as email, news, social media and gaming. In terms of the gaming experiences, 9 participants reported previous experiences of playing digital games; with 5 participants affirmed that they play digital games every day. The participants generally played digital games on their personal computer, laptop, tablet or smartphone. Games such as monopoly, solitaire, Sudoku, and scrabble are some of the games that they are familiar with.

4.2 Participants Perspectives on Different Platforms

Figure 2 illustrates the views from the participants after interacting with both platforms, which address 6 criteria evaluated through game-play on both platforms. *Mann–Whitney U* test was conducted and showed a significant difference between console and tablet for two items; *Player Enjoy Playing the Game* (U (25) = 35.5, Z = −2.671, p = 0.008), *Player in Total Control* (U (25) = 44.5, Z = −2.130, p = 0.033). The result reveals that when the older people were in a total control of utilising the platform, they found enjoyment and engagement in playing the game. This is tally to our finding in Sect. 4.3.1, when the older people found it was easy to operate console which also offer appropriate user interfaces (i.e. better graphic, big screen), indirectly it brought fun (i.e. social aspect) and enjoyment to them. This result is directly proportional to the andragogical perspective in terms of the older people's need to take control over their learning (i.e. utilising the platform) and enthusiasm towards learning activities they are participating in (i.e. playing games) [15]. Meanwhile, no significant difference is found for the rest of the criteria.

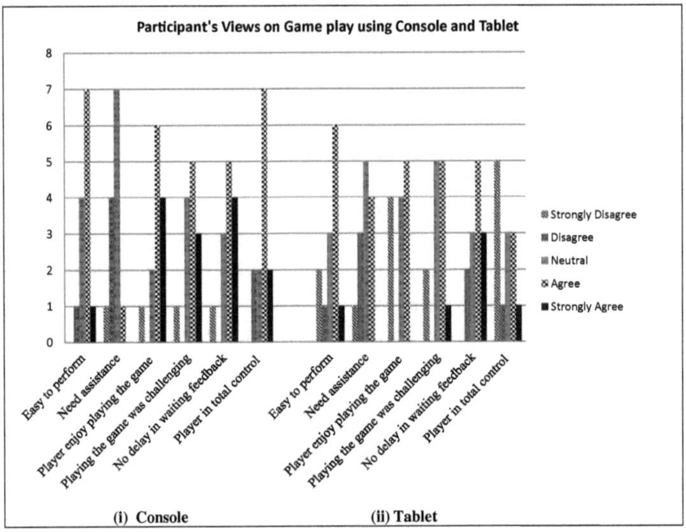

Fig. 2. Participant's view on game-play using *console* and *tablet*

4.3 Group Discussion on the Game-Play Experience

Based on the findings, there are 3 main components that we want to highlight; the view on interacting with the different platforms, views on digital games and change of perspective.

4.3.1 Platform

After the game-play sessions, there was a balanced number of participants (n = 7 each) choosing either platform; console and tablet. Based on the findings, both platforms have their own advantages and disadvantages and this contributed to the selection of platform to the participants – on which they favour the most.

Half of the participants prefer to play games on a tablet; the main reasons being that they can play alone (i.e. when they want to), its portability (can play anywhere at any time) and easy to use and play (less setup process). Pointed out by one participant, *"I prefer using a tablet. If you've got pain or disabilities, much easier to use a tablet. You don't have to be home to do that. It's much portable. You can do it on a train or bus, or sitting and waiting"*. The other half of the participants stated that they found that the console platform has comprehensive displays (better graphics, big screen), which enabled better control, more fun (i.e. social aspect) and provided immersion (i.e. flow), as well as offer physical movement. One participant stated, *"I like to play on that Xbox because you can immerse yourself in the game. And it's not dangerous and you don't need special equipment... You're in the flow and you're doing exercise while doing it. It's easy to understand what you're doing"*. Despite of the advantages of both platform, several disadvantages also been highlighted. For console, the downfall due to the cost barrier and it requires participant to learn some technical skills prior to playing the actual game. *"That one (Xbox), I would hate to do that (setting up). Anything technical like that I'll dumb foul. If somebody set it up, shows how to do it ... then I got it, and I can do it"*.

While participants indicated that tablet has smaller screen and lack of physical elements compared to console make them lost interest in continue playing. One participant mentioned that she needs more time to understand the instruction (not clear on tablet screen) and sometimes delay in response from the system made the tablet games boring and frustrating to her.

The participants aged 66–70 showed higher level of engagement during gameplay using console due to the comprehensive displays and social interaction it offered. *"Console games were very attractive to me – greater possibility of whole body interaction than I previously thought."* However, tablet technology has gained place and widely accepted among the participants. This may be due to its relatively lower price and portability factor. The participants perceived the technology as difficult. *"Identifying controls may have taken a bit of time, but that would be expected for a first time with a particular item of equipment."* However, upon discovering some real life benefits to the game-play, their perceptions towards the technology changed. One participant stated, *"They were generally stimulating and relaxing at the same time"*.

4.3.2 Games

In general, 64% of participants classified as non-gamer, who played games occasionally or not at all; and only 36% were considered gamer, who played games every day (n = 5; 61–65 (40%), 66–70 (60%)). 90% of the participants prefer interacting with the console games (*Kinect Sports – Bowling and Skiing*), because these games were fun, challenging and involve body movement, indirectly leading to some form of exercising. Participants also pointed out they could relate those games with real life experience. Mentioned earlier in Sect. 2, to capture the adequate interaction between players and the games, the aspect of user experience, needs and interests should be considered and examined.

Feedback and suggestions from the participant's interaction and experiences were taken into consideration. Similar to findings by [2–4], age-related declines such as in physical and cognitive functions could influence gameplay (i.e. needs, preferences) for older people. Participants emphasised that simple and clear instructions are important (i.e. written, auditory) and should be included in the game. One participant mentioned that, *"...be viable both ways because actually when you looking at screen, something in your ear telling what to do is good, for me... There are people don't hear very well. So they got to have it and on the screen"*. Simple and less elements in interface design was preferable (i.e. not require too much working memory), appropriate information *"They must not be written in a lot of technical jargon..."*, adjustable interfaces (i.e. font type and size, screen resolution) *"Need to make sure the printing is big. I couldn't see so that straight. My glasses need changes. Older people needed big, bold print"*. Lastly, no timer should be included in the game, as suggested by two participants *"I don't like time limited thing. Because some people take longer to learn things than other"*.

4.3.3 Change of Perspectives

From our findings, we observe that the perspectives on the perceived difficulties and benefits of digital gaming are influenced by their confidence barriers related to their first impression, their perception of engaging with something new (i.e. technology) and their perspective towards the relevance of technology.

4.3.3.1 Something New or Beneficial

As mentioned earlier, some of the participants owned a tablet due to the portability and affordability of the device. The participants demonstrated interest in playing games on the device after participating in the study. For example, one participant (who has 'hand tremor') was impressed to see that he could play car racing using tablet which he never thought of before. He learned playing the games by tilting the tablet to right and left as steering a real car. *"I was pleasantly surprised by some features on the tablet (mainly the steering by tilting it – I hadn't thought of that as an option before the session), and the details visible were better than I would have thought beforehand"*. It showed that the participant learned new knowledge and learning new thing, when playing the car-racing game on the tablet and learned new skills by discovering the functions on the tablet (tilting to imitate steering a wheel).

Based on the andragogical perspective, it would be easier for someone to learn something or use something new if it has relevance or beneficial to them. People will only interact with something familiar, interest them, meaningful and beneficial to them. As mentioned one participant, *"... if you would to offer me a serious driving... to improve your driving skills or an aircraft simulation or something. I might be more interested. But, that's maybe because I am an engineer and more interested in that type of thing"*.

4.3.3.2 Social Aspect: Peer Support

From the findings, 76.9% of participants like to play digital game alone compare to 15.4% preferred having companies. Several studies show that older people like to play digital games with their family members and friends, which encourage social interaction and reduce the digital divide among the intergeneration [17, 18]. They changed their perspectives when they had seen their family members or friends playing it. Responses from two participants regarding playing digital game (i.e. crosswords) together:

> A: *"... I notice my newspaper is part of the package that you get a guide in it and you get the crosswords. Now, at the moment, we have one paper - newspaper and if we both do the crosswords... I have to do in the little piece of paper before"*
> B: *"And one of us can do it online...that's true. I never thought of that"*

As described in Sect. 4.3.1, one of the reasons why older people like to play game using the console is because of the social aspects (interaction) it offers. Older people will perceive playing games with family members (i.e. grandchildren) and friends could be used as a social support (medium for social interaction). Another participant stated she enjoyed the social interaction with family members while playing games. *"I had played a console game before at my brother's house on Christmas day. I think it was very funny to play with them (playing tennis games). And we have a situation that is funny... ask another person to move a little bit... *laugh*"*.

This is in line with the andragogical perspective, where adult learners are more interested in learning or do something that has immediate relevance to them (work or personal life). In other words, they prefer to engage in something that is important or beneficial to them. However, such perspectives can change based on our findings. As for example, 5 participants reluctance of using new technology such as games changed once they realised the benefits and observed the practice of others. One participant who mentioned had a knee problem and would not join game-play session (using console), changed her mind and joined the session once she saw her friends having fun and enjoying themselves. Other participants mentioned that they will play the game again as they find it fun and at the same time the game was perceived to stimulate their brain and lead body movement associated to some form of exercising.

5 Conclusion

The study shows that older people's initial perspectives and perceptions towards digital gaming are influenced by perceived difficulties, relevance and benefits. The results of our study indicate that there are three main components that should be considered when investigating the interaction and experience of older people with digital games; the perspectives of engaging with different platforms, views on digital games and the factors that could change their perspectives. However, there are other components, which are not addressed in this paper, i.e. challenges faced by the older people around ergonomics issues. The other components will be addressed in our future work, including the mapping of these components with our findings in this paper.

Acknowledgments. This research is funded by Universiti Malaysia Sarawak (UNIMAS) and the Ministry of Education Malaysia. Thanks to all participants for taking part in the study.

References

1. Weisman, S.: Computer games for the frail elderly. Gerontologist **23**(4), 361–363 (1983)
2. Whitcomb, G.R.: Computer games for the elderly. ACM SIGGAS Comput. Soc. **20**(3), 112–115 (1990). Rosenberg, R.S. (ed.). ACM, New York
3. Ijsselsteijn, W., Nap, H.H., de Kort, Y., Poels, K.: Digital game design for elderly users. In: Proceedings of the 2007 Conference on Future Play, pp. 17–22. ACM (2007)
4. Flores, E., Tobon, G., Cavallaro, E., Cavallaro, F.I., Perry, J.C., Keller, T.: Improving patient motivation in game development for motor deficit rehabilitation. In: Proceedings of the 2008 International Conference on Advances in Computer Entertainment Technology, pp. 381–384. ACM (2008)
5. Gamberini, L., Raya, M.A., Barresi, G., Fabregat, M., Ibanez, F., Prontu, L.: Cognition, technology and games for the elderly: an introduction to ELDERGAMES project. Psychnology J. **4**(3), 285–308 (2006)
6. Gerling, K.M., Masuch, M.: When gaming is not suitable for everyone: playtesting wii games with frail elderly. In: 1st Workshop on Game Accessibility: Xtreme Interaction Design (GAXID 2011) (2011)
7. Gerling, K.M., Schild, J., Masuch, M.: Exergame design for elderly users: the case study of SilverBalance. In: Proceedings of the 7th International Conference on Advances in Computer Entertainment Technology, pp. 66–69. ACM, November 2010
8. The Entertainment Software Association (ESA), Essential Facts about the Computer and Video Game Industry (2011). http://www.theesa.com/facts/pdfs/ESA_EF_2011.pdf
9. Pearce, C.: The truth about baby boomer gamers a study of over-forty computer game players. Games Cult. **3**(2), 142–174 (2008)
10. Nap, H.H., Kort, Y.D., IJsselsteijn, W.A.: Senior gamers: preferences, motivations and needs. Gerontechnology **8**(4), 247–262 (2009)
11. Nacke, L.E., Nacke, A., Lindley, C.A.: Brain training for silver gamers: effects of age and game form on effectiveness, efficiency, self-assessment, and gameplay experience. CyberPsychol. Behav. **12**(5), 493–499 (2009)
12. De Schutter, B., Vanden Abeele, V.: Meaningful play in elderly life. In: Proceedings of ICA (2008)
13. Gerling, K.M., Schulte, F.P., Smeddinck, J., Masuch, M.: Game design for older adults: effects of age-related changes on structural elements of digital games. In: Herrlich, M., Malaka, R., Masuch, M. (eds.) ICEC 2012. LNCS, vol. 7522, pp. 235–242. Springer, Heidelberg (2012). doi:10.1007/978-3-642-33542-6_20
14. Romero, N., Sturm, J., Bekker, T., De Valk, L., Kruitwagen, S.: Playful persuasion to support older adults' social and physical activities. Interact. Comput. **22**(6), 485–495 (2010)
15. Knowles, M.S.: Associates: Andragogy in Action. Applying Modern Principles of Adult Education. Jossey Bass, San Francisco (1984)
16. Tanaka, K., Parker, J.R., Baradoy, G., Sheehan, D., Holash, J.R., Katz, L.: A comparison of exergaming interfaces for use in rehabilitation programs and research. J. Can. Game Stud. Assoc. **6**(9), 69–81 (2012)
17. Khoo, E.T., Lee, S.P., Cheok, A.D., Kodagoda, S., Zhou, Y., Toh, G.S.: Age invaders: social and physical inter-generational family entertainment. In: CHI 2006 Extended Abstracts on Human Factors in Computing Systems, pp. 243–246. ACM (2006)
18. Keyani, P., Hsieh, G., Mutlu, B., Easterday, M., Forlizzi, J.: DanceAlong: supporting positive social exchange and exercise for the elderly through dance. In: CHI 2005 Extended Abstracts on Human Factors in Computing Systems, pp. 1541–1544. ACM (2005)

A Serious Game for Digital Skill Building Among Individuals at Risk, Promoting Employability and Social Inclusion

Hariklia Tsalapatas[1,2], Olivier Heidmann[1,2](✉), and Elias Houstis[1,2]

[1] University of Thessaly, Argonafton & Filellinon, 38221 Volos, Greece
htsalapa@inf.uth.gr, olivier.heidmann@gmail.com, enh@uth.gr

[2] I.RE.TE.TH, Dimitriados 95 & Pavlou Mela, 38333 Volos, Greece

Abstract. The EMPLOY project addresses the development of digital skills among young learners with the objective of enhancing their future employment opportunities in innovation-related sectors that are expected by policy makers to drive economic growth. Digital skills are considered among the basic and transversal competencies that are necessary in wide economic sectors and as such must be developed among individuals with diverse professional and career aspirations, independently of area. It also promotes the strategic deployment of ICT in education as a learning tool, and the development of ICT applications for learning and the integration of digital tools as complementary educational content within wider, blended learning and teaching processes. The integration of proposed technology and pedagogies offer broad learning benefits to both students and teachers by enhancing motivation, promoting long-term engagement with the learning process, providing timely and constructive feedback, and promoting critical and entrepreneurial thinking mind sets.

Keywords: Serious games · Digital skills · Employability · Inclusion

1 Introduction

According to the Grand Coalition for Digital Jobs [1] in the coming decade there will be a shortage of 900.000 ICT professionals in Europe in the ICT sector and ICT using sectors. This shortage is seen as a threat to economic growth as it may be an obstacle to business development activities of corporations and SMEs alike that cannot find skilled personnel to pursue entrepreneurial expansion. According to the Coalition, economic recovery and growth in Europe is expected to be driven by the knowledge economy, which has elevated needs on skilled personnel, especially in relation to digital skills. Some argue that for every job that opens in ICT 5 more jobs open in other sectors. Recognizing the potential threat to economic growth and sustainability of business activities in broad sectors, the European Commission has introduced a number of initiatives, including the Grand Coalition for Digital Jobs and the New Skills for New Jobs Agenda [2], that identify digital skills as core, basic competencies to which priority is given in the context of ET2020 [3] and other educational and development strategic initiatives.

C. Vaz de Carvalho et al. (Eds.): SGAMES 2016, LNICST 176, pp. 91–98, 2017.
DOI: 10.1007/978-3-319-51055-2_12

On the other hand, it is expected that there will be a loss of jobs with low skills that may reach as high as 16 M positions in Europe in the coming decade. This trend in the job market may be a contributing factor to rising unemployment rates and threaten social cohesion. Low skilled individuals, who in the present may be attracted by jobs that have low entry level requirements, may face increasing challenges in becoming employed as the demand for highly skilled professionals is expected to rise.

The EU-28 unemployment rate was 10.8% in January 2014 according to Eurostat [4]. This is the result of an increasing trend in unemployment which was 8.5% in 2001 and has been exaggerated during the crisis in the years following 2008. Youth unemployment rates are significantly higher exceeding 50% or even reaching 60% in southern Europe. The retraining or refocusing of unemployed individuals in relation to digital skills may contribute to closing the gap between competence availability and demand, reducing unemployment, and facilitating sustainable economic growth.

Individuals who are at risk of exclusion, including persons who are not employed and/or not in education or training (NEETs), have dropped out of school early, are of low social economic status, are migrants, constitute minorities, and others are at increased risk of facing employment challenges as a result of ineffective or misaligned skill sets and inadequate digital competences. This is a consequence of vicious cycles in which any of the above factors or combinations of two or more drive individuals at risk of exclusion, i.e. at the fringes of social networks, out of educational channels in pursuit of jobs with low skill requirements with the objective of covering day to day needs. The missed training opportunities further exasperate the mismatch between available skills in those individuals and ones demanded by the market resulting to further reduced possibilities of becoming socially included, active citizens pursuing broad options for personal and professional fulfillment.

The above point to the urgent need for interventions in education and training practices towards strengthening the digital skill profiles of individuals at risk of exclusion, with an emphasis on the next generation that will become professionally active in the coming years. Enhanced digital skill sets, driven by market demands, will increase the employability of this group for their own benefit by enhancing their ability to follow dreams, for the benefit of their communities through enhanced social cohesion, and for businesses through enhanced capacity of businesses to support economic activity in an evolving, knowledge-driven economy. It will further strengthen the competitiveness of Europe in the global economic environment through a highly trained work force that can support innovation-related economic activities.

2 EMPLOY, A Game-Based Learning Approach

The EMPLOY project aims at building the digital skills among young learners at risk of exclusion through strategic use of ICT, and specifically game-based learning that facilitates exposure to work-driven activities that require digital competencies, problem-solving capacity, and analytical thinking. The advantages of the proposed active learning, game-based approach are linked to increased knowledge retention, ability to transfer knowledge to the real-world, and learning games that drive inspiration from the needs of the world of work thus broadening professional options through awareness of market needs and enhancement of skill sets.

EMPLOY is innovative by addressing the issue of digital skill building among individuals that are at risk of social exclusion early in life, in primary and lower secondary school, through activities that are linked to real world needs. By addressing digital skill development among youngsters aged 10 to 15, the project aims at preventing the issue of less than adequate digital skills among individuals at risk of social exclusion, which is often a result of reduced access to learning opportunities and services, from ever arising, thus promoting equity and inclusion in education. The project promotes the broadening of career options for individuals at risk of exclusion by raising awareness on professional profiles that will be in demand in the coming years and by building the skills that are necessary for entering the knowledge economy by:

- Increasing access to learning resources through openly available serious games
- Empowering learners to take control of their lives by addressing core digital competencies early, in school education
- Deploying and evaluating serious games as learning tools towards building skills among individuals at risk of social exclusion that will enhance their employability and as a result their capacity to be socially included and civically active
- Raising awareness on broadened professional development paths related to innovation

The project uses ICT in a strategic manner by introducing serious gaming as a means for exposing young learners to activities that simulate the real world but are age appropriate. Research shows that students remember only 10% of what they read; 20% of what they hear; 30% if they see visuals; 50% if they watch someone doing something and explaining it; and 90% of what they do themselves, even only as a simulation [5]. There is a wide consensus in the scientific community on the educational value of serious games towards enhancing motivation, engagement with learning processes, and knowledge scaffolding. However, scientists also agree that the educational effectiveness of serious games in specific learning contexts still needs to be tested. Serious games evaluation efforts are so far scattered and no common evaluation approach appears to be broadly adopted. Often, failure of serious games as learning tools is related to implementation that does not address all aspects of serious games, i.e. pedagogical design, gaming design, and user-game interaction design. EMPLOY contributes to research related to serious gaming evaluation in learning contexts by designing and executing an extensive evaluation strategy for establishing the added value of the learning games.

The project also innovates at the learning intervention level:

- EMPLOY promotes active learning by doing, which has been seen to significantly contribute to knowledge retention (FAS)
- It links gaming to specific learning objectives tied both to school activities (e.g. STEM education) and work practices
- It contributes to linking learning activities to desired learning outcomes through immediate feedback

- It empowers learners to transfer new knowledge to other educational and life activities through real-world inspired learning scenarios
- It promotes knowledge transferability through role playing
- It promotes analytical thinking skills, which are gradually favored in the job market as compared to routine manual and cognitive ones [6]
- It stimulates entrepreneurial thinking and creativity by encouraging learners to come up with original solutions
- It nurtures the development of latent digital skills that to a certain degree young individuals possess towards advanced digital literacy relevant in the world of work
- It exploits gamification features including competition, collaboration, and awards towards learning through activities that are inclusive and encourage participation

3 Design Goals of the EMPLOY Serious Game

Learning digital skills is sometimes resumed in learning how to use the most common digital tools in the market, focusing on a more mechanical and technical aspect rather than a more global approach.

In order to avoid this dry approach and to go beyond the simple use of a spreadsheet or a word processor, the EMPLOY Serious Game aims at presenting in an interesting way digital skills themselves rather than how to simply implement them. In other terms, detach the user from the digital tool to teach them how to use any tool in any circumstances.

Here is a list of a series of digital skill the game aims to cover:

- Understanding the concept of databases
- Using a search engine to find the desired information
- Understanding the concept and the management of digital identities
- Knowing how to use email
- Knowing how to use instant messaging
- Knowing how to use video calls
- Knowing how to use social media
- Shopping online
- Managing your bank account
- Using government online services and saving time
- Using accurate sources of support
- Teaching yourself simple tasks using video lessons
- Using feedback from other internet users to solve common problems
- Identifying and assessing accurate sources of information
- Getting quick, effective solutions to problems from safe, accurate sources
- Recognizing scams, phishing, and other types of cyber malevolence
- Protecting yourself from fraud or scams by recognizing secure websites
- Protecting your personal data
- Respecting the privacy of others/third parties
- Using secure websites for financial transactions
- Being aware about the notions of copyright and knowing the available solutions
- Protecting personal data

4 Design and Implementation of the EMPLOY Serious Game

By playing the game, the users of the software will be placed in an office environment where they will need to solve daily tasks of varying difficulty. All the tasks presented will require a certain digital skill or a combination of several of them to be performed adequately. Each in-game day correspond to a certain amount of game time and at the end of the game day in-game currency will be earned according to the successes and failures of the players in the given tasks. A certain amount of currency (fixed or variable according to some events) will also be deduced from the players' accounts every day for up-keeping/maintenance/etc. purposes.

The overall goal of the game is being able to keep playing, with the earnings from the successes in the daily tasks outweighing the general costs incurred.

The Unity engine and development tools will be used to create this game, ensuring a multi-platform reach for the EMPLOY product. A 2D perspective has been selected while retaining the full capacities of the 3D Unity Engine.

The game can be used both inside and outside of the classroom. The software needs to be used in the context of a course, and its design has been adapted to the constraints of classrooms and courses by warranting playtimes of various lengths, anywhere between 5 min and several hours.

Each game in the EMPLOY Project corresponds to the work life of an employee or entrepreneur or any worker faced with having to deal with computers and digital challenges in their everyday work life. The goal of the game is to keep playing, which in game terms means keep working. A savegame will be automatically created at the end of every in-game day, in order to allow the player to go back in time if they need or want to do so. At the beginning of every in game day, the player will start at a desk or in an outdoor environment. The tasks will be exactly similar in both cases, the main difference being that in the outdoor environment the player will have to use mobile devices instead of computers to complete the assigned tasks. Every in-game working day will last the exact same real time duration. Once the player arrives in the daily environment, he/she will be presented a general briefing for the day. There will be an infinite number of tasks presented to the player, in a serial fashion. The next task is only presented once the last one has been completed.

The player will be able to drag and drop important information from the task given to his/her work environment in order to achieve the task. For example, if the task is to send an email, the body, subject, recipients of the email can be dragged and dropped from the task zone to the work environment zone, here an email client.

The tasks could be presented by colleagues or clients, either in the flesh if the player is in an indoor environment or through email or text messaging if the player is outdoors.

Some task might require a combination of different skills. For example if an email is to be sent to the CEO of a company the player doesn't have the email address of, then it means that the player will need to do an Internet research in order to find it. Alternatively, the user could also use instant messaging to ask a colleague. Several approaches could be possible to solve a certain given task. As the whole game is based

Fig. 1. An early version of the main menu

on time performance, the amount of time each sub-task and task will take has to be carefully weighed for game balancing purposes.

A visual and/or audio cue will signal in advance the end of the in-game work time. Once it is over, the player environment freezes and a new screen appear, summing up the performance of the day. The daily summary of the players' successes and failure

Fig. 2. A later version of the game design, where the three zones described in Fig. 1 are still present but blend better into the environment

could be presented either as a detailed lists of all tasks undertaken or in a more simple fashion a screen to transform each success into a credit in the form of the game internal currency. Each failure could be transformed into a debit of in-game currency, but this might be a bit harsh as it is a double punishment. After the summary of the player's daily action, a certain amount of in-game currency will be deducted from the player's account. The screen detailing the successes and failures and the one summing up the daily costs could be merged into one.

This means that the players are obliged to succeed in a minimum amount of tasks per day; the exact number of those successful tasks will be ironed out during a game balancing phase later on during the game development (Fig. 2).

5 Conclusions

The EMPLOY projects foresees the creation of a methodological learning framework that exploits emerging ICT, and specifically active, explorative, and collaborative learning through serious games, for enhancing key digital and STEM competencies of school learners so that they are in-line with industry and market demands fostering employability. The framework will take into account analyses on the training requirements of school learners as well as needs for building the competencies of teachers and will be designed for integration into existing school practices enriching learning experiences and learning outcomes.

The project consortium will also author a proof-of-concept serious game for the development of ICT skills among individuals at risk of exclusion. The game will draw inspiration from real-life activities that deploy ICT for work purposes and will build digital capacity among young learners in primary and lower secondary education; the game interface will be available in all languages represented in the consortium through project partners, i.e. Turkish, Greek, Estonian, French, and Italian, as well as in English. An accompanying user guide on the proposed ICT-skill building serious game, acting as a reference on game use; will be available in Turkish, Greek, Estonian, French, and Italian, as well as in English.

Instructional support content in the form of good practice videos will facilitate the integration of proposed methodologies and tools into existing school practices, enriching learning for the benefit of the ultimate end-users, i.e. learners and teachers.

Acknowledgements. This work is funded with support from the European Commission, Life Long Learning Programme. The publication reflects the views of the authors only and the Commission cannot be held responsible for any use made of the information within.

References

1. European Commission website: https://ec.europa.eu/digital-single-market/en/grand-coalition-digital-jobs
2. European Commission website: http://ec.europa.eu/social/main.jsp?catId=958
3. European Commission website: http://ec.europa.eu/education/policy/strategic-framework/

4. Eurostat website: http://ec.europa.eu/eurostat/statistics-explained/index.php/Unemployment_statistics/
5. Federation of American Scientist, Harnessing the Power of Videogames for Learning (2006). http://fas.org/programs/ltp/publications/summit/Summit%20on%20Educational%20Games.pdf
6. Levy, F., Murnane, R.J.: The New Divisions of Labor: How Computers Are Creating the Next Job Market. Princeton University Press (2005)

Learning and Long-Term Retention of Task-Specific Training in a Non-injured Population Using the Computer Assisted Rehabilitation Environment (CAREN)

Amanda E. Markham(✉), Kathrine A. Service, John-David Collins, and Pinata H. Sessoms

Warfighter Performance Department, Naval Health Research Center, 140 Sylvester Rd., San Diego, CA 92106, USA
{amanda.e.markham2.ctr, kathrine.a.service.ctr, john.d.collins1.ctr, pinata.h.sessoms.civ}@mail.mil

Abstract. Task-specific training in virtual environments (VEs) can provide practice for skills that are transferred to real-world settings. The present study examined skill acquisition and retention of a non-injured population performing a sensorimotor navigation task in the Computer Assisted Rehabilitation Environment (CAREN). Seventeen subjects participated twice weekly for 6 weeks, with follow-up visits at 3-month intervals for one year. Subjects performed a navigation task, where they drove a virtual boat through a scene using weight shifting and body movement. Subjects improved over time on all outcome measures. A significant effect was observed for visit number on total score, time to complete the task, number of buoys navigated successfully, and number of penalties incurred. No differences were observed between the last training visit and any follow-up visit. Task-specific training in immersive VEs may be effective for warfighter operational skills training and rehabilitation of wounded warriors, by utilizing tasks that lead to long-term retention.

Keywords: CAREN · Virtual environment · Task-specific training · Retention · Operational tasks

1 Introduction

Task-specific training has been used successfully in a variety of injured and healthy populations [1–4] and can serve as a method of providing practice before applying the skills in real-world settings. Various studies have analyzed the effect of different methods of training a motor skill and demonstrated that mentally practicing a motor skill provides some improvement in performance [5], but does not serve as a replacement for physical practice [6]. Virtual environments (VEs) have been used to augment practice of motor tasks by simultaneously challenging physical and mental performance, particularly in the field of rehabilitation [7, 8]. VEs can provide feedback to the subject such as body positioning and can even incorporate physiological measurements like heart rate and muscle activity. Some research has shown that augmented

C. Vaz de Carvalho et al. (Eds.): SGAMES 2016, LNICST 176, pp. 99–108, 2017.
DOI: 10.1007/978-3-319-51055-2_13

feedback in a VE has a direct effect on performance of a real task, indicating that the components of the VE can directly relate to rehabilitation or training performance [9]. Distributing practice of a skill across multiple days is an important factor in optimal motor skill learning and retention [10]. Constant training is more effective for skill acquisition, while variable training is more effective for skill retention [11]. Previous work studying task-specific training of the wounded warrior has shown improvements in skill learning and retention in VEs [4]. Additionally, in military and law enforcement populations, more realistic training scenarios have a greater physiological effect on subjects compared with less realistic training on the same skill. These scenarios have also produced greater motivation to succeed in subsequent trainings [12, 13]. The relevance of the training task and multisensory cues are important [14] to its transference to actual task performance.

The Computer Assisted Rehabilitation Environment (CAREN; Motek-Forcelink BV, Amsterdam, The Netherlands) is a VE that has the capability to provide relatively realistic training scenarios. The CAREN consists of a force plate-instrumented treadmill that sits atop a six-degrees-of-freedom motion platform. Visual displays are projected on a large screen and can be synchronized with the platform and/or subject movement. Although previous work has studied task-specific training of motor skills in a variety of environments among healthy and injured populations [15], including patients with stroke, traumatic brain injury (TBI), and lower-limb amputation, little is known about skill learning and retention using the unique CAREN platform. The purpose of this study was to understand the adaptation of healthy, non-injured adults performing a navigation task in an immersive VE and to determine the long-term retention of this task-specific training over time.

2 Methods

2.1 Subject Population

Seven male and 10 female subjects participated in this study. The mean$\pm$standard deviation age for the subjects was 29.24 ± 4.41 years and body mass index was 22.97 ± 3.04 kg/m^2. Subjects were healthy and had no known orthopedic injury or other injury affecting their balance, learning, or vision. Volunteers gave written informed consent. This study was approved by the Naval Health Research Center (NHRC) institutional review board.

2.2 Task-Specific Training Program

The task on the CAREN involved a virtual boat navigation course in which subjects stood on the motion platform facing forward and navigated through a slalom course of 50 buoys. Subjects were instructed to use body movement to control the direction and speed of the virtual boat by shifting their body forward, backward, and side-to-side. Reflective markers placed on the subjects' shoulders and captured using an optical motion capture system (Motion Analysis Corporation, Santa Rosa, CA) allowed them to interact with the VE and navigate the virtual boat through the course (Fig. 1).

Fig. 1. A subject navigates a boat through a virtual scene in the CAREN

Platform motion mimicked the movement of the boat through the course and over the waves. Subjects participated in the training twice a week for 6 weeks, for a total of 12 visits. The initial training session occurred at visit 1 and the final training session occurred at visit 12. Follow-up tests were also conducted up to 1 year later at 3, 6, 9, and 12 months following the 12th training visit, for a total of 16 testing sessions.

2.3 Measurements

A total score was calculated using an algorithm that accounted for the number of buoys that were navigated successfully, the number of objects (buoys [−1 point] and islands [−5 points]) hit, the time to complete the task, and specific course parameters (held constant for the sessions in this study: i.e. maximum wave height = 3 m and maximum boat speed = 15 m/s). Study outcomes included total score, number of buoys successfully navigated, penalties for objects hit, and time to complete the course.

2.4 Statistical Analyses

A multiple regression analysis was conducted to evaluate how well each performance variable predicted the overall score. The predictors were completion time, penalties, and buoys successfully navigated, while the criterion variable was the overall task score.

A one-way repeated-measures analysis of variance (ANOVA) was conducted to determine if there were differences in outcome measures over the 12 training visits. When Mauchly's test indicated assumption of sphericity was violated, Greenhouse-Geisser corrected tests were reported. Post hoc tests using Bonferroni correction were conducted to determine if there were significant differences between visits. Only sequential visit-to-visit scores (i.e., visit 1 compared with visit 2, visit 2 compared with visit 3, and so on) and comparisons between visit 1 and all subsequent visits were reported.

Paired t tests were conducted on available total scores between visit 12 and the four follow-up visits (3, 6, 9, and 12 months) to determine if the skills of navigating through the virtual boat task were retained. Not all subjects were able to attend all four follow-up sessions, resulting in different N values for each follow-up pairwise comparison. Data analyses were conducted using SPSS statistical software, version 19 (IBM, Armonk, NY). Significance was defined as $p \leq .05$.

3 Results

3.1 Multiple Regression Analysis

All variance inflation factors were between 1 and 2, indicating that multicollinearity was not an issue. The linear combination of the performance variables was significantly related to the overall task score, $F(3, 193) = 923.0$, $p < .005$, $R^2 = .935$, $R^2_{adjusted} = .934$, indicating that the model explains more than 93% of the variance in overall score. Evaluation of each of the variables indicates that all three variables significantly contributed to the prediction of the dependent variable (score) in the model. Overall score was significantly predicted by the number of penalties (beta = −.30, $t(193) = -14.81$, $p < .005$), task completion time (beta = −.45, $t(193) = -21.85$, $p < .005$), and buoys successfully navigated (beta = −.49, t(193) = 22.89, $p < .005$). From these results, the number of buoys successfully navigated made the strongest unique contribution to total score, followed by task completion time, and lastly, number of penalties.

3.2 Total Score

Total scores ranged from 1006 to 1440 points. Improvements were shown in all individuals over the 12 training visits (Fig. 2). Results showed a significant effect for visit number, $F(4.40, 70.36) = 29.975$, $p < .001$. Post hoc comparisons indicated no significant difference in total score for any sequential visits. Average total scores over the 12 training visits significantly improved, displaying an increase of 241 points between visit 1 and visit 12 ($p < .001$). Between visits 1 and 2, mean score on the task increased by 109.71 points, the largest difference in score between consecutive visits, but was not significant ($p = .138$). Other consecutive visit differences were between 0.47 and 33.18 points. All other visits (3 through 12) were significantly different from visit 1 (comparison of visits 1 and 3, $p = .011$; all other visits, $p < .001$). No significant differences in scores were reported between the final training visit and any of the follow-up visits (Table 1).

3.3 Time to Complete the Task

Time to complete the course improved over the 12 training visits. Results showed a significant effect for visit number, $F(2.75, 43.92) = 74.297$, $p < .001$. Post hoc comparisons revealed significant differences in number of seconds to complete the boat task

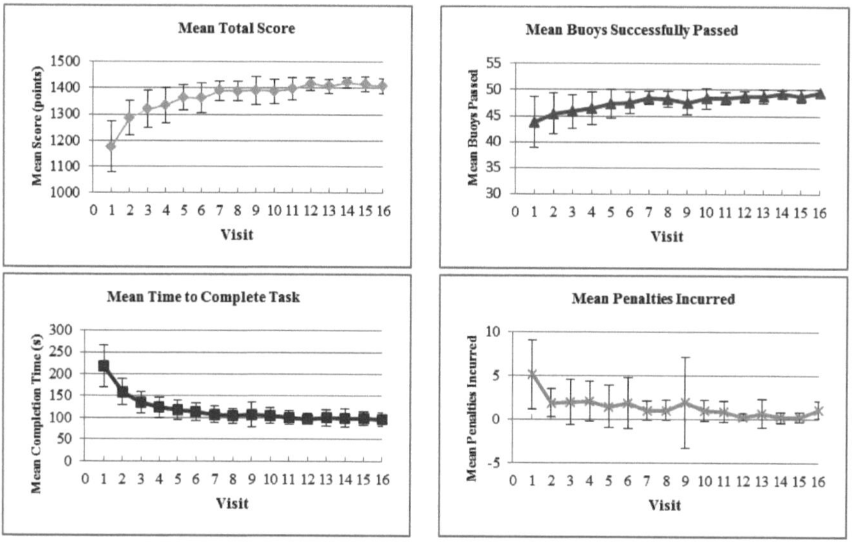

Fig. 2. Mean and standard deviations of total score, time to complete, buoys passed, and penalties incurred across the 16 visits. Follow-up visits at 3, 6, 9, and 12 months are labeled as Visit 13, 14, 15, and 16, respectively.

Table 1. Comparison of Visit 12 with follow-up visits for total score.

Pair	Variable	*N*	Total Score *M* (SD)*	*t* Score	*p* Value	95% CI
1	Visit 12	9	1416.44 (28.07)	0.67	.525	−21.66 to 39.22
	3-month follow-up		1407.67 (27.51)			
2	Visit 12	10	1414.50 (27.02)	−0.80	.445	−29.53 to 14.13
	6-month follow-up		1422.20 (19.61)			
3	Visit 12	15	1416.13 (24.84)	0.05	.958	−18.16 to 19.09
	9-month follow-up		1415.67 (27.33)			
4	Visit 12	16	1415.38 (24.38)	1.00	.332	−9.08 to 25.21
	12-month follow-up		1407.31 (28.11)			

Note: CI, confidence interval; M, mean; SD, standard deviation.

between visits 1 and 2 ($p < .001$), visits 2 and 3 ($p = .003$), and visits 3 and 4 ($p = .032$). Pairwise comparisons for additional sequential visit pairs yielded no significant results. The largest decrease in time for consecutive visits was between 1 and 2 (mean difference = 83.47 s). In one comparison (visits 8 and 9) mean time *increased* between visits by 3.47 s. Mean completion time decreased by 120.7 s and was significantly different ($p < .001$) between visits 1 and 12. No significant differences were observed between the final training visit and any of the follow-up visits (Table 2).

Table 2. Comparison of Visit 12 with follow-up visits for time to complete boat navigation task.

Pair	Variable	N	Time to Complete Task, M (SD)*	t Score	p Value	95% CI
1	Visit 12	9	95.54 (12.16)	−0.78	.456	−19.29 to 9.51
	3-month follow-up		100.33 (19.41)			
2	Visit 12	9	98.44 (15.80)	−0.18	.862	−12.30 to 10.52
	6-month follow-up		99.33 (21.98)			
3	Visit 12	16	98.19 (13.22)	0.04	.969	−6.56 to 6.81
	9-month follow-up		98.06 (15.76)			
4	Visit 12	16	98.06 (13.34)	0.43	.674	−5.20 to 7.82
	12-month follow-up		96.75 (15.99)			

Note: Time is in seconds. CI, confidence interval; M, mean; SD, standard deviation.

3.4 Number of Buoys Navigated Successfully

The number of buoys navigated successfully increased over the 12 training visits from a mean of 43.57 to 48.57 ($p = .147$) (Fig. 2). Number of buoys successfully passed for individual subjects ranged from 35 to 53. Results showed a significant effect for visit number, $F(3.89, 50.60) = 4.372$, $p = .004$. Post hoc results indicated no significant difference in number of buoys passed for any visit pairs (Table 3).

Table 3. Comparison of Visit 12 with follow-up visits for number of buoys passed.

Pair	Variable	N	Buoys Passed, M (SD)*	t Score	p Value	95% CI
1	Visit 12	8	48.75 (1.16)	.55	.598	−0.82 to 1.32
	3-month follow-up		48.50 (1.07)			
2	Visit 12	8	48.63 (1.06)	−1.49	.180	−1.62 to 0.37
	6-month follow-up		49.25 (0.71)			
3	Visit 12	14	48.64 (1.15)	−0.33	.745	−1.07 to 0.79
	9-month follow-up		48.79 (1.25)			
4	Visit 12	14	48.79 (1.05)	−2.59	.022	−1.18 to −0.11
	12-month follow-up		49.43 (0.65)			

Note: CI, confidence interval; M, mean; SD, standard deviation.

3.5 Number of Penalties Incurred

The number of penalties incurred by individual subjects ranged from 0 to 20. Results showed a significant effect for visit number, $F(3.77, 60.43) = 4.060$, $p = .006$, though post hoc comparisons indicated no significant difference in the number of penalties incurred for any sequential visit pairs. Average number of penalties incurred over the 12 training visits improved, decreasing by 4.82 penalties between visits 1 and 12 (p = .006). Significant decreases occurred between visits 1 and 7 (p = .025), 1 and 8 (p = .013), 1 and 10 (p = .016), and 1 and 11 (p = .013). No significant decreases were observed for any other pairs or the follow-up visits (Table 4).

Table 4. Comparison of Visit 12 with follow-up visits for number of penalties incurred.

Pair	Variable	N	Penalties, M (SD)*	t Score	p Value	95% CI
1	Visit 12	9	0.44 (0.53)	−0.45	.665	−1.36 to 0.92
	3-month follow-up		0.67 (1.66)			
2	Visit 12	10	0.30 (0.48)	0.56	.591	−0.31 to 0.51
	6-month follow-up		0.20 (0.63)			
3	Visit 12	15	0.33 (0.49)	0.37	.719	−0.32 to 0.46
	9-month follow-up		0.27 (0.59)			
4	Visit 12	16	0.31 (0.48)	−2.78	.014	−1.43 to −0.19
	12-month follow-up		1.13 (1.02)			

Note: CI, confidence interval; M, mean; SD, standard deviation.

4 Discussion

The results of this study indicate that task-specific sensorimotor skills improved with regular exposure to a navigation task in an immersive VE. Additionally, these skills were retained without practice for up to one year following the training program. Total score and the elements that comprised the total score (time to complete the boat navigation task, number of buoys navigated successfully, and number of penalties incurred) improved as a function of visit number across the 12 training visits. Although significant differences were not observed in sequential visits, there were significant improvements across the visits as a whole.

The greatest improvements in time to complete the task were observed between the first three visits, with smaller improvements thereafter. This is similar to previous work in which two groups showed improvements on a timed motor sequence task between days 1 through 4 of training, reaching a plateau in performance by days 4 through 5 [10]. Other work shows improvements in military operational performance after at least 3 visits using VE training [16], including significant improvements in driving performance of military personnel who had suffered a TBI after 4 to 6 training sessions of simulated driving in a VE [17]. Our results match published work, showing most learning occurs within the first four sessions of training. Work in other areas related to the CAREN has shown that six training sessions is sufficient for motor training [4], but more research is needed. No significant differences in scores, time to complete the boat navigation task, number of buoys navigated successfully, or number of penalties incurred were observed between visit 12 compared with any of the four follow-up visits. This indicates that the task-specific skill was retained long-term and provides support that the 12-visit program over the 6-week period was effective for providing the necessary training to teach and retain this specific skill for up to a year. This matches well with previous reports that suggest there are few declines in performance after a motor skill task is well-learned, even after a long delay with no practice [10, 18, 19]. Although VEs are widely used in military operations training (e.g., flight simulators, infantry immersive trainers), further research demonstrating the effectiveness of training in VEs compared with other types of instruction, such as field-based and classroom-based training, is needed.

The results from this study are useful for comparison with injured populations. Recently, researchers at NHRC and Naval Medical Center San Diego have used the same boat navigation task in the CAREN VE as a method of vestibular physical therapy for wounded warriors with TBI. Preliminary findings show patients who underwent 12 training sessions over a 6-week period started out with significantly lower scores than the non-injured control group, but were able to achieve similar scores by visit 12 [20]. This work provides support for the 12-visit training protocol in the CAREN VE as an effective program for providing task-specific training for patient populations, and it may be used to inform rehabilitation programs for other injuries such as musculoskeletal injury or amputation. Use of VEs for training injured warfighters is not meant to replace traditional therapies, but rather to provide patients with an alternative form of therapy that supports current strategies and is relevant to real-world scenarios [21]. In addition to providing a safe and controlled learning atmosphere for training healthy and injured warfighters, the CAREN platform also provides a tool for measurement and assessment of performance.

5 Conclusions

After training in an immersive VE, the acquisition of a novel skill seems to be quickly acquired and retained in a healthy, non-injured population. Task-specific training in an immersive VE can be useful for warfighters to acquire and practice skills before applying those skills in an operational setting. Task-specific training in the immersive VE may also be useful for rehabilitating injured populations, since specific movements can be practiced while the patient is within a safe, controlled setting. Capabilities of this VE training have implications for returning injured warfighters to duty due to the potential for positive physical and cognitive performance gains. Details of this work can be used to plan duration of training programs in the immersive VE for subjects or patients to obtain maximal performance results.

Acknowledgments. We thank LCDR Jose Dominguez, LCDR Seth Reini, Genieleah Padilla, and Jordan Sturdy for their contribution to this research, as well as Sarah Kruger from the National Intrepid Center of Excellence for her initial work on the scoring for the boat navigation task.

This work was supported by the Bureau of Medicine and Surgery Wounded, Ill, and Injured grant R116, under Work Unit No. 60818. The views expressed are those of the authors and do not reflect the official policy or position of the Department of the Navy, Department of Defense, or the U.S. Government. Approved for public release; distribution is unlimited. U.S. Government Work (17 USC 105). Not copyrighted in the U.S. This research was conducted in compliance with all applicable federal regulations governing the protection of human subjects (Protocol NHRC.2010.0012).

References

1. Nadeau, S.E., Wu, S.S., Dobkin, B.H., Azen, S.P., Rose, D.K., Tilson, J.K., Cen, S.Y., Duncan, P.W.: The LEAPS Investigative Team: effects of task-specific and impairment-based training compared with usual care on functional walking ability after inpatient stroke rehabilitation: LEAPS Trial. Neurorehabil. Neural Repair **27**(4), 370–380 (2013)
2. Grabiner, M.D., Bareither, M.L., Gatts, S., Marone, J., Troy, K.L.: Task-specific training reduces trip-related fall risk in women. Med. Sci. Sports Exerc. **44**, 2410–2414 (2012)
3. Ross, J.C., Trainor, J.L., Eppich, W.J., Adler, M.D.: Impact of simulation training on time to initiation of cardiopulmonary resuscitation for first-year pediatrics residents. J. Grad. Med. Educ. **5**(4), 613–619 (2013)
4. Kaufman, K.R., Wyatt, M.P., Sessoms, P.H., Grabiner, M.D.: Task-specific fall prevention training is effective for warfighters with transtibial amputations. Clin. Orthop. Relat. Res. **472**(10), 3076–3084 (2014)
5. Feltz, D.L., Landers, D.M.: The effects of mental practice on motor skill learning and performance: a meta-analysis. J. Sport Psychol. **5**, 25–57 (1983)
6. Hird, J.S., Landers, D.M., Thomas, J.R., Horan, J.J.: Physical practice is superior to mental practice in enhancing cognitive and motor task performance. J. Sport Exerc. Psychol. **8**, 281–293 (1991)
7. Holden, M., Todorov, E., Callahan, J., Bizzi, E.: Virtual environment training improves motor performance in two patients with stroke: case report. Neurol. Rep. **23**(2), 57–67 (1999)
8. Holden, M.K.: Virtual environments for motor rehabilitation: review. Cyberpsychol. Behav. **8**(3), 187–211 (2005)
9. Todorov, E., Shadmehr, R.: Augmented feedback presented in a virtual environment accelerates learning of a difficult motor task. J. Mot. Behav. **29**(2), 147–158 (1997)
10. Savion-Lemieux, T., Penhune, V.B.: The effects of practice and delay on motor skill learning and retention. Exp. Brain Res. **161**, 423–431 (2005)
11. Memmert, D.: Long-term effects of type practice on the learning and transfer of a complex motor skill. Percept. Mot. Skills **103**, 912–916 (2006)
12. Taverniers, J., De Boeck, P.: Force-on-force handgun practice: an intra-individual exploration of stress effects, biomarker regulation, and behavioral change. Hum. Factors **56**(2), 403–413 (2014)
13. Oudejans, R.R.: Reality-based practice under pressure improves handgun shooting performance of police officers. Ergonomics **51**(3), 261–273 (2008)
14. Meyer, G.F., Wong, L.T., Timson, E., Perfect, P., White, M.D.: Objective fidelity evaluation in multisensory environments: auditory cue fidelity simulation. PLoS ONE **7**(9), 1–14 (2012)
15. Collins, J.D., Markham, A., Service, K., Reini, S., Wolf, E., Sessoms, P.: Computer assisted rehabilitation a systematic literature review of the use and effectiveness of the environment for research and rehabilitation as it relates to the wounded warrior. Work **50**(1), 121–129 (2015)
16. Pleban, R.J., Matthews, M.D., Salter, M.S., Eakin, D.E.: Training and assessing complex decision-making in a virtual environment. Percept. Mot. Skills **94**, 871–882 (2002)
17. Cox, D.J., Davis, M., Singh, H., Barbour, B., Nidiffer, F.D., Trudel, T., Mourant, R., Moncrief, R.: Driving rehabilitation for military personnel recovering from traumatic brain injury using virtual reality driving simulation: a feasibility study. Mil. Med. **175**(6), 411–416 (2010)

18. Shadmehr, R., Brashers-Krug, T.: Functional stages in the formation of human long-term motor memory. J. Neurosci. **17**(1), 409–419 (1997)
19. Fleishman, E.A., Parker Jr., J.F.: Factors in the retention and relearning of perceptual-motor skill. J. Exp. Psychol. **64**(3), 215–226 (1962)
20. Sessoms, P.H., Gottshall, K.R., Collins, J.D., Markham, A.E., Service, K.A., Reini, S.A.: Improvements in gait speed and weight shift of persons with traumatic brain injury and vestibular dysfunction using a virtual reality computer-assisted rehabilitation environment. Mil. Med. **180**(3S), 143–149 (2015)
21. Isaacson, B.M., Swanson, T.M., Pasquina, P.F.: The use of the Computer Assisted Rehabilitation Environment (CAREN) for enhancing wounded warrior rehabilitation. J. Spinal Cord Med. **36**(4), 296–299 (2013)

Sign Language Support – Adding a Gesture Library to the Leap Motion SDK

Tiago Lopes, Tiago Cardoso(✉), and José Barata

Faculdade de Ciências e Tecnologia,
Universidade Nova de Lisboa, 2829-516 Caparica, Portugal
tm.lopes@campus.fct.unl.pt, {tomfc,jab}@uninova.pt

Abstract. There are several research initiatives that tackle gesture recognition. Nevertheless the interaction between the input devices and an application level is still a hard task that has to be accomplished each time a new system is being developed. The objective of this research work is to facilitate that endeavor by introducing a new generic software layer between the gesture capture device and the application level. This layer will provide the introduction of a gesture library and a set of functionalities both to feed this library and pursue gesture recognition afterwards. The objective is to hinder lower-level software/hardware details from a developer towards letting him or her to focus directly at the Application Level. This article presents the created architecture for this new layer. The validation was made using the Leap Motion, at the Sensor Level, and creating a Serious Game devoted to Sign Language exercising, at the Application Level.

Keywords: Natural user interface · Gesture recognition · Serious games · Leap motion · Middleware

1 Introduction/Motivation

Serious Games might be seen as a knowledge distribution method that keep the players focused on a problem and allows them to overcome it. This gives a reward satisfaction and a background knowledge that continues with the player long after the game session ends. The interaction between the user and an application is a factor to have in account, especially in the particular case of Serious Games that expect the player to feedback through gestures. Several examples of this need may be identified, especially when one consider games focused on teaching Sign Languages (SL). These do require the player to make gestures that a typical input devices, like a game controller, a keyboard, or a mouse are not able to capture.

There are already some sensors in the market that have the ability to capture hand position information, facilitating the interaction between users and software applications. Nevertheless two major drawbacks may still be identified: 1 - this information is provided in a proprietary schema dependent on the sensor Software Development Kit (SDK) and 2 – too few gestures are provided at the firmware level and a mechanism to store and recognize new gestures is not provided. In other words, this data, comes with a low abstraction level, introducing the need to implement a gesture recognition algorithm to translate raw data in known gestures. The developer, by choosing a sensor,

C. Vaz de Carvalho et al. (Eds.): SGAMES 2016, LNICST 176, pp. 109–116, 2017.
DOI: 10.1007/978-3-319-51055-2_14

locks himself in a dilemma that obligates him into modifying the low level data alongside with the implementation of an interpretation algorithm and the creation/maintenance of a database storing known gestures.

This research work proposes a solution for such dilemma by creating a SDK extension that hides the low level information by transforming it into a known and common format with a higher level of abstraction that can then be used in the Application Level. This solution is not only responsible for the representation of the sensor data but also for managing a gesture library and the usage of a classification algorithm for the data it is working with. This means that an Application Level developer only needs to choose a sensor, add this SDK extension and use its common gesture information for classification/recognition to develop his or her application. This is explained in more detail on Sect. 3.

The research work presented in this article is three-folded: 1st the sensors that form the basis for the gesture SDK extension proposed, in Sect. 2.1; 2nd the role of the games in serious purposes like education, Sect. 2.2 and 3rd the Portuguese Sign Language, on Sect. 2.3, that was used at the Application Level.

To validate the Proposed Architecture a Serious Game to exercise Portuguese Sign Language was developed. This game was tested with six Portuguese SL static signs achieving satisfactory results, for further detail refer to Sect. 4.

2 Related Work

In compliance with the proposed objective, this section provides an overview on some sensors that can be used to capture gestures, the role of Serious Games as a teaching aid and how the Portuguese Sign Language is structured.

2.1 Natural User Interfaces

As stated in [1] "The mouse and the keyboard are being replaced by touch and motion based interfaces, increasingly known as Natural User Interfaces (NUI)". Some NUI sensors that have the required capabilities to solve some of the objectives proposed for this research work include:

The Microsoft Kinect – This sensor is capable to detect and track hand and body movements. This features were explored in detail in various projects such as the ones developed by [2–4]. Currently this sensor has an SDK that allow development in applications for Microsoft's Windows OS and Xbox game consoles.

Leap Motion – Leap Motion was particularity design to capture hands and small tools in its field of view. It also has greater precision than the Microsoft's Kinect as studied in [5], with some issues with finger occlusion in certain hand configurations. Leap Motion comes with a very small form factor (80 mm × 30 mm × 11,25 mm). The current SDK provides support for Windows, Mac OS X, Linux and a beta version for Android. One project that demonstrates its capabilities is the communication tool (gesture - sound) provided by the company MotionSavvy [6].

Myo - Myo is an armband that captures gestures by measuring electrical activity from the user's muscles, through the use of electromyography sensors, and data provided by accelerometers, gyroscopes and magnetometers [7]. Being an armband it has a circular shape with a circumference that can go from 19 to 34 cm and it connects to a computer (Windows or Mac OS X) or a smartphone/tablet (iOS or Android) wirelessly over Bluetooth.

2.2 Role of Games as a Learning Tool

As early as 1992 there are research works that show the importance and impact of Serious Games as a learning tool. As stated in [8] "Because games require the active participation of students, the material has a greater chance of being integrated into the cognitive structures of the individuals and thus being retained". A game is not just a tool for entertaining but one with value for teaching its users about different types of subjects. There have been multiple studies, [9–11], that demonstrate the success of games as a teaching tool.

Nowadays games are not restricted to boards, fixed consoles or computers but available everywhere, facilitated by the wide spread of smartphones and tablets increasing the ease of access to games even more. Because of this wide potential the development of Serious Games for teaching purposes gained increasing attention, namely to teach sign language. [2, 3, 12], show two examples exercising the gestures of the Portuguese Sign Language (PSL) through a game.

2.3 Portuguese Sign Language (PSL)

The PSL is the aggregation of different types of gestures [13] which involve:

- The hand configuration, the shape that the hand assumes during a gesture;
- Hand movement, the motion involving the hand and/or fingers;
- Non-hand expressions, marking made with the cheek, mouth, tongue or teeth;
- Localization, the local were the gesture is being made;
- Orientation, the direction the gesture hand is facing during its movement.

For a gesture to be classified in gender, number or verb form, a classifier type gesture is used [13]. This gesture is preceded by the gesture to classify. In PSL it is also possible to state an interrogation, a declaration, or an exclamation by using non-hand expressions [13], normally this is achieved by using face or shoulder expression.

The PSL also has signs that represent the individual letters and numerals. This is commonly used to spell names [14].

3 Proposed Architecture

The proposed architecture for solving the mentioned problem makes use of three modules and two support classes that are integrated in a single layer – SDK Extension. The placement of this architecture in an application can be observed in Fig. 1. A class diagram with some of the most important routines can be found on Fig. 2.

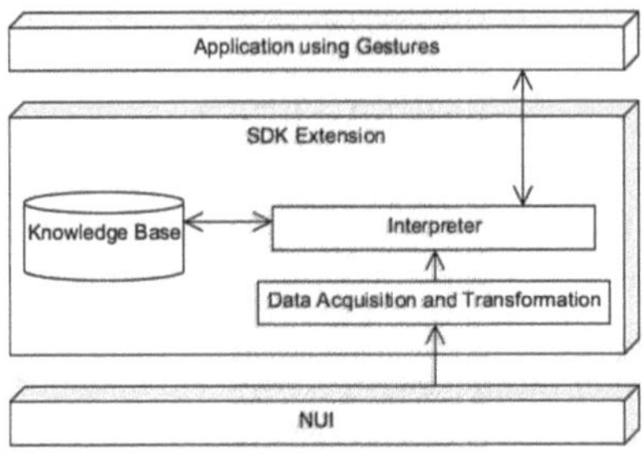

Fig. 1. Use case of the proposed architecture.

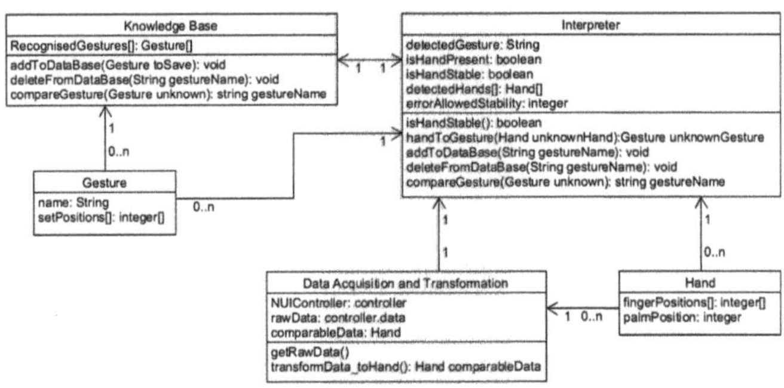

Fig. 2. Class Diagram for the proposed solution.

3.1 Knowledge Base Module

This module is responsible for managing the known gesture patterns in a pre-set format (Gesture Class) in a database. It is also responsible for storing the rules that allow a gesture to be classified, meaning that the gesture recognition algorithm (GRA) should be set in this module. The chosen GRA (the `compareGesture` function) is a Nearest Neighbor algorithm that receive has inputs the unknown Gesture and compares it to all the stored Gestures, returning the name of the most similar gesture.

3.2 Data Acquisition and Transformation Module

The DAT module is the one responsible for direct interaction with the chosen NUI. It requests raw data using `getRawData()`, in the case of the Leap Motion, by polling the most recent Frame captured by the sensor. This Frame is then processed by `transformData_toHand()` which creates a Hand information holder with the 3 dimensional positions of the fingertips and palm of the captured hand. This data is then made available to the Interpreter module.

The transformation made by this module hides the NUI raw information from the Interpreter and by extension to all the higher abstraction level applications. With the proposed architecture this is the only module that needs to be changed if it is to be used with a different NUI.

3.3 Interpreter Module

This is the nuclear module that aggregates and processes all the available data into a meaningful information to be later used. It is the liaison between the processed data and the Application level.

The Interpreter receives the processed data from the DAT module and uses it for multiple objectives:

- Transforming the received Hand data into a Gesture format. This is done by the method: `handToGesture(Hand unknownHand)` which takes the fingertip positions and calculates the distances between all the fingers returning a Gesture with no classification but ready to be compared.
- Classifying the captured gesture through the Knowledge Base `compareGesture` method and making this classification available to the Application level through the `detectedGesture` object. Alongside this gesture classification it also provides information about the hands stability, by using the `isHandStable()` method, judging the stability by calculating the differences between the captured Hand and the previously stored Hands. If, and only if, the difference is smaller than a pre-defined threshold the hand is stable.
- Adding, deleting or modifying the gesture data in the Knowledge Base. This allows the Application level to add new specific gestures. Making it more versatile by not locking the developer to a set of pre-established gestures. Adding a new gesture requires the user to choose a name and make that gesture multiple times capturing multiple Hand data sets. These are then averaged and transformed into a single Gesture object to be added to the KB.

3.4 Support Classes

For support and information exchange, in this solution, two support classes were defined:

- Gesture class – responsible for storing the gesture information. This support class stores an array of values, representing distances between fingers, which are the key values to a gesture. It also has a text field to hold the gesture name.
- Hand class – this class contains all the data required for a loyal representation of the hand to be used by the Application level. It provides the information of the fingertips and palm positions in a 3 dimensional environment. This class makes the representation of captured hands independent from the NUI.

4 Validation

To validate the proposed solution a prototype application has been developed for Android with the objective of exercising PSL. This prototype uses the Leap Motion NUI (LM NUI) because of its precision, the availability of an Android SDK, and the portability given by its reduced dimensions.

4.1 Proposed Architecture Validation

The validation of the proposed architecture was done by implementing the architecture as a middleware. This was later tested by executing multiple gesture to test the interaction and recognition capabilities.

The DAT module transforms the data polled from the Leap Motion and recovers from it the fingertips and palm x, y and z coordinates of the hand captured in the Frame, which are then made available to the Interpreter as a Hand Object as explained in Sect. 3.2. In the KB module a Nearest-Neighbor algorithm has been implemented as the GRA and a set of five gestures (the PSL letters: 'b', 'i', 'm', 't' and 'u') were saved for comparisons. These values that are to be compared against and stored in the KB are the ten distances between every two fingers. The stored values were obtained by averaging multiple Hand objects of the same gesture done at various distances from the NUI. The Interpreter modules polls, at each frame of the game, the hand information (Hand object) made available by the DAT module and queries the KB for the gesture classification. This information, is then made available to the Application level.

The tests which this prototype was submitted to, consisted on a user performing one of six gestures, chosen randomly, ten times at different distances from the sensor. The six gesture set consisted on the five gestures that can be classified plus one not loaded in the KB, the 'v' sign, due to its similarities with 'u' and 'm'.

The results can be seen in Table 1. As one can observe, the results are satisfactory, with the lowest success rate being 70%. It is noteworthy that the results were obtained after the hand is stable which, in a small subset of gestures, due to the workings of the Leap Motion SDK, took a reset of the gesture (a reset consists on the user taking his hand from the LM capture field and putting it back in it). The gesture 'i' is an example of this, which due to the hand being somehow closed, made the tracking software lose the hand.

Table 1. Confusion Matrix with the test results.

		Gesture performed					
		b	i	m	t	u	v
Gesture recognised	b	8	0	0	0	0	0
	i	0	7	0	0	0	0
	m	0	0	8	0	0	0
	t	0	0	0	9	0	0
	u	0	0	0	0	10	2
Not recognised		2	3	2	1	0	8
Success rate (%)		80	70	80	90	100	80

4.2 Game Validation (Application Level)

The developed game consisted on a simple gesture detection, with which the user interacts with the game by placing his/hers hand in the air near the Leap Motion, and performing gestures. These gesture are compared in real time with the ones loaded on the KB and the player is informed of what PSL letter it represents. This evaluation type game is not very interesting or challenging for the player, a situation to be solved in future work with more challenging and educational game modes.

However it can be evaluated that the user only needs to load the game in the smartphone, plug the Leap Motion to it and make a gesture near its sensor. This demonstrates the ease of use of this solution, refer to Fig. 3 and you can observe the application being used.

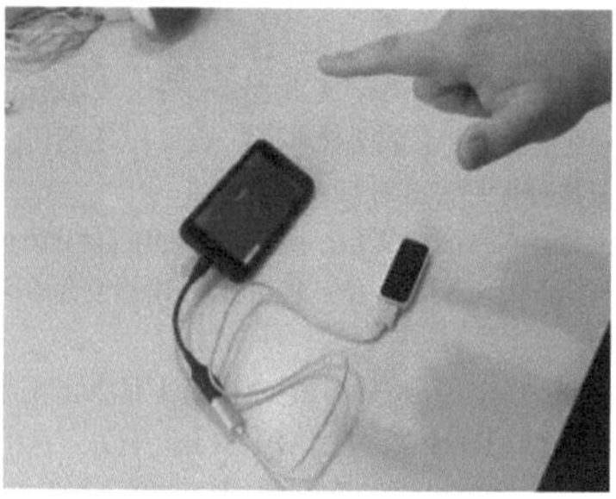

Fig. 3. User interacting with the developed prototype (by making the gesture ‘t’).

The game, with this solution implemented, had a satisfactory response time between the user making a gesture and its classification. There are some cases where the hand was not detected by the NUI. This latter issue is due to the beta stage of the LM Android SDK as it performs better in a laptop version with a stable LM Windows SDK.

5 Conclusion and Future Work

The work presented here intends to demonstrate the increase in value that is brought by the proposed architecture. It has been demonstrated that the proposal can be implemented and that a prototype application can be built upon it. The objective of gesture recognition, as demonstrated in the validation section, is within acceptable values. Managing a knowledge base with gestures has been made transparent to the application developer completing another objective of this proposal, but there is still work to be done as this is an ongoing project.

5.1 Future Work

To improve on the gesture recognition the rest of the static gestures of the PSL will be added to the KB and there are improvements to be made to allow the recognition of gestures that involve motion. The game will also be improved to be more appealing and interactive for its players.

After these improvements, this prototype will be deployed for tests in a real use case scenario. This will be made possible with the help of the *Instituto Jacob Rodrigues Pereira*, a school dedicated in teaching Portuguese Sign Language to children and young adults based in Lisbon.

References

1. Câmara, A.: Natural User Interfaces. In: Campos, P., Graham, N., Jorge, J., Nunes, N., Palanque, P., Winckler, M. (eds.) INTERACT 2011. LNCS, vol. 6946, p. 1. Springer, Heidelberg (2011). doi:10.1007/978-3-642-23774-4_1
2. Gameiro, J.M.F.: About using Serious Games to teach (Portuguese) Sign Language (2014)
3. Galveia, B.M.G.D.: Extensão do SDK do Kinect : Criação de uma Biblioteca de Gestos (2014)
4. Zhang, Z.: Microsoft kinect sensor and its effect. IEEE Multimed. **19**(2), 4–10 (2012)
5. Weichert, F., Bachmann, D., Rudak, B., Fisseler, D.: Analysis of the accuracy and robustness of the leap motion controller. Sens. (Basel) **13**(5), 6380–6393 (2013)
6. MotionSavvy, Uni. http://www.motionsavvy.com/. Accessed 06 May 2016
7. Thalmic Labs Inc., Tech Specs | Myo Gesture Control Armband. https://www.myo.com/techspecs. Accessed 02 Feb 2016
8. Randel, J.M., Morris, B.A., Wetzel, C.D., Whitehill, B.V.: The effectiveness of games for educational purposes: A review of recent research (1992)
9. Papastergiou, M.: Digital game-based learning in high school computer science education: impact on educational effectiveness and student motivation. Comput. Educ. **52**(1), 1–12 (2009)
10. Camerer, C.F.: Sophisticated experience-weighted attraction learning and strategic teaching in repeated games. J. Econ. Theory **104**(1), 137–188 (2002)
11. Erhel, S., Jamet, E.: Digital game-based learning: impact of instructions and feedback on motivation and learning effectiveness. Comput. Educ. **67**, 156–167 (2013)
12. Gameiro, J., Cardoso, T., Rybarczyk, Y.: Kinect-sign, teaching sign language to 'listeners' through a game. Proc. Technol. **17**, 384–391 (2014)
13. Escola Virtual de Língua Gestual Portuguesa, Introdução à Língua Gestual Portuguesa. http://www.lgpescolavirtual.pt/index.php?module=modulo&m=1. Accessed 06 May 2016
14. Associação Portuguesa de Surdos, Informação - Língua Gestual. http://www.apsurdos.org.pt/index.php?option=com_content&view=article&id=41&Itemid=56. Accessed 24 Oct 2015

VirtualSign Game Evaluation

Paula Escudeiro, Nuno Escudeiro, Marcelo Norberto(✉), and Jorge Lopes

Informatic Engeneering Department, Instituto Superior de Engenharia do Porto, Porto, Portugal
{pmo,nfe,matno,jolbl}@isep.ipp.pt

Abstract. This paper presents the evaluation methods and techniques applied to the serious game developed within the VirtualSign project as well as the results achieved through those methods. VirtualSign is a Portuguese sign language bi-directional translator with three main components. The components are a gesture to text translator, a text to gesture translator and a serious game. The serious game aims to make the process of learning sign language easier and enjoyable using the VirtualSign bi-directional translator. The method used to evaluate the VirtualSign was the Quantitative Evaluation Framework (QEF). The translator undertakes a rigid validation process by both sign language experts and the deaf community. The evaluation process was also supported by questionnaires. The precision of the translator has a direct impact on the game performance. To evaluate the precision of the automatic translator we have used QEF and 10-fold cross validation to estimate the accuracy of the translator. The experimental results show a precision above 90%. In the identification of the Portuguese Sign Language terms As for the game the quality rate is 88% based on the QEF evaluation.

Keywords: VirtualSign · Serious game · Results · Sign language · Translator

1 Introduction

The interest in Portuguese Sign Language (PSL) has shown a remarkable growth over time, not only by the deaf community - which now accounts for nearly 100000 persons in Portugal - but also for the whole community involved, such as relatives, educators, teachers, and many more.

The Virtualsign project aims to improve the social inclusion of this community. In order to do so a bi-directional translator of PSL was created. It allows the translation from gestures to text using a pair of sensor gloves and the Microsoft Kinect which provides the necessary data for the sign recognition. Also, it allows the translation from text to gesture using an animated 3D avatar that performs the gestures received by text. After the creation of the translator an additional component was added to the project, a serious game.

Serious games provide a remarkable opportunity to overcome the lack of educational digital content available for the hearing impaired community. A well-designed game entices players into the "reality" of the game world and keeps them there until the

C. Vaz de Carvalho et al. (Eds.): SGAMES 2016, LNICST 176, pp. 117–124, 2017.
DOI: 10.1007/978-3-319-51055-2_15

goals of the game have been met [1]. Therefor there is a need to validate the performance and design of any serious game.

The method used to validate the Virtual sign game was the QEF [2], however to improve the evaluation process additional validations were performed by both sign language specialist and the deaf community through questionnaires. The Virtualsign game depends on the translator for both recognition of the gestures and the performing of the gestures through an avatar inside the game [3]. In the game the player will control a 3D avatar that will perform gestures corresponding to sign language and the user himself has specific areas where he will be prompt to perform a gesture. This dependency means that the game is affected directly by the bi-directional translator performance. The bi-directional translator uses the QEF for evaluation just as the game but has an additional technique named 10-fold cross-validation that estimates the accuracy and precision of the classifiers. The results of both the translator and the game account for the overall quality of the game.

2 Related Work

Despite the lack of content related to this area there are a few projects under development but there is yet very little information about them.

The most similar project to the one mentioned in this paper is the CopyCat. The project CopyCat [4] is an interactive adventure and educational game with ASL recognition. Colorful gloves equipped with accelerometers are used in order to simplify the segmentation of the hands and allow the estimation of motion acceleration, direction and the rotation of the hands. The data is classified using Hidden Markov Model (HMM) [5], yielding an accuracy of 83%.

Another application related to this work is ProDeaf [6], although it is not a serious game it is very similar to one of the main components used on the VirtualSign game, which is the text to gesture translation.

ProDeaf is an application that does the translation of Portuguese text or voice to Brazilian Sign language named Libras. The objective of the ProDeaf is to make the communication between mute and deaf people easier by making digital content accessible in Libras. The translation is done using a 3D avatar that performs the gestures. This software is already used by over 130 000 users.

There is also the application Handtalk [7] which is very similar to the prodeaf, it translates Portuguese text or voice to Libras using a 3D avatar. It's available for mobile and there is also a plugin for websites.

As for the sign recognition there are several models.

Celal Savur et al. [8] suggests a real-time American Sign Language recognition system using the surface Electromyography (EMG). Surface EMG data is acquired from subject's right forearm domain information. The experiment result of offline system is reaching a accuracy rate of 91.1% and real-time system has an accuracy rate of 82.3% using Support Vector Machine.

Nicolas Pugeault et al. [9] suggest a system for recognition of the hand configuration in the context of ASL, using the Microsoft Kinect to collect information about appearance and depth, and the OpenNI + NITE framework to detect and track the hand. The collected data is classified by applying a random forests algorithm, yielding an average accuracy rate of 49.5%.

3 Evaluation Methodology

3.1 Game Quantitative Evaluation Framework

QEF is a generic quality evaluation framework. This framework may also be applied in other settings. The QEF evaluates the educational software quality (ISO 9126 is the standard of reference) Scalet et al. [10] in a three dimensional space. A dimension aggregates a set of factors. A factor is a component that represents the system performance from a particular point of view. The dimensions of the Virtualsign Game Cartesian quality space are: Pedagogical (P); Ergonomic (E) and Technical (T), represented in Fig. 1.

Fig. 1. Cratesian quality space of the game

The quality q, of a given system is defined in our tri-dimensional Cartesian quality space, Q, and measured, in percentage, relatively to a hypothetically ideal system, I.

The Pedagogical dimension reflects the characteristics of the educational software related to its learning aspects. It aggregates two factors: learning and assessment.

The Ergonomic dimension aggregates two factors: usability and gameplay. Those factors measure the system's ability of presenting its content with minimum effort.

The Technical dimension for this case only has one factor which is the Support.

For each system being developed we will have to identify the importance of each factor to the dimension, pn in Eq. 1. The dimension coordinate is them computed as the weighted mean of these factors:

$$\mathrm{Dim_i} = \sum_n (p_n \times factor_n), \sum_n (p_n) = 1 \mathrm{e}\, p_n \in [0, 1] \quad (1)$$

Where n is the number of relevant factors for the dimension at hand.

The ideal system has a set of requirements that indicates what the system must do. Those requirements have an associated weight according to a scale from 0 to 10 where 0 is irrelevant and 10 fundamental. The weight of a given criterion is the relevance of the criterion to the factor, which have been assigned previously. These weights define the ideal system.

$$\mathrm{Factor}_{n=} \frac{1}{\sum_m pr_m} \times \sum_m (pr_m \times pc_m) \tag{2}$$

In the Eq. 2 pr_m is the weight of the criterion m for the factor under evaluation. The pc_m represents the fulfillment percentage of the requirement m.

The global deviation of the real system – represented by the three dimensional coordinates in the quality space – with regards to the ideal system – represented by the coordinates (1,1,1) – is computed by the Euclidean distance between these two points in quality space.

The real system quality is then computed as seen in Eq. 3.

$$\mathrm{Q} = 1 - \frac{D}{\sqrt{n}}, \mathrm{Q} \in [0, 1] \tag{3}$$

QEF has previously been applied to control the quality of several products throughout their lifecycle with very good results.

3.2 VirtualSign Translator Evaluation

The Virtualsign bi-directional translator was also evaluated using the QEF. However, the set of dimensions used for the translator were Functionality, Adaptability and Efficiency. The 10-Fold Cross-Validation was used in order to estimate the accuracy of the classifiers responsible for the analysis and classification of the gestures. The cross-validation is a model validation technique used to assess how the results of a statistical analysis vary according to an independent data set. The model is usually given a dataset of known data to be used in the training of the classifier (training dataset), and a dataset of unknown data (or first seen data) against which the model is tested (testing dataset). This validation allows the prediction of how accurate the classifiers are.

Besides the QEF and the cross-validation, several questionnaires were delivered to deaf users who tried the text to gesture component of the Virtualsign translator. Each user translated 275 words on the translator and replied whether the translation performed by the avatar was correct, wrong or they could leave a comment. The total number of deaf users who replied the questionnaires were four, two male and two female, and their ages are ranged from 39 to 64 years old.

4 Results

4.1 QEF Requirments and Results of the Game

The VirtualSign game main goal is to aid those who are willing to learn sign language. In order to do so its content had to be validated and the game design had to be the adequate for a serious game. The QEF was used for those validations along with other tools and experts. A set of requirements were chosen aiming to evaluate the main aspects that should be part of any serious game.

In Table 1 there is the list of requirements for the pedagogical dimension of the game. The learning factor has a weight of 0.75 and the assessment has a weight of 0.25. All the requirements are essential to the game and therefore all have the same weight of 10.

Table 1. Requirement list for the pedagogical dimension of the QEF.

Factors	Requirements
Learning	PL01 - The story line promotes interactive learning curve
	PL02 - The game promotes an incremental educational guide
	PL03 - The game elements represent clearly the educational objects in the real world
	PL04 - The game evaluates and awards the player that capture more educational content information
	PL05 - The checkpoints use clear language for the target group
	PL06 - In the end of the checkpoints the player is awarded by its performance
Assessment	PA01 - The game promotes self-assessment
	PA02 - The game provides a screen to check out the top player results

The ergonomic dimension has the most requirements as it contains the usability factor, which weight is 0.55 and the gameplay factor with a weight of 0.45. Those two factors are the core of any game thus having such a large amount of requirements associated with each. Those requirements are listed in Table 2.

Finally, the technical dimension of the QEF for the game is listed in Table 3, it contains only the support factor with a weight of 1.

The pedagogical dimension has a completion rate of 100% whilst the ergonomic is at 84.9% and the Technical at 70%.

In the ergonomic dimension the usability factor is at 78.1% as the game is missing the help button and difficulty adjustment. As for gameplay is at 93.2% lacking some audio feedback the pace could be improved. Finally the technical dimension is missing a verification upon a game crash to save the game state and the game is not easily updated thus the 70% only.

Based on the set of requirements for the game it has a quality percentage of 88% according to the QEF. The game performance also depends on the translator therefore the results of the translator have been also evaluated and described in this paper.

Table 2. Requirement list for the ergonomic dimension of the QEF.

Factors	Requirements
Usability	EU01 - The game is easy and does not require a large learning curve
	EU02 - The user should be able to retry a level to try to achieve a better result
	EU03 - A help button is provided
	EU04 - The game difficulty is increased by level
	EU05 - The common element's colors used in the game were consistent throughout it
	EU06 - Written/spoken content is free of grammatical and syntactical errors.
	EU07 - Feedback for users action is quick and effective
	EU08 - Main game menus and in game menus are easy to use
	EU09 - Options in game menu correctly do what their supposed to
	EU10 - A user can leave and restart the adventure (level) anytime during the gameplay
	EU11 - The controls of the game are easy to use
	EU12 - The graphics were recognizable to the players and it was clear what items were by looking at them.
	EU13 - All user input actions with active objects in game set result in audio feedback, visual feedback or both.
	EU14 - The color palate used is clear and lean avoiding health problem for people with epilepsy
	EU15 - The player can set an initial difficulty for the game
	EU16 - The game should provide a cooperative mode for multiplayer
Gameplay	EG01 - The game story is well represented in the game sets
	EG02 - The game is original
	EG03 - The effects of the player's actions can clearly be seen in the game environment
	EG04 - Audio usage enhances gameplay
	EG05 - The game pace is quick and pleasing
	EG06 - The game is challenging and defies the user to beat his own best results
	EG07 - Game content enhances the game play
	EG08 - Application allows the recognition of patterns
	EG09 - The characters design are representative of the real elements that they represent
	EG10 - Game navigation and actions capture is quick and fluid
	EG11 - The game story creates an educational immersive context for the players

Table 3. Requirement list for the techincal dimension of the QEF.

Factors	Requirements
Support	TS01 - The game is easy updatable
	TS02 - Usage statistics and user history is saved
	TS03 - There is a unique entry point to the game
	TS04 - In case of crash the game should be able to be set to the latest valid state without data loss
	TS05 - The connection with the VS translator is stable and fast

4.2 Results of the Translator

Based on the QEF the Virtualsign translator has a quality of 89%. The dimension with the lowest quality percentage is the adaptability with 66.6%. As for the efficiency it's at 100% and the functionality is at 92% as the misspellings and syntax correction system is not yet fully functional.

According to the questionnaires about the text to gesture translation, an average of 74% of the words were correct, 6% could use some improvements and 20% were incorrect, however, based on the comment section of the questionnaires it's possible to conclude that some of the incorrect words are synonyms or differ of the dialect of the person who answered.

As for the performance of the gesture to text component six classification algorithms were compared using 10-fold cross validation, namely Random Trees (RT) [11], Boost Cascade (BC) [12], Neural Networks (NN) [13], K-Nearest Neighbors (KNN) [14], Naive Bayes (NB) [15] and Support Vector Machine (SVM) [16]. To evaluate their performance a dataset composed of 40 samples was used for each hand configuration (1680 samples in total). In Table 4 the results of the evaluation are presented.

Although RT shows a slightly higher precision the SVM classifier became the default of the VirtualSign yielding a precision of 98,6 for the left hand and 98,1 for the right as in this test it obtained an accuracy of 100%.

Table 4. Classification results of the 1680 samples, obtained with the sensor gloves.

%	RT	BC	NN	KNN	NB	SVM
Precision Left	98,6	82,0	98,1	98,8	97,5	98,6
Accuracy Left	85,5	95,4	78,1	97,3	97,1	100,0
Precision Right	98,8	86,1	97,2	98,0	98,0	98,1
Accuracy Right	87,3	96,6	80,4	98,2	96,8	100,0

5 Conclusion

According to the QEF the game shows a quality rate of 88%. The game is complete but a multiplayer cooperation system is under development for it and also the fact its performance is influenced directly by the translator makes it hard for the game to reach the 100% quality rate that we are aiming for. However even though the translator precision is not 100% it's still higher than any current alternatives. For instance the CopyCat is currently the only similar game and its translator shows a lower accuracy rate than the Virtualsign. The Virtualsign translator accuracy overall stands above 90% which is a very impressive result compared to the existing models. Both the translator and the game are being continuously improved to ensure the best user experience. So far the feedback from those who tested it has been very positive and many of the improvements came from it. As for future work there is a cooperation module under development to be added to the game. There is also in progress a parameterization application that will fill the gesture database using very limited amounts of data which will improve the game performance. We are also looking for alternatives to the sensor gloves in order to improve the usability of the game.

References

1. Salen, K., Zimmerman, E.: Rules of Play: Game Design Fundamentals. MIT Press, Cambridge (2004)
2. Escudeiro, P., Bidarra, J.: Quantitative evaluation framework (QEF). Conselho Editorial/Consejo Editorial, p. 16 (2008)
3. Escudeiro, P., Escudeiro, N., Norberto, M., Lopes, J.: VirtualSign in serious games. In: de Carvalho, C.V., Escudeiro, P., Coelho, A. (eds.) Serious Games, Interaction, and Simulation, pp. 42–49. Springer, Heidelberg (2016)
4. Zafrulla, Z., Brashear, H., Yin, P., Presti, P., Starner, T., Hamilton, H.: American sign language phrase verification in an educational game for deaf children. In: 2010 20th International Conference on Pattern Recognition (ICPR), pp. 3846–3849. IEEE (2010)
5. Blunsom, P.: Hidden markov models. Lecture notes, pp. 18–19, 15 August 2004
6. Prodeaf. http://www.prodeaf.net/en-us/Solucoes
7. HandTalk. https://www.handtalk.me/sobre
8. Savur, C., Sahin, F.: Real-time american sign language recognition system using surface EMG signal. In: 2015 IEEE 14th International Conference on Machine Learning and Applications (ICMLA), pp. 497–502. IEEE, December 2015
9. Pugeault, N., Bowden, R.: Spelling it out: real-time ASL fingerspelling recognition. In: 2011 IEEE International Conference on Computer Vision Workshops (ICCV Workshops), pp. 1114–1119. IEEE, November 2011
10. Scalet, D., Yokohama, A., Koscianski, A., Rêgo, C.M., Asanome, C., Romero, D., Vostoupal, T.M.: ISO/IEC 9126 and 14598 integration aspects: a Brazilian viewpoint. In: The Second World Congress on Software Quality (2000)
11. Le Gall, J.F.: Random trees and applications. Probab. Surv. **2**(245), 10–1214 (2005)
12. Viola, P., Jones, M.: Rapid object detection using a boosted cascade of simple features. In: Proceedings of the 2001 IEEE Computer Society Conference on Computer Vision and Pattern Recognition, CVPR 2001, vol. 1, pp. 1–511 (2001)
13. Haykin, S.: Neural Networks: A Comprehensive Foundation, 2nd edn. Prentice Hall, Upper Saddle River (2004)
14. Cover, T.M., Hart, P.E.: Nearest neighbor pattern classification. IEEE Trans. Inf. Theor. **13**(1), 21–27 (1967)
15. Rish, I.: An empirical study of the naive Bayes classifier. In: IJCAI 2001 Workshop on Empirical Methods in Artificial Intelligence, vol. 3, pp. 41–46. IBM, New York (2001)
16. Steinwart, I., Christmann, A.: Support vector machines. In: Izenman, A.J. (ed.) Modern Multivariate Statistical Techniques: Regression, Classification, and Manifold Learning. Springer Texts in Statistics. Springer, New York (2008)

Towards an Ontology of Requirements for Pervasive Games Based Learning Systems: A Requirements Engineering Perspective

Yemna Mejbri[1,4(✉)], Maha Khemaja[2,4], and Kaouther Raies[3,4]

[1] National School of Computer Science, University of Manouba, Manouba, Tunisia
mejbriyemna@yahoo.fr
[2] Higher Institute of Applied Sciences and Technology, University of Sousse, Sousse, Tunisia
maha_khemaja@yahoo.fr
[3] Faculty of Economic Sciences and Management, University of Sfax, Sfax, Tunisia
kaoutherraies@yahoo.fr
[4] Prince Research Group, Isitc, Sousse, Tunisia

Abstract. The ludic, the pervasive and the educational aspects of pervasive games based learning systems (PGBLSs) have huge impact on understanding, developing, validating, reasoning and managing requirements. We propose in this paper a computation independent model (CIM) driven requirements engineering process in order to improve the development of PGBLSs. This model is based on an ontology of requirements (RO). RO addresses the development of an ontology of requirements (RO) as a powerful formalism to assist requirements' analysts in order to fulfill changing requirements in the PGBLSs dynamic context.

Keywords: Pervasive games · Learning systems · Ontology · Requirements engineering

1 Introduction

The integration of ubiquitous computing in game industry, the intersection of urban phenomena such as mobile technology, fiction, reality and taking into account the context allows producing the pervasive games. These offer a game experience combining real and virtual worlds. According to Markus Montola [1], "Pervasive game is a game that has one or more salient features that expand the contractual magic circle of play socially, spatially or temporally". The spatial aspect means that the game can be played at different places and the location of the game can affect the game play. The temporal aspect means that the game can be played during the daily activities of the player. The social aspect means that the player may change his/her role in a flexible manner, because he/she switches from non-participant or a spectator to an active performer and vice versa. The spatial, temporal and social dimensions of pervasive games distinguished by Montola [2], are supposed to be built for fun and educational

C. Vaz de Carvalho et al. (Eds.): SGAMES 2016, LNICST 176, pp. 125–132, 2017.
DOI: 10.1007/978-3-319-51055-2_16

dimensions into an instrument promoting learning systems, hence the birth of pervasive games based learning systems (PGBLSs).

Due to the emergence of studies on technologies enhanced learning systems, the capacity to build pervasive games based learning systems that process dynamic context information and adapt the knowledge to meet the requirements of users, has attracted quite a bit of attention. A computation independent model (CIM) based on an ontology of requirements is considered necessary. As requirement engineering process consists on establishing the services that the user requires from a system and the constraints under which it operates and is developed. This paper intends to use the ontology of requirements within the requirements engineering process which is suitable for continually updating the user's changing requirements.

The rest of this paper is organized as follows: the Sect. 2 presents background and motivation. Section 3 presents the related works. Section 4 presents the proposed approach. Finally the Sect. 5 reports on the progress and the future works.

2 Background and Motivation

One of the challenges which encounter PGBLSs developers is requirements definition. This task, considered as essential step, treated at an advanced stage of the development process, completely changed status; it becomes a task to be considered throughout the development process of PGBLSs.

Requirements Engineering (RE) is the first fundamental step of any project of system development. According to GTIE (Working Group on Requirements Engineering) of the AFIS (French Association of Systems Engineering) [3], RE means all activities to discover, analyze, validate and evolving a set of requirements for a system. RE is essentially based on communication between different participants. The main objective is to enable a common understanding by the various project stakeholders, to design the system. In general, this understanding is represented in the form of written and graphical models, corresponding to the requirements specification.

Moreover, the PGBLSs requirements are requested by players. They want, for example and not for limitation, to play with real human beings in the same way that they would interact with them in the real world. Sometimes, the player needs to move in all location-based games like Can You See Me Now [4] and Uncle Roy All Around You [5]. Often, their needs change. QuaGauntlet [5] is a good example of a game in which the players need to change their postures to aim, fire, and activate their shields.

Since ontologies [6] allow formally presenting knowledge, describe the reasoning on that knowledge, sharing and reusing, we propose, in this research, using ontologies in the process of requirements engineering for PGBLS development. An ontology is an explicit specification of a conceptualization [7]. It can be used for both, to describe requirements specification documents [8, 9] and formally represent requirements knowledge [10, 11]. In contrast to traditional knowledge-based approaches, e.g. formal specification languages, ontologies seem to be well suited for an evolutionary approach to the specification of requirements and domain knowledge [11]. Moreover, ontologies can be used to support requirements management and traceability [8, 10]. Automated validation and consistency checking are considered as a potential benefit compared to semi-formal or informal approaches providing no logical formalism or model theory. Finally, formal specification may be a prerequisite to realize model-driven approaches in the design and the implementation phase.

3 Related Works

Only little research concerning the modeling of PGBLSs requirements is found. Chen and Shih [12] proposed a prototype of a meta-model which puts together several partial perspectives of the Instructional Pervasive Games (IPG) and made a set of checklist as the reference for IPG developers. Context requirement, pedagogy requirement, and design requirement form the main body of the meta-model. With this mega model, a structured guideline for IPG designers can be drawn. The guideline consists of three sets of checklists: Context Requirement Checklist, Pedagogy Requirement Checklist, and Design Requirement Checklist. Tang [13] introduced a new game content model that can aid game designers document specification of game design. The content Model covers all the essential game design concepts for documenting serious game design in the role-playing and simulation genres initially (but this can be easily expanded upon to support other genres). The top level of the game content model consists of ten interrelated key concepts that best represent the rules, play and aesthetic information of a computer game. These are Game Structure, Game Presentation, Game Simulation, Game Rules, Game Scenario, Game Event, Game Objective, Game Object, Game Player and Game Theme. Laine, Sedano, Joy and Sutinen [14], illustrated a "technology integration model" for game-based pervasive learning systems, stated that an IPG needs to meet the following requirement: (1) Pedagogical requirements, (2) Game design requirements, and (3) Context requirements.

Other approaches exist in the domain of RE, some of them are designed specifically for pervasive systems. Those approaches take into account the characteristics of ambient intelligence and ubiquitous computing as context awareness, personalization or dynamics, etc. Sitou and Spanfelner [15] presented a model based on requirements engineering to analyze and specify the basic behavior of the system and the adaptive behavior based on the needs of the customers. The approach is based on the elicitation, analysis and specification of different parts of the context adaptive systems. The model enriches the context with aspects of participants, activities, changing behavior change, etc. This model consists of a user model, a task model, a domain model, a platform model, a model of dialogue and a presentation template.

Most of the works described previously don't exploit ontologies like the work of Chen. Tang used the ontologies but he doesn't take into account the key role of ontologies for the definition, the specification and the requirements management. Although ontologies have attracted much attention recently [13–15], the various existing approaches, using ontologies, are characterized by specificity and limits of developed ontologies. Generally, developers define domain ontologies which vary in their degree of generality (business level) and in their degree of specificity (technical level). They also vary in their coverage of aspects of the modeled systems. As we know, none of those approaches has considered the use of requirements ontologies in the PGBLSs development process which causes a generic and an incomplete definition of requirements and requires the participation of actors with different skills (Analysts, Architects, etc.). Stakeholders in the PGBLSs development process don't provide a detailed and directional semantic model that explains the system, or how changing context affect users' requirements. A changing context essentially means that developers can't rely on reassuring assumptions by analyzing the requirements. That is why we also proposed a semantic formalism to represent, define, specify and adapt to PGBLSs requirements.

4 Proposed Approach

We aim to take advantage of ontologies and propose mechanisms and techniques to use them in a guiding approach in order to define and analyze PGBLSs requirements. Our ontology of requirements intended to reduce the ambiguity of needs and avoid incomplete requirements definition. In this context, Castaneda et al. [16] describes the benefits and challenges of using ontologies in the process of requirements engineering (RE). This is exactly the basis of our approach. Indeed, RE imposes a systematic series of activities to be conducted on the requirements. It contains the activities of elucidation, analysis, specification, validation and management [17]. Our approach takes those activities [18] but adapts them for the definition of PGBLSs requirements.

4.1 The Requirements Elicitation

The elicitation of the requirements consists on the collection, the capture, the discovery and the development of requirements from a variety of resources including human stakeholders. To do this, we suggest reviewing the literature to study the areas of learning systems and pervasive games. The result of this step consists of a first set of textual PGBSLSs requirements. Since the PGBLSs is characterized by the overlapping of two areas: Pervasive games and learning, we have broken the requirements into two categories of requirements which are pervasive games requirements and learning requirements. Literature review was conducted to get requirements for the development of PGBLSs. Unfortunately, no publications dealing with requirements for PGBLSs could be found in scientific literature. Instead, a list of PGBLSs influencing factors could be identified, which have an effect on the learning success and motivation of players like the works of [19–22]. In another hand, understanding of "learning" is the first step towards defining requirements of learning. Indeed, Learning is the activity or process of gaining knowledge or skills by studying, practicing, being taught, or experiencing something. In this context, Quintin et al. [23] defined a learning scenario as the scenario whose role is to describe the learning activities, their articulation in the training sequence and the productions which are expected. Paquette [24] defined the scenario as linking the activities of learners with the resources used and produced.

4.2 The Requirements Analysis

The analysis focuses on reviewing, understanding of elicited requirements and their verification for the quality in terms of accuracy, completeness, clarity and consistency in order to remove inconsistencies and to ensure completeness and non redundancy. The result of this step is a set of identified requirements but they aren't formalized. So, these factors have been analyzed and at the current stage of our research we have deducted twenty requirements for the development of PGBLSs. Table 1 shows an extract of the requirements list.

Table 1. Requirements list for the development of PGBLSs

Requirements of pervasive games
A PGBLS must pervades the real world in an undefined manner, and thus blends with it,
A PGBLS must be with a persistent presence in the real world, and thus available to the players at all times,
A PGBLS should make a specific setting of the game world within the real world,
A PGBLS should allow the gameplay to interact with elements of the real world, thus challenging standard gameplay conventions,
A PGBLS must make a mutual interaction among players and elements in the real world;
A PGBLS should blend with everyday experiences.
A PGBLS must allow movement,
A PGBLS allow the players to act,
A PGBLS allow the players to play in fixed time and fixed round or open ended time or open ended round,
A PGBLS allow the player to focuses on a clear goal,
A PGBLS can be played fixed in one place as most traditional computer games are,
A PGBLS can be played in large-scale outdoor places anywhere (often also played in everyday life),
A PGBLS can be played where the player must move in one place and physical actions are needed to change gesture, posture, etc. due to the requirements of gameplay,
A PGBLS should precise players relationships which can be Individually, A Simple Collaborative/Competitive/Opposed relationship, The Combined option, The Community, free relationship.
Requirements of learning
A PGBLS should allow the participation of learners,
A PGBLS must allow interaction,
A PGBLS should allow perception,
A PGBLS must offer a content to learn,
A PGBLS must offer a structured content,
A PGBLS should dispose players with resources,
A PGBLS can allow repeated activity,
A PGBLS should allow a feedback,
A PGBLS should define prerequisites,
A PGBLS should precise an objectives for learning,
A PGBLS should let formative and normative evaluation.

4.3 The Requirements Specification

The specification is the registration and the documentation of requirements so that they are usable by stakeholders, in particular, for developers who need to design and build the system. It is to establish the final list of requirements by organizing them according to categories. Here we suggest an ontology of requirements that represents the requirements and the relations between them and the relationships with the system.

There are a number of methods and methodologies one can employ to develop their own ontology in a domain. Among those methods [25] we find CyKB, Uschold and King's method, Grüninger and Fox's method, etc. For starting point, Noy & McGuinness's presented a guide to create ontologies. In this paper, we have adopted Noy & McGuinness's method to build our ontology of requirements due to the simplicity of the method. Noy & McGuinness's seven steps method requires one to [26]: 1. Determine the domain, scope and purpose of the ontology; 2. Consider reusing existing ontologies; 3. Enumerate important terms in the ontology; 4. Define the classes and the class hierarchy; 5. Define the properties of the classes – slots; 6. Define the facets of the slots; and finally 7. Create the instances. The next figure illustrates an extract of the requirements classifications (Fig. 1).

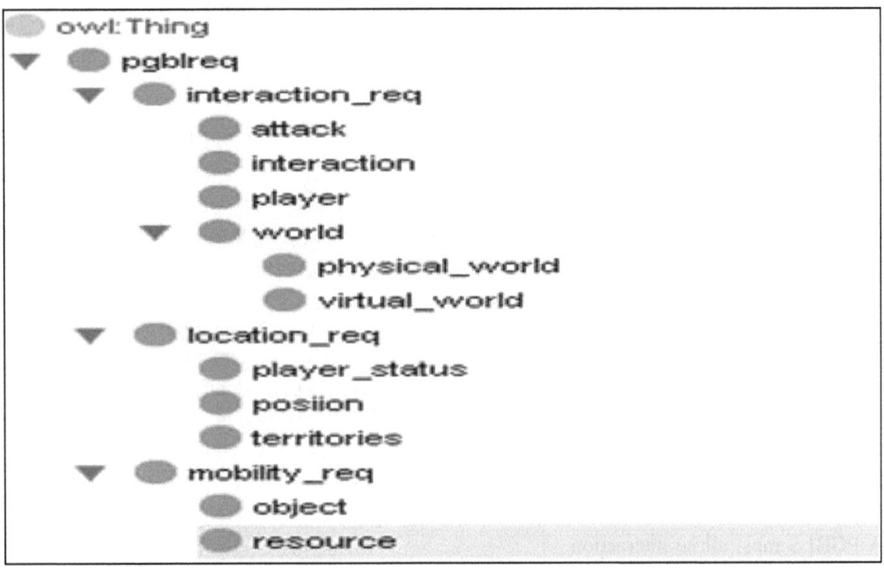

Fig. 1. An extract from the PGBLSs requirements ontology

4.4 The Requirements Validation

The validation is the confirmation of the quality of requirements and their compliance with the needs and desires of stakeholders. The requirements are tested using a prototype. Indeed, a validation of the quality attributes of those requirements (consistency, accuracy, completeness, wholeness) must be conducted.

We have modeled until now the ontology via protégé 4.3. Currently, we are inferring the requirements from a domain ontology in order to validate our computation independent ontology. We aim to test the incorporation of ontologies in the process of defining PGBLSs requirements. We focus on a case study in order to validate the feasibility of our proposed approach.

5 Conclusion

We presented in this paper our vision regarding an explicit classification of PGBLSs requirements following the two dimensions which are pervasive games and learning systems. The main idea of our approach is an ontology of requirements following the requirements engineering process. The guidelines of the ontology of requirements help developers to capture user requirements, to facilitate the updating of dynamic requirements due changing context and allow reuse of the ontology when the learning environment varies.

In future works, we plan to provide a formalized version of the current work with detailed axioms. Following that, an ontology of requirements is developed, focusing on different kinds of context changes. We hope that our work could be used as a foundation for the relating domains.

References

1. Montola, M.: Exploring the Edge of the Magic Circle: Defining Pervasive Games. University of Tampere - Game Research Lab (2005)
2. Montola, M., Stenros, J., Waern, A.: Pervasive Games: Theory and Design (2009)
3. AFIS, Modèle de données AFIS, version 2.0, groupe de travail Méthodes et Outils (2005)
4. Benford, S., Crabtree, A., Flintham, M., Drozd, A., Anastasi, R., Paxton, M., et al.: Can you see me now? ACM Trans. Comput. Hum. Interact. **13**, 100–133 (2006)
5. Magerkurth, C., Cheok, A., Mandryk, R., Nilsen, T.: Pervasive games: bringing computer entertainment back to the real world. Comput. Entertainment (CIE) **3**, 4 (2005)
6. Guarino, N., Carrara, M., Giaretta, P.: An ontology of meta-level categories. In: Doyle, J., Sandewall, E., Torasso, P. (eds.) Principles of Knowledge Representation and Reasoning: Proceedings of the Fourth International Conference (KR 1994), pp. 270–280. Morgan Kaufmann, San Mateo (1994)
7. Gruber, T.R.: A translation approach to portable ontologies. Knowl. Acquisition **5**(2), 199–220 (1993)
8. Mayank, V., Kositsyna, N., Austin, M.: Requirements engineering and the semantic web, Part II. Representation, Management, and Validation of Requirements and System-Level Architectures. Technical report. TR 2004-14, University of Maryland (2004)
9. Decker, B., Rech, J., Ras, E., Klein, B., Hoecht, C.: Selforganized reuse of software engineering knowledge supported by semantic wikis. In: Proceedings of Workshop on Semantic Web Enabled Software Engineering (SWESE), November 2005
10. Lin, J., Fox, M.S., Bilgic, T.: A Requirement Ontology for Engineering Design. Enterprise Integration Laboratory, University of Toronto, Manuscript, September 1996

11. Wouters, B., Deridder, D., Van Paesschen, E.: The use of ontologies as a backbone for use case management. In: European Conference on Object-Oriented Programming (ECOOP 2000), Workshop: Objects and Classifications, a Natural Convergence (2000)
12. Chen, C., Shih, J.: A prototype on a Meta-model for designing instructional pervasive games. In: Fourth IEEE International Conference on Digital Game and Intelligent Toy Enhanced Learning (2012)
13. Tang, S., Hanneghan, M.: A model Driven Serious Games Development, School of Computing and Mathematical Sciences, Liverpool John Moores University Byrom Street, United Kingdom (2013)
14. Laine, T.H., Islas Sedano, C., Joy, M., Sutinen, E.: Critical factors for technology integration in game-based pervasive learning spaces. IEEE Trans. Learn. Technol. **3**(4), 294–306 (2010)
15. Sitou, W., Spanfelner, B.: Towards Requirements Engineering for Context Adaptive Systems, Technische Universitat Munchen, Department of Informatics, Boltzmannstr.3, 85748 Garching/Munich, Germany (2007)
16. Castañeda, V., Ballejos, L.C., Laura Caliusco, M.: Improving the quality of software requirements specifications with semantic web technologies (2012)
17. Kotonya, G., Sommerville, I.: Requirements Engineering – Processes and Techniques. John Wiley & Sons, UK (1998)
18. Wiegers, K.: Software Requirements. Microsoft Press (2003)
19. Hong, G., Trætteberg, H., Wang, A.I., Zhu, M.: TeMPS: a conceptual framework for pervasive and social games. In: Third IEEE Information Conference on Digital Game and Intelligent Toy Enhanced Learning Kaohsiung, Taiwan (2010)
20. Jegers, K.: Pervasive game flow: understanding player enjoyment in pervasive gaming. ACM Comput. Entertainment **5** (2007)
21. Gentes, A., Guyot-Mbodji, A., Demeure, I.: Gaming on the move: Urban experience as a new paradigm for mobile pervasive game design. Multimedia Syst. **16**, 43–55 (2010). doi:10.1007/s00530-009-0172-2
22. Walther, B.K.: Notes on the methodology of pervasive gaming. In: Kishino, F., Kitamura, Y., Kato, H., Nagata, N. (eds.) ICEC 2005. LNCS, vol. 3711, pp. 488–495. Springer, Heidelberg (2005). doi:10.1007/11558651_47
23. Quintin, J.-J., Depover, C., Degache, C.: Le rôle du scénario pédagogique dans l'analyse d'une formation à distance. Paper presented at the Actes de la conférence EIAH, Paris, INRP, pp. 335–340 (2005)
24. Paquette, G.: Ingénierie Pédagogique. Presses de l'Univesité du Québec, Québec (2002)
25. Corcho, O., Fernandez-Lopez, M., Gomez-Perez, A.: Methodologies, tools and languages for building ontologies. Where is their meeting point? Data Knowl. Eng. **46**(1), 41–64 (2003)
26. Noy, N.F., McGuinness, D.L.: Ontology development 101: a guide to creating your first ontology, Stanford Medical Informatics (2001)

Social Mpower: An Educational Game for Energy Efficiency

Aikaterini Bourazeri[1(✉)], Jeremy Pitt[2], and Sylvester Arnab[1]

[1] Disruptive Media Learning Lab, Coventry University, Coventry CV1 5DD, UK
{ac2601,aa8110}@coventry.ac.uk
[2] Imperial College London, London SW7 2BT, UK
j.pitt@imperial.ac.uk

Abstract. A number of serious games have been developed for energy systems that act as an educational tool and help energy consumers to better understand concepts such as resource allocation, electricity prices and grid sustainability. In such gamified environments, players use technology to solve environmental problems including greener environment, optimised energy and water infrastructure, sustainable resources and reduced energy use. *Social Mpower* game is a representation of an autonomous energy community for local power generation and distribution in which the participants have to avoid a collective blackout by individually reducing their energy consumption by synchronising and coordinating their actions. Our experimental hypothesis is that collective awareness can be enhanced by appropriate features of the game interface, and therefore to increase the opportunities and prospects for successful collective action (e.g to avoid a blackout).

Keywords: Educational game · Energy efficiency · Serious games

1 Introduction

Collective awareness has been informally defined as "an attribute of communities that helps their members to solve collective action problems" [2]. In this paper, we investigate the proposition that collective awareness can be enhanced by Information and Communication Technologies (ICT) with the appropriate affordances, therefore increasing the opportunities and prospects for successful collective action. This investigation is based on the development of a serious game, *Social Mpower*, in which participants have to avoid a collective blackout in a community energy system, by individually reducing their energy consumption through synchronisation and coordination of their actions.

Accordingly, this paper is structured as follows. In Sect. 2 we go deeper into the background and motivation for this research where we define collective awareness and we present serious games. Section 3 describes the design of the game interface which focuses on different interface features; interface cues, visualisation, social networking, feedback and incentives. Section 4 presents the *Social*

C. Vaz de Carvalho et al. (Eds.): SGAMES 2016, LNICST 176, pp. 133–140, 2017.
DOI: 10.1007/978-3-319-51055-2_17

Mpower game and in Sect. 5 we report the results of the experiments, which show that the more cues for collective awareness that are added, the more often the users can coordinate their behaviour to avoid a blackout. Section 6 describes how this game can be used as an educational tool. Finally, we conclude with some remarks on the experimental results in Sect. 7.

2 Background and Motivation

In this section we present the background and motivation for our research. Collective awareness is a pre-requisite for successful collective action in communities and has to be shaped through affordances of the 'human-infrastructure interface'. Serious games are extensively used to simulate real-world events and they are designed to train or educate people on science, health care, management, engineering and so on. Energy systems are a particular area where serious games have been widely deployed to achieve a desired progress or change in players' behaviour.

2.1 Collective Awareness

Collective awareness is informally defined as "an attribute of communities that helps them solve collective action problems", i.e. analogous to the way that social capital is defined by Ostrom and Ahn [12] as "an attribute of individuals that helps them solve collective action problems". Collective awareness is a critical aspect within communities which promotes collective action; members of communities take the necessary actions as a synchronised and accumulated body to reach a desirable outcome for collective resources and services – water, electricity and data [13].

Collective awareness is the common knowledge that comes from social networking, self-organisation and coordination, and it is the essential link between self-organising communities and successful collective action [14]. In communities in which collective awareness is absent, individuals are generally less willing to obey the norms or the rules, or able to understand that their actions have an effect on the community [5]. Individuals may understand the situation they are in from a micro-level perspective (e.g. reducing individual energy consumption) and might additionally recognise the macro-level requirement (e.g. meeting national carbon dioxide emission pledges); however, they might not be aware of interactions occurring at the meso-level which are critical for mapping one to the other [16]. There are communities where common resources are not sufficient for all their members, and the lack of collective awareness may prohibit individuals from changing their community behaviour or even taking actions that may lead to depletion of those resources [2]. Collective awareness can contribute to an efficient resource allocation within a community, ensuring at the same time the long-term sustainability of that community [1,15].

2.2 Serious Games

Games are activities among two or more independent decision-makers who want to achieve their goals in a specific environment. In the context of a game there are rules, and players compete against their adversaries to meet their objectives. But not all games are competitions; there are games where players cooperate to achieve a common goal and there are no individual objectives. Games may be played just for fun but there are games, called serious games, which have a clear and intentional educational purpose and they are not intended primarily for entertainment [9].

Serious games are extensively used to simulate real-world events, inform or make players aware, and trigger their problem-solving skills. These games prepare people to work smarter by enabling them to visualise their actions and explore different events in an intuitive way. Serious games are games in which education in various forms is the primary goal rather than entertainment, and they help users to develop skills such as decision-making, critical thinking and analytical skills [3,6,8]. They are experiential environments that use characteristics of games to deliver a message, teach a lesson or provide an experience. The main goal of these games is to educate players while they entertain them. Serious games are very effective in teaching and training players despite their age and they can communicate their concepts in a very efficient way. Players, through their roles, solve problems, set strategies and make decisions without facing the cost of real world consequences. Serious games allow players not only to learn but also to apply and show what they learned during the gameplay [11].

3 Interface Design

Five interface features have been identified as sufficient conditions to promote collective awareness for successful collective action, and the design of the *Social Mpower* interface focused on them; interface cues, visualisation, social networking, feedback and incentives [2].

1. Interface cues: In *Social Mpower* interface, different interface cues are introduced to induce users to participate in a collective-action situation. Interface cues are used to guide the user interface interaction and communicate different behaviours to users. Users are informed about the different tasks they should complete and receive feedback regarding their actions. Specifically, users become members of a virtual energy community whose objective is the resolution of a collective-action problem; within a specific amount of available energy, users should complete specific tasks. The graphical cues inform users (e.g. send alerts) about upcoming problems and emphasise users' actions and states of the system. A SmartMeter display board is used as a graphical cue whose objective is to inform users about their energy consumption both on individual and common basis, and displays the limit of the available energy. Textual cues are used to link the illustrated information available on the SmartMeter display board with text messages that users receive regarding

their energy consumption. Users can also get advice on how to solve potential problems, i.e. help information.
2. Visualisation: *Social Mpower* interface provides appropriate presentation and representation of data, making what is conceptually significant, perceptually prominent. Every house in *Social Mpower* has a SmartMeter display board. These boards display the energy consumption of every individual house and the total community consumption. The energy consumption is clearly illustrated through a line graph, where the lines have different colours depending on the information displayed each time, and they fluctuate based on the consumed power. There is another board in every home which shows the consumption of the most common kitchen appliances in percentage. This board helps users to estimate how much electricity each appliance is using.
3. Social networking: *Social Mpower* supports fast and convenient communication channels to support the propagation of data. Users could take advantage of the different types of text chat to communicate upcoming energy problems and coordinate with others a plan or schedule to avoid them. Communication helps in self-organisation and resolution of collective-action problems.
4. Feedback: In *Social Mpower*, users should know that their ('small', individual) action X contributes to some ('large', collective) action Y which achieves beneficial outcome Z. In many collective-action situations, individual users may not recognise that their small actions can contribute to resolve a problem, especially if the effect is indirect, undetectable or long-term (e.g. climate change). Real-time feedback includes all the necessary information (e.g. power consumption of electrical appliances) that users should know to proactively coordinate their behaviour and take collective actions to prevent energy problems.
5. Incentives: Rewards and incentives typically in the form of social capital (itself identified as an attribute of individuals that helps them with solving collective action problems [12]) give to users a sense of achievement when they avoid energy problems. The rewards are assessed at the end of the game and are given to players who have completed their tasks without having exceeded their energy limit. Introducing social capital mechanisms and rewards in form of prizes to *Social Mpower* interface, benefit users both in individual and group level, as these mechanisms and rewards support and promote successful collective action.

4 Social Mpower: An Overview

Social Mpower game is a representation of a community energy system for local power generation and distribution, true to detail and as realistic as possible. This game creates a unique experience to players who can observe the immediate weather changes and the use of renewable energy. We wanted to create a game which is easy-to-understand and portrays the energy community of the future. Power generation results from Photovoltaic (PV) cells which are the only energy sources for the community and they are installed on the roofs of the

Fig. 1. Social Mpower virtual world

virtual residences. The virtual residences are connected so that they consume the produced power and eventually share any remaining energy with the rest of the residences. The produced energy is stored in each residence in appropriate energy storage systems. *Social Mpower* challenges the player to sustain the energy system of the community, where the player takes the role of a consumer in a rural area and whose task is to avoid the depletion of the available resources.

Figure 1 presents a screen capture of *Social Mpower* interface; PV cells installed on the roofs of the residence generate the required power for the community, whereas the home devices use the produced electricity. Bedrooms are included in the house to make players feel like home, and animals (i.e. cat) increase the game recreation. The graphical representation of the user, avatar, can be customised to meet user's requirements, while the 'build' option enables users to personalise their virtual environment. In the inventory, players can save and store their virtual assets and objects, and via chat they can communicate with other in-world avatars. Users can listen to music while playing, and with the world map option they can see in miniature the whole virtual world.

The virtual community consists of three types of residences; single, couple and shared house. These houses accommodate the same electrical appliances, but the number of appliances in every house may vary.

5 Experimental Results

87 players took part in the experiments, separated into groups of 2 or 3 players, and each experiment lasted about 30 min. Our proposition (experimental hypothesis) was that the more interface features we added to the game interface that increased collective awareness, the more our players would cooperate to avoid a collective action problem. Logistic regression, a direct probability model, was used to calculate the percentage that players, given the different

Table 1. Percentage of players who coordinated their actions

Interface features	Percentage of coordination
No Interface Feature	43.7 %
SmartMeter	55.2 %
Chat	73.6 %
Rewards	42.5 %
Real-Time Feedback	55.2 %
SmartMeter & Real-Time Feedback	57.5 %
SmartMeter & Chat	62.1 %
SmartMeter & Rewards	56.3 %
Chat & Rewards	73.6 %
Chat & Real-Time Feedback	73.6 %
Real-Time Feedback & Rewards	55.2 %
SmartMeter, Rewards & Feedback	57.5 %
SmartMeter, Feedback & Chat	73.6 %
SmartMeter, Rewards & Chat	74.7 %
Real-Time Feedback, Rewards & Chat	73.6 %
SmartMeter, Real-Time Feedback, Rewards & Chat	73.6 %

interface features, managed to coordinate their actions and avoid a blackout. Table 1 presents a summary of the results; percentage of players who managed to coordinate their actions and thus avoid an energy problem given different combinations of the interface requirements enabled on the game interface.

When no interface feature was enabled on the *Social Mpower* interface, only 43.7 % of players managed to coordinate their actions and avoid an energy problem. Adding the different interface features, this percentage increased. Just by adding social networking in the form of chat, we found that we could achieve a successful collective action (e.g. avoid a blackout). However, the other interface features were having another effect. Players avoided fragmentation and re-built community spirit for long-term engagement, and the educational purposes prior to gamification prepared players for the 'real-thing'; they learned to trust each other before they are let loose on a real life community energy system.

Based on the experimental results, we can now use *Social Mpower* in an educational context and as a stepping stone to gamification and real community energy systems.

6 Social Mpower: An Educational Game

In *Social Mpower*, players are members of a community and their goal is to prevent energy problems. The use of a simulated environment helps in educating players fast and effectively. There are no consequences when players do something wrong during the gameplay as they learn how to avoid problems and take better actions and decisions regarding real life problems. With *Social Mpower* game, players develop social and cognitive skills, and they gain the required confidence to engage with virtual worlds.

Players explore new activities and experiences, communicate with other in-world players and practise new skills [7,17]. At the end of each game, players receive feedback in the form of instant messages and advices regarding their energy use which challenge their critical thinking and understanding of electricity [10]. *Social Mpower* enables players to understand how the power generation and distribution network works, and through different tasks they learn how energy communities can actually use the different technologies to become energy sustainable and efficient.

Social Mpower combines learning with fun and recreation. Through voluntary play and without extrinsic goals that force learning, this game actively engage players. Creativity is promoted tremendously as players can be involved in constructing buildings and objects, personalising their avatars and residences, or even using the different engaging elements that are available in the virtual world to enhance their game experience. *Social Mpower* game is a process to learning rather than a predicted outcome, and it raises strong motivation for energy efficiency [4]. Using the experience from a virtual world, players can build new knowledge and understanding in different energy-related contexts which stimulate and support their skill development.

The educational aim of *Social Mpower* is not only to make the energy system that serves the virtual community more efficient, but also to enable players to understand that they should unite into a group to effectively resolve a collective action problem. Players should recognise that they are impacted in a collective action situation, and that any small individual action will contribute to resolving any upcoming problems. Especially in the energy sector, if players are "collective aware" of an incipient energy problem they can proactively coordinate their behaviour to take a collective action to prevent it. *Social Mpower* awares individuals to take actions regarding common resources that are suboptimal from a community-wide perspective without leading to the depletion of those resources. Players are led towards successful action through self-organisation and social networking promoted via the game interface.

7 Summary and Conclusions

In this paper we presented the *Social Mpower* game, a serious game in which players have to avoid a collective energy problem (e.g. blackout) by individually reducing their energy consumption. The design of the *Social Mpower* interface is based on five interface requirements which enhance collective awareness; interface cues, visualisation, social networking, feedback and incentives. The experimental results gave us empirical evidence on whether the proposed interface features were successful to promote collective awareness for successful collective action in an energy community system or not. Based on statistical analysis and received feedback, visualisation, social networking, feedback and incentives enabled users to successfully coordinate their behaviour and avoid potential energy problems. Rewards in the form of prize were not a strong incentive for players to change their behaviour during the gameplay and thus, in future work new incentives/rewards should be examined and introduced to *Social Mpower* game.

References

1. Bourazeri, A., Pitt, J.: Serious game design for inclusivity and empowerment in smartgrids. In: First International Workshop on Intelligent Digital Games for Empowerment and Inclusion (2013)
2. Bourazeri, A., Pitt, J.: An agent-based serious game for decentralised community energy systems. In: Dam, H.K., Pitt, J., Xu, Y., Governatori, G., Ito, T. (eds.) PRIMA 2014. LNCS (LNAI), vol. 8861, pp. 246–253. Springer, Heidelberg (2014). doi:10.1007/978-3-319-13191-7_20
3. Bulander, R.: A conceptual framework of serious games for higher education: conceptual framework of the game innov8 to train students in business process modelling. In: Proceedings of the International Conference on e-Business (ICE-B), pp. 1–6 (2010)
4. Dietze, B., Kashin, D.: Playing and Learning in Early Childhood Education. Pearson, Canada (2012)
5. Fogg, B.: Persuasive technology: Using computers to change what we think and do (interactive technologies) (2002)
6. van der Hulst, A., Muller, T., Besselink, S., Coetsier, D., Roos, M.C.: Bloody serious gaming-experiences with job oriented training. In: The Interservice/Industry Training, Simulation & Education Conference (I/ITSEC), vol. 2008
7. Kahn, J., Wright, S.E.: Human Growth and the Development of Personality: Social Work Series. Elsevier, Amsterdam (2013)
8. Marks, S., Windsor, J., Wünsche, B.: Evaluation of game engines for simulated clinical training. In: New Zealand Computer Science Research Student Conference, pp. 92–99 (2008)
9. Marsh, T.: Serious games continuum: between games for purpose and experiential environments for purpose. Entertainment Comput. **2**(2), 61–68 (2011)
10. Martlew, J., Stephen, C., Ellis, J.: Play in the primary school classroom? the experience of teachers supporting children's learning through a new pedagogy. Early Years **31**(1), 71–83 (2011)
11. Michael, D.R., Chen, S.L.: Serious Games: Games That Educate, Train, and Inform. Muska & Lipman/Premier-Trade, New York (2005)
12. Ostrom, E., Ahn, T.K.: Foundations of Social Capital. Edward Elgar, Cheltenham (2003)
13. Pitt, J., Bourazeri, A., Nowak, A., Roszczynska-Kurasinska, M., Rychwalska, A., Santiago, I.R., Sanchez, M.L., Florea, M., Sanduleac, M.: Transforming big data into collective awareness. Computer **46**(6), 40–45 (2013)
14. Pitt, J., Nowak, A.: The reinvention of social capital for socio-technical systems (special section introduction). IEEE Technol. Soc. Mag. **33**(1), 27–80 (2014)
15. Pitt, J., Nowak, A.: Collective awareness and the new institution science. In: Pitt, J. (ed.) The Computer After Me. IC Press, Iowa City (2014). Chap. 11
16. Sestini, F.: Collective awareness platforms: engines for sustainability and ethics. IEEE Technol. Soc. Mag. **31**(4), 54–62 (2012)
17. Tickell, C.: The early years: foundations for life, health and learning (2011)

Gamification at Scraim

Diogo Silva[1(✉)], António Coelho[1], César Duarte[2], and Pedro Castro Henriques[2]

[1] DEI/FEUP, INESC TEC, Porto, Portugal
diogoemsilva@gmail.com, acoelho@fe.up.pt
[2] Strongstep, Porto, Portugal
{cesar.duarte,pedroch}@strongstep.pt

Abstract. Software developers usually work as a team and in order to improve the team organization and performance several companies use agile methodologies. The efficiency of this methodologies can be improved by the use of project management tools. Several software developers are difficult to motivate on the usage of these tools, as they often claim being disruptive to their workflow.

This paper presents the use of gamification to incite software developers to use this kind of tools with the necessary regularity. The main focus of this work is on the tasks completion and the regular use of the project management tool, while insuring the respect of the values proposed by the agile manifesto to software development.

The gamification process is described in detail, followed by an application the project management software SCRAIM.

Keywords: Gamification · Game design · Software management tools · Agile manifesto

1 Introduction

The use of project management tools based on Agile methodologies for software development brings benefits to the project members. While the project manager can distribute the work efficiently, the development team knows what to do in every moment.

Towards a correct use of these tools, the development team is often forced to disrupt their workflow to fill in the required information on these tools. Although this is not a negative factor by itself it may affect the efficacy of these tools in such manner that the use may not be the desirable. In this research project we use SCRAIM, an online project and process management platform that has the goal to promote better organizational practices.

To engage software development teams on the use of the project management tools we applied gamification, in order to incorporate game elements and game design techniques to motivate them.

The problem identified is how to create a gamification strategy that engages software developers to make a better use of these tools.

C. Vaz de Carvalho et al. (Eds.): SGAMES 2016, LNICST 176, pp. 141–147, 2017.
DOI: 10.1007/978-3-319-51055-2_18

To do this we considered the following research questions:

- What's the most suitable combination of game elements?
- How to mitigate the risks associated to gamification?
- How to ensure the values of the manifesto for agile software development?

Following these research questions we defined the following goals:

- Develop a survey to help understanding the motivating/blockers aspects of the use of project management tools.
- Design a gamification approach for SCRAIM
- Develop a prototype to integrate this gamification approach in SCRAIM.
- Test and validate the developed strategy.

2 State of Art and Related Work

This section presents the manifesto for the agile software development and the concept of gamification and also some related work.

Software development undergoes several steps since the requirements identification to the product release. It is necessary to have a plan, although usually this plan may be adjusted if and when necessary. Agile software development is an adaptive process that considers [1]:

- Individuals and interactions over processes and tools
- Working software over comprehensive documentation
- Customer collaboration over contract negotiation
- Responding to change over following a plan

Gamification is defined as the use of game elements and game design techniques in non-game contexts [2]. Different combination of game elements may offer different user experiences. One particular common combination is PBL (points, badges and leaderboards) [3].

Gamification has a strong component of psychology, particularly related to motivation. Intrinsic activities are the ones where the user does something in order to fulfil personal goals while extrinsic activities uses external motivators as money [4]. Extrinsic motivators can be a strong motivational tool but may bring some risks [3].

Although it may bring several benefits, gamification has some critics that is necessary to be aware. First the rewards may be a problem if misused or overused. We should be aware that rewards usually are extrinsic motivators so they must be used as a mean to a end (usually intrinsic motivators as personal goals) [2]. Secondly gamification may be used to explore users (exploitation), not only by replacing tangible rewards by intangible ones with less value but it may also incite an unfavorable behavior [5]. At least some game elements uses in gamification strategies may cause law issues. So it is necessary to be aware about laws that may be applied as privacy laws or gambling laws.

Gamification in the workplace has some aspects that are necessary to be considered as the organization hierarchical structure and the motivation mechanics already implemented. Money as a motivational factor must be used with care, always to promote the professionalism without disrespecting the people and promote quality over quantity. [4]

In terms of related work, StackOverflow is a very famous programming assistive platform. The mechanic is simple, the user just asks questions and answers questions from other users. It may also classify answers if they are good or not. Through this actions, the user earns reputation points. This points may be used to unlock new features as moderation tools. The user may also earn some badges if certain conditions are met.

Another example of gamification is RedCritter Tracker. It's an agile project management tool that uses gamification as differential factor. In this tool the users earn points by doing tasks. This points may be used to buy items in the virtual shop and the users may also earn badges if certain condition are met.

As we can see, there are some game elements that are used often such as points (reputation points or virtual currency), badges and leaderboards, known as the PBL triad.

SCRAIM is the project and process management tool in which this research is focused. It follows an agile methodology and has several features as project planning, work distribution, project overview showing statistics as burdown chart and risks management.

3 Gamification Process

In order to create the gamification process to incorporate it on SCRAIM, we followed the Werbach's "six D" step process:

- Define business objectives. They must be clear and objective and not a mean to an end. The identified objectives were: engagement of the correct use of SCRAIM by software developers, improve its efficiency and provide mutual aid.
- Delineate target behaviours and define metrics to evaluate them. The identified behaviours were: fill task details and check for the main fields, complete tasks, collaboration between project elements, improve workplace culture through the use of surprise element, consult leaderboards, promote mutual aid and access gamification options.
- Describe the players. Identify who are the players that will play and try to understand their point of view. To do this several personnel were developed in order to understand the different kinds of users (according to Kim's model (2010)[1]).
- Devise activity cycles. Be aware that there is different game phases that need to be considered. The cycles identified were the daily challenge system where a

[1] http://amyjokim.com/blog/2012/09/19/social-engagement-whos-playing-how-do-they-like-to-engage/.

new challenge is presented every day to user when he access SCRAIM for the first time, the help request system where a user can answer help requests and make new ones and a competition for best team using SCRAIM in a sprint.
- Don't forget the fun. It's a fundamental aspect of the games. The fun factor is present in daily challenges, help requests, competition of good practices and the mascot (this element serves as a mean for the user to access gamification options outside the default workflow of SCRAIM).
- Deploy the appropriate tools. This step must be the logic result of all the previous steps.

In order to find the motivating and blockers aspects of this kind of tools, interviews were done to nine students of Masters in Informatics of FEUP. These happened before the beginning of the conception of the strategy and it served as a starter point. During the interviews users were asked about what motivates them for use this kind or tools or not. Most of the users said that this tool is great for work distribution and planning. That is great for the users to organise themselves and in a work team. About the blocking aspects, several users pointed the interface as the main blocking aspect.

As a result of several iterations of this process, the following game elements where integrated on SCRAIM:

Daily challenge system
: Users propose challenges to each other and one of them is chosen each day challenge. That offers a playful space in the tool while promoting surprise to entice a regular use by the users.

Helping system
: This system allows users to help each other. Besides facilitating the problem resolution, the answers can be consulted later in such manner that helps similar problems in the future.

Good practices of using SCRAIM
: In order to promote a better use of the tool, we developed a competition between existing projects. Each task has a score depending on how well it is filled. The collection of task's scores grants an overall score to the project.

Mascot
: Given the enterprise context of the tool, the proposed components were developed in such manner that are not intrusive to the user (an example is the use of pop-ups to view challenges and help requests). On the other hand, a mascot was created that, through notifications, works as a connection between the tool and the gamification components while keeping the user's autonomy.

While developing the gamification process, a second series of interviews were performed in order to validate the strategy. These interviews were done to five students of Masters in Informatics of FEUP. The main aspects of the strategy were discussed towards finding what would be possible to improve. In the interviews, the users were presented with several mock-ups and they are asked to give their opinion about them. The main conclusions were:

- It is interesting to use feedback mechanisms
- Simple and non intrusive game elements must be used in order not to disrupt the workflow
- Gamification options must be outside of the main workflow of the tool
- Avoid the use of negative connotations on user evaluations (e.g. leaderboards).

4 Evaluation and Results

In order to validate the developed strategy, the test methodology consisted in two parts: an interview using think-aloud protocol and a quiz.

The interviews were conducted to collaborators of Strongstep because they already knew the product so they could measure the impact of gamification in SCRAIM. Besides these collaborators other people were included from different areas such as informatics, management, design and economy so they could act differently regarding their experience and skill.

In the first part, several tasks were presented to the interviewed for them to execute and to express everything that they feel. This follows a think-aloud protocol that allows to capture and evaluate the user experience. The tasks asked consisted in the user to interact with the developed system in order to:

- Examine the gamification mascot.
- Open the daily challenge, answer it and give some feedback.
- Open the notifications center.
- Open a notification and check its content.
- Open a help request and answer it.
- Create a challenge.
- Create a help request.
- Check the gamification area for challenge and help request's statistics and hall of fame.
- Check task's gamification bar (it is a progress bar that shows if the task has the main fields properly filled).
- Check the project view for the members contribution table.

The second part of the interview was a survey with the purpose to evaluate the user experience in parameters such as simplicity and necessity. This survey was also a complement to the think-aloud protocol since it would capture details that users did't express. The survey asked the user to grade the components of the developed strategy (Daily challenge system, helping system, "Good pratices of using SCRAIM" and notifications) using parameters as "it is useful?", "it is fun?", "it is necessary?" and "Would you use it regularly?" in classification such "Strongly disagree", "Disagree", "Neither disagree or agree", "Agree" and "Strongly agree". Besides, it was asked if the use of gamification encourages a better use of SCRAIM.

The results showed that in general the developed strategy had a positive impact in SCRAIM. The number of collaborators interviews was six. This may be a small number of results but they are valuable to a future development of this work. All of the users knew SCRAIM and the concept of gamification and they agree that it is a potential way to improve and increase the use of the tool.

Regarding the challenge system, it showed up simple and intuitive in a general way, where the surprise factor attracts the user to use the tool at least daily. The users suggest improvement in the creation of the challenge regarding mainly the way that the correct answer is chosen.

Regarding the help system, the users identified the necessity of this system on SCRAIM. It was interesting the fact that half of the users don't agree that this system was fun. This can be explained by the existence of several perspectives of fun [4]. The work environment also may contribute to this review since helping a team member is part of the job.

Regarding the presence of gamification in the tasks, the users considered as a good way to promote the good pratices of using SCRAIM mainly because it is fun and provides a quick feedback.

Regarding the presence of the mascot with notifications in SCRAIM, it was considered as a bridge that connects the developed solution with the scope of the rest of the tool. Some users were confused with notification at first. One possible solution would provide a greater information about notification and their purpose.

5 Conclusions

Considering the results, it is possible to conclude that the developed prototype had a positive impact on the tool. The strong points identified were:

- The use of simple and intuitive elements. That way, the users don't need additional time to learn how to use the tool.
- Use of non-intrusive elements. This gives the user the choice of using the gamification component without disrupting his workflow in the tool.
- Promotion of the interaction between users though mutual aid.
- Use of the surprise element as a way to attract the user to use the tool at least daily.
- Promotion of the correct way to use the tool.

In this paper several research questions were answered in order to solve the identified problem. At this point we can present some conclusions:

- What's the most suitable combination of game elements? At this context the chosen combination of game elements must be simple and intuitive in such manner that allows a simple interaction with a user without being intrusive, promotes the user autonomy and respects the enterprise environment.
- How to avoid the hazards associated to gamification? Defining simple and fair metrics, design a simple feedback mechanics, avoids negative connotation and promotes interaction between users.
- How to ensure the proposed values of the manifesto to agile software development? In order to respect these values, the strategy was designed in such manner that the good use of the tool is a mean to the improvement of users relationships.

Acknowledgements. The research leading to these results has received funding from the European Union's Horizon 2020 - The EU Framework Programme for Research and Innovation 2014–2020, under grant agreement No. 687676.

References

1. Manifesto for Agile Software Development. http://www.agilemanifesto.org/
2. Deterding, S., Dixon, D., Khaled, R., Nacke, L.: From game design elements to gamefulness. In: Proceedings of the 15th International Academic MindTrek Conference on Envisioning Future Media Environments - MindTrek 2011 (2011)
3. Werbach, K., Hunter, D.: For the Win: How Game Thinking Can Revolutionize Your Business. Wharton Digital Press, New York (2012)
4. Dale, S.: Gamification: Making Work Fun, or Making Fun of Work? Business Information Review. SAGE Publications Ltd, New York (2014)
5. Bogost, I.: Persuasive games: exploitationware. Gamasutra (2011). http://goo.gl/jK1VR

The LabRint Serious Game: A New Intelligence Analysis Methodology

Michel Rudnianski, Olivier Heidmann, Raphael Attias(✉), and François Mohier

ORT FRANCE, 24 Rue Erlanger, 75116 Paris, France
michel.rudnianski@wanadoo.fr, {olivier.heidmann, raphael.attias, francois.mohier}@ort.asso.fr

Abstract. LabRint provides intelligence analysts with a set of learning experiences The game focuses on three stages of intelligence analysis: information collection and structuring, inference schemes development, and determination of inferences about the issue under scrutiny. To that end LabRint innovative approach implements two methodologies: the W^4HW information structuring, and the association of two graphical models for inference determination: Graphs of Deterrence and Bayesian Networks.

Keywords: Bayesian Networks · Graphs of Deterrence · Inference · Inference schemes · Information structuring · Intelligence analysis · Serious games · Strategies playability

1 Introduction

The fast development of digital technologies increases exponentially the generation of information coming from multiple sources. It thus makes a priori the work of intelligence analysts more complex. In this context, the FP7 European project LEILA (law Enforcement and Intelligence Learning Applications) provides law enforcement organizations with innovative learning methodologies for improving Intelligence analysis (IA) capabilities like [1]):

- filtering and analyzing massive amounts of data
- awareness of cognitive biases
- critical and creative thinking
- decision making in a complex environment generating cognitive biases, and under social and time pressure.
- communication and collaboration.

To this end, LEILA elaborates learning experiences, offering the possibility to actively acquire the IA skills (learning by doing), and computerizes them under the form of serious games like LabRint. In the present paper, Sect. 2 lists some of the core conceptual foundations considered in LabRint and how their consideration translates into the game workplan. Section 3 focuses on the issue of information structuring. Section 4 describes the technique that LabRint players must apply in order to develop in a visualizing manner the inference scheme on which the conclusions drawn will be

C. Vaz de Carvalho et al. (Eds.): SGAMES 2016, LNICST 176, pp. 148–155, 2017.
DOI: 10.1007/978-3-319-51055-2_19

based. Section 5 considers various possible types of game play. Last, Sect. 6 defines the players performance indices used in the game.

2 Core Conceptual Foundations and Work Plan

Intelligence analysis requires a variety of skills and competences, including knowledge of various factors or tools like:

- psychological and cultural factors explaining specific behaviors
- cognitive and decision making biases generating errors in data interpretation and related decisions
- preferences elicitation stemming from past choices
- formal logic connecting various facts or data with each other, providing in particular argumentation assessment
- rational decision-making techniques enabling to draw appropriate conclusions

LabRint, addresses these issues in an interrelated manner, covering both the associated theoretical and practical perspectives. This translates into a work plan based on an iterative and action oriented user-centered approach that involves different actors and guarantees the substantive quality of the technological research. The actors include:

- end-users
- experts in the different domains of conceptual foundations
- specialists in education
- technological and learning game designers having the ability to translate the theoretical issues into engaging learning experiences.

The work plan also includes the development and implementation of pilot sessions providing demonstration and evaluation of these learning experiences.

3 Information Representation

Information representation and analysis is a core issue in many domains of human societies, like education, business intelligence or intelligence analysis, sociology, psychology and medicine. For instance, some pedagogical models, like the successful Finnish one according to the PISA ranking, have introduced the usage of concept maps [2], even at the level of primary schools. The pupils receiving raw information from the teacher use these maps to structure the information and give it an appropriate meaning. The structuring process enables them to memorize that meaning more easily than if it had been entirely and directly given by the teacher.

The standard approach is often to let the learner or the trainee develop inference schemes, i.e. schemes representing causal relations between various evidences, and enabling thus to draw a meaningful conclusion (inference). To that end, in various domains like medicine [3] or intelligence analysis [4], a particular type of inference schemes, called Bayesian Networks (due to the use of conditional probabilities according to the so called Bayes Rule) has been applied. Although quite successful in several domains, Bayesian Networks raise two kinds of problems:

- They assume that some probabilities at least are available
- The complexity of the techniques used might increase exponentially with the size of the issue at stake, and is in the overwhelming majority of cases out of reach of the trainee or the learner, especially if the latter is a pupil in a primary school.

On the other hand, many issues, like the ones addressed in the Finnish education model, do not deal with probabilities, but rather with argumentation. Now argumentation has been the subject of significant development, especially for legal applications through resorting to what is known as Dialog Games, in which one player, the defender, makes a statement and tries to justify it, while the other player, tries on the opposite to refute all the defender's arguments. More recently, another alternative has been developed, based on a particular type of qualitative games (in the sense of Game Theory), called Games of Deterrence [5]. These games provide inference schemes under the form of graphs in which, given two nodes A and B representing each one some information, there is arc of origin A and of extremity B, if and only if A true implies that B is false. Several applications have already been developed, like the serious game called LabRint, developed within the framework of the EU FP7 LEILA project (Law Enforcement and Intelligence Learning Applications) in which the trainees have to draw conclusions from a set of raw data, some of them purposely generating cognitive or decision biases.

4 The LabRint Serious Game

The LabRint game includes two core elements: a structuring method for standard information analysis and inference schemes that connect different chunks of information and enable to draw conclusions about the issue under scrutiny.

The LabRint game provides a scenario in which the players will have to develop an intelligence analysis process, through using the toolbox in order to answer a question or a set of questions.

4.1 Structuring Method for Standard Information Analysis

The method used in LabRint for standard information analysis, is very well known in the field of marketing under the denomination W4HW meaning:

WHO does WHAT, WHERE, WHEN, HOW and WHY

So each data set provided to the player, will have to be transformed by the latter into a W4HW structure, which will be called an evidence. Figure 1 shows on the example of the first chunk of information made available to the player, how this player should proceed.

This first chunk of information has the label I01. To break it down into the W4HW structure, the player has to click on each column and select the element that

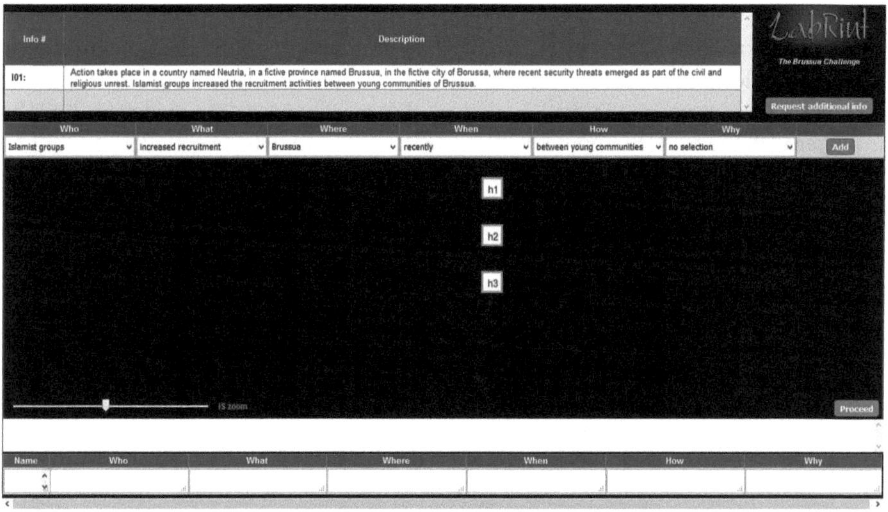

Fig. 1. The LabRint interface

appropriately represents the issue in the chunk of information. Just to give an example, in the column WHO the appropriate selection should be "islamist groups". As in real life sometimes, the information provided to the player may be incomplete. In particular, it may not enable him/her to completely fulfill the W4HW structuring process. This is fully taken into account by the system supporting the game. This means for instance that if for a given chunk of information, no date appears, then the item that appropriately describes the situation in the column WHEN is "no selection". But of course if the chunk of information included a date, then choosing "no selection" in the column WHEN, will trigger an error message from the system. When all 6 dimensions of the W4HW have been addressed, the player clicks on "add" and the system will reply by providing on the screen an icon "Ev x" where Ev stands for evidence and x stands for the evidence number.

5 Inference Schemes and Conclusions

Determining the inference schemes associated with the case under consideration is a core task of the LabRint game. Following the Oxford Dictionary, one can define an inference as "a conclusion obtained on the basis of facts and reasoning". On its side the United Nations Office on Drugs and Crimes considers that "in any criminal investigation, the objective of the analysis is to find an explanation of what the information means. This explanation is called inference". To find an inference, one needs to: gather data which concern the issue under scrutiny, analyze the consistency of the data set (i.e. determine the possible contradictions between the data composing that data set) and finally determine the conclusion/inference that can be drawn from this consistency analysis. One important point that must be stressed upon is that, in the present version of the LabRint game, for the sake of simplicity, a fact or a data which is the subject of no denial, is considered true (of course, such assumption might be questioned). So, in order to be able to draw conclusions on the basis of all the information collected, the player will first determine the denial relations that exist between the evidences built by the player with the W4HW approach. Thus, let Ev x and Ev y be two evidences built by the player. Let us suppose that if Ev x is true, then Ev y is false. This denial relation may be represented as follows (Fig. 2):

Fig. 2. Denial relation

In a figurative sense, this is as if Ev x was "shooting" on Ev y. Now of course, this does not necessarily mean that Ev x is true and Ev y is false. Imagine for instance a third evidence Ev z such that if EV z is true, then Ev x is false. The associated representation is then (Fig. 3):

Fig. 3. Three evidences

This means that if the three evidences are the only ones to be considered, then: Ev z is true, Ev x is false and Ev y is true.

Let us last consider that the issue at stake is to determine if a given assumption H is true or false, given that the inference scheme is the following (Fig. 4):

Fig. 4. Three evidences and an assumption

It stems from what precedes that Ev z true implies Ev x false which implies Ev y true, which in turn implies H false. Of course not all inferences schemes are linear paths like the ones above. Consider for instance the following inference scheme (Fig. 5):

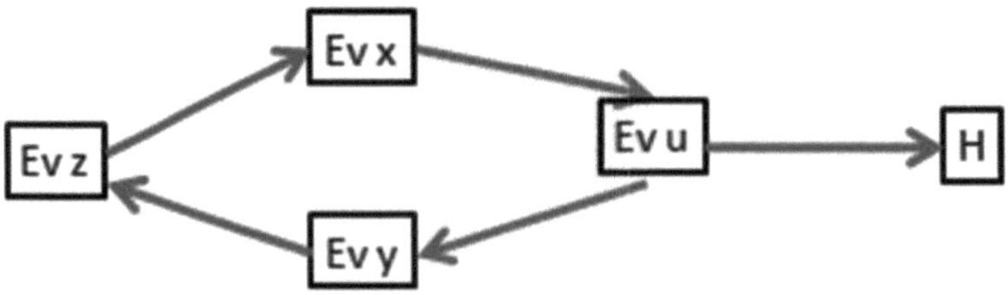

Fig. 5. Non-linear evidences path

There are in fact two possibilities, either Ev x and Ev y are true, in which case Ev u and Ev z are false and H is true. Or Ev u and Ev z are true, in which case Ev x and Ev y are false, and H is false.

If we generalize, in the LabRint framework, an inference scheme is a graph which vertices are the evidences and the conclusions to be drawn, and which edges represent the denial relations existing between evidences.

As seen in the elementary example here above, building that graph enables to draw conclusions about the truth or falsity of assumptions. This is precisely what LabRint is about. The player has three tasks:

- Structure the raw information into evidences
- Build the inference scheme associated with these evidences
- Use that inference scheme to draw conclusions about the truthfulness or falsity of hypotheses

To build inference schemes in the LabRint Game, each time that after having appropriately structured a chunk of additional information, the user clicks on the "add" button, a new evidence appears on the screen. The player may then move the evidence by clicking on it except on its extremities (for reasons that will be given hereunder) and then move the cursor. After all structuring has been made, then by clicking on the extremities of an evidence, the player will generate an arrow (with a red cross in its middle). By moving the extremity of that arrow with his/her cursor, the player will be able to connect the former evidence to another one, or to a hypothesis that, according to him/her, the former evidence defeats (Fig. 6).

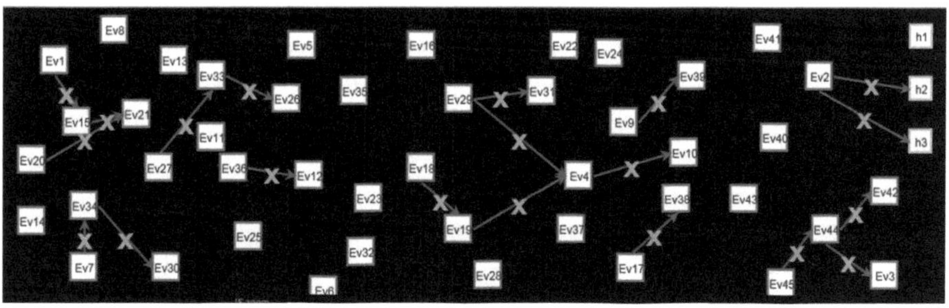

Fig. 6. A schema in LabRint

6 Performance Assessment

The game is played under time constraint, which is fixed by the trainer on the basis of: the players' experience and the informational complexity of the game.

Given that constraint, the player's analysis performance is assessed at two levels: the inference scheme and the conclusions. As far as the inference scheme is concerned, the system supporting the game assesses the player's analysis performance as a percentage of the appropriate inference scheme that is being represented by the inference scheme developed by the player. With respect to the conclusions, the system supporting the game assesses the player's analysis performance as a percentage of the conclusions that are true.

To perform these analyses, the player has to click on the Proceed button, and the following screen will appear, asking him/her to confirm his/her decision to proceed, since the player will then not be able to redo the proceed without re-creating all the evidences, that is to say without re-playing the game from the beginning (Fig. 7).

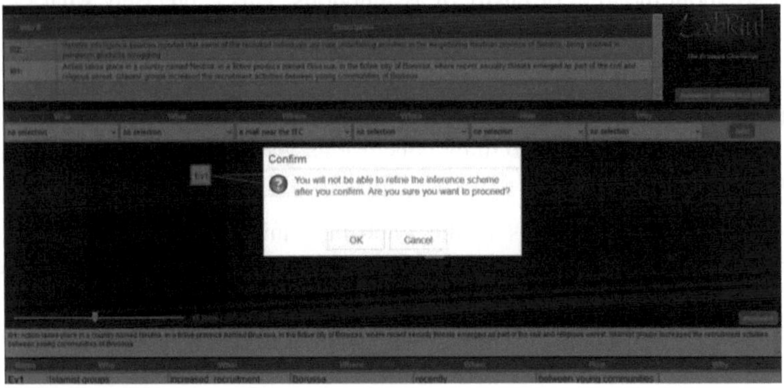

Fig. 7. Confirmation screen

If the player confirms, he/she will be asked to give his/her answers to the questions asked by the system. In the present scenario, the player will thus need to: decide whether each of the hypotheses submitted to him/her is TRUE or FALSE and then click on the Proceed button. Once the Proceed button has been clicked, the engine analyses the inference scheme developed by the player and the player's conclusions. The engine will then give the player the numerical assessment of his/her performance, as shown here below (Fig. 8).

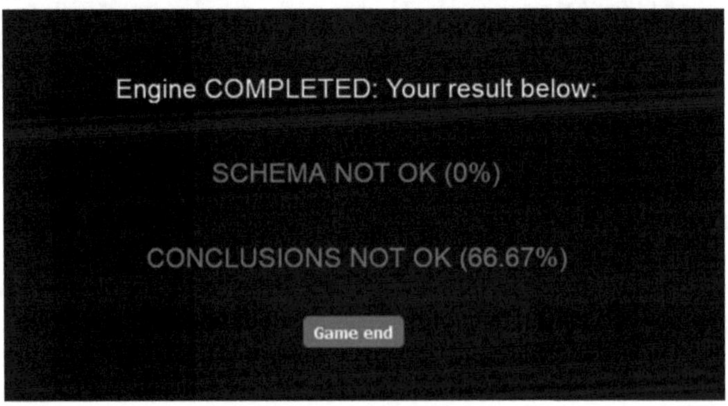

Fig. 8. Assessment screen

7 Conclusions

Serious games are an effective way for users to safely make decisions in different scenarios, even incorrect ones, and see their possible effects. Situations which are impossible to represent in the real world for reasons of cost, safety or time constraints could be accessible for users through the LEILA serious game. Serious games are a powerful tool for acquiring knowledge, training skills or changing behavior, and they can be the ideal means for intelligence analysts' training.

The LEILA learning experience will help the Intelligence Analyst to be aware of the cognitive biases, to realize when they take place, to be able to prevent or mitigate their impact in the analysis process and to dampen their effect. Through the cycle of experiential learning (exploration, experience, reflection, conceptualization) embedded in the game, the knowledge is consolidated into an experience and can be transferred (conceptualized) to several domains, enabling the intelligence community to become proactive and deploy efficient efforts to prevent criminal and/or terrorists acts.

Numerous pilots sessions have been held and will be held in many countries this year.

References

1. The LEILA project website. http://www.leila-project.eu/
2. Pernaa, J., Akse, M.: Concept maps as meaningful learning tools in a web–based chemistry material. In: Cañas, A.J., Reiska, P., Åhlberg, M., Novak, J.D. (eds.) Proceedings of the Third International Conference on Concept Mapping, Tallinn, Estonia & Helsinki, Finland (2008). http://citeseerx.ist.psu.edu/viewdoc/download?doi=10.1.1.412.4412&rep=rep1&type=pdf
3. Lucas, P.: Bayesian Networks in Medicine: a Model-based Approach to Medical Decision Making. https://www.cs.ru.nl/~peterl/eunite.pdf
4. McNaught, K., Sutovsky, P.: Representing variable source credibility in intelligence analysis with bayesian networks. In: 2012 Australian Security and Intelligence Conference (2012). http://ro.ecu.edu.au/cgi/viewcontent.cgi?article=1021&context=asi
5. Rudianski, M.: From Argumentation to Negotiations: The Game of Deterrence Path, i-lex. Scienze Giuridiche, Scienze Cognitive e Intelligenza artificiale, Rivista quadrimestrale on-line, 17 Novembre 2012. www.i-lex.it

Author Index

MIX
Papier aus verantwortungsvollen Quellen
Paper from responsible sources
FSC® C105338

If you have any concerns about our products,
you can contact us on
ProductSafety@springernature.com

In case Publisher is established outside the EU,
the EU authorized representative is:
Springer Nature Customer Service Center GmbH
Europaplatz 3, 69115 Heidelberg, Germany

Printed by Libri Plureos GmbH
in Hamburg, Germany